# A Thousand Hearts' Devotion

## A HISTORY OF
# Monmouth College

"From out thousands of earnest, devoted hearts, let daily petitions rise to our Father in Heaven, that we all, Board of Trust, Faculty and Students, may be blessed and made a blessing…"

*David Alexander Wallace
Inaugural Address,
Monmouth, Illinois,
September 1, 1857*

"A thousand hearts to-day hold high
The treasures of thy love.
How proudly glows the oriflamme
Of red and white above!"

*Anonymous Poet, 1900
Monmouth College
Ravelings*

"A flame of white and crimson
Weaves mem'ries, shadows spell;
And a thousand hearts' devotion,
To the school we love so well."

*Elizabeth Farell
Zumstein '25*

# A Thousand Hearts' Devotion

## A HISTORY OF
# Monmouth College

*By Daniel Meyer and Jeffrey D. Rankin*
Monmouth College, Monmouth, Illinois 2002

Library of Congress Cataloging-in-Publication Data

Meyer, Daniel, 1950-
  A thousand hearts' devotion: a history of Monmouth College / by Daniel Meyer and Jeffrey D. Rankin.
     p. cm.
  Includes bibliographical references (p.   ) and index.
     ISBN 0-9720303-0-1 (hardback)
  1. Monmouth College (Monmouth, Ill.)—History. 2. Education, Higher—Illinois—History. I. Rankin, Jeffrey D., 1957- II. Title.
     LD3501.M62 M49 2002
     378.773'415—dc21

            2002006678

© 2002 by Monmouth College. All rights reserved. No part of this book may be reproduced in any form or by any means, electronic or mechanical, including photocopying, without written permission from Monmouth College. Inquiries should be addressed to: Monmouth College, 700 E. Broadway, Monmouth, IL 61462-1998.

First printing
First edition

Produced by Kim Coventry The Coventry Group, Chicago.

Designed by The Grillo Group, Inc., Chicago. Typeset in Bembo and Bodoni Poster Italic.

Color separations by Professional Graphics, Rockford, Illinois.

Printed on Furioso Matt 150 gsm by Snoeck-Ducaju & Zoon, Belgium.

Front jacket illustration: Overlooking Monmouth College's scenic campus for nearly a century, the cupola of Wallace Hall is a familiar landmark to all alumni.

Back jacket illustration: Without the benefit of modern machinery, Wallace Hall rises from the ashes of the Old Main in the summer of 1908, just months after Monmouth College's venerable recital hall was destroyed by fire.

Photo Credits

Dust jacket Rick Kessinger.

Pages iii-ix, xiii, xvi, xix, 121, 166-167, 168, 175, 176-177, 186 by Hedrich Blessing.

Pages 2, 4, 7 (left), 9 (lower), 18 (upper), 21 (upper), 25, 26 (upper), 32, 42, 45, 68, 69 (cap), 79, 103 (cap), 115 (caps), 160 (lower), 179 by Michael Tropea.

Page 8, 14-15, 21 courtesy Library of Congress.

Page 18 courtesy Hendershott Museum Consultants.

Page 19 (left) courtesy U.S. Naval Historical Center.

Page 19 (right) © 2002 David A. Luff.

Pages 142 (top left, lower left, and right), 143 (lower left, lower right), 145, 146, 150-151, 157, 158 by James L. Ballard.

Page 172 by Ray Mendez.

Page 184 by Kent Kriegshauser.

| | | |
|---|---|---|
| ***Introduction*** | | xi |
| ***Chapter 1*** | A College on the Frontier 1853–1860 | 3 |
| ***Chapter 2*** | Monmouth in Peace and War 1860–1878 | 17 |
| ***Chapter 3*** | Victorian Monmouth 1878–1903 | 31 |
| ***Chapter 4*** | Monmouth Comes of Age 1903–1920 | 49 |
| ***Chapter 5*** | The College Community 1920–1936 | 67 |
| ***Chapter 6*** | The Era of Challenge: The Depression and World War II 1936–1952 | 83 |
| ***Chapter 7*** | Monmouth in Transition 1952–1964 | 101 |
| ***Chapter 8*** | The Impact of Change 1964–1974 | 119 |
| ***Chapter 9*** | A Decade of Renewal 1974–1985 | 139 |
| ***Chapter 10*** | Securing Foundations 1985–1994 | 153 |
| ***Chapter 11*** | Into the Twenty-First Century 1994–2002 | 169 |
| | List of 25-Year Faculty and Staff | 188 |
| | Acknowledgments | 190 |
| | Index | 191 |

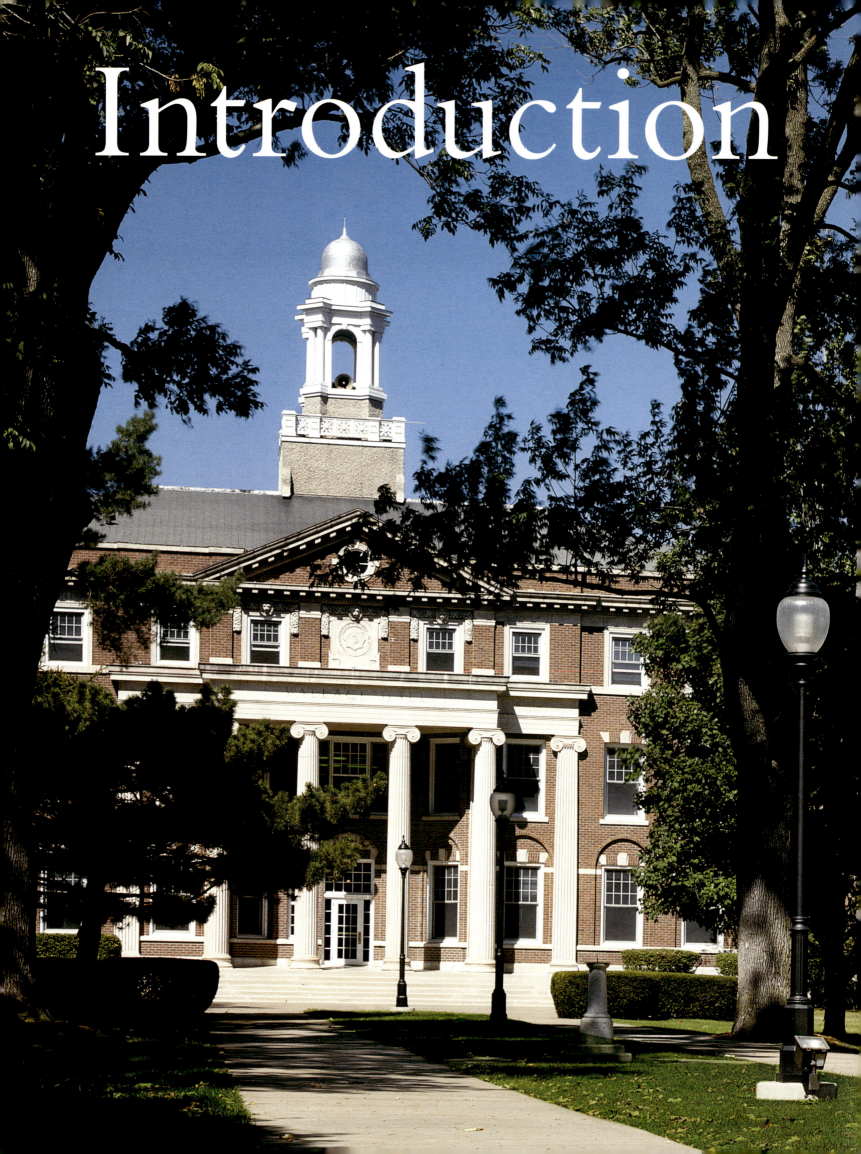
# Introduction

# *Introduction*

Acknowledged as one of America's distinguished small colleges, Monmouth College ushered in the new millennium anticipating its sesquicentennial celebration in 2003. This history offers a portrayal of the dedicated people and colorful events that helped shape the institution from a fledgling Presbyterian academy, founded on little more than faith, to the nationally ranked liberal arts college it is today.

To put in perspective the dynamic growth Monmouth has experienced over 15 decades, it is necessary to begin this history with an overview of Monmouth College today.

Nestled in the heart of a quiet, residential neighborhood in Monmouth, Illinois (population 9,800), the college's 75-acre campus is home to 1,100 students from 18 states and 22 foreign nations. New facilities include Bowers Hall, a contemporary suite-style residence opened in 2001, and the Huff Athletic Center, featuring a gymnasium, natatorium, and fieldhouse, scheduled to open in 2003. In recent years, the former Carnegie Library was transformed into an elegant student services building named Poling Hall, while a former fraternity house was remade into the Mellinger Teaching and Learning Center.

All the academic buildings and the football field are located on the rolling, tree-crowned campus on the east side of the city of Monmouth,

PRECEDING PAGES *Wallace Hall, completed in 1909, is named in honor of Monmouth's first president, David Alexander Wallace.*

OPPOSITE PAGE *Kyle Duane (left), Pat DuMais, and Emily Delaney enjoy their moment in the sun at commencement 2001.*

the Warren County seat. Peacock Memorial Athletic Park, a state-of-the-art soccer and baseball complex, was recently constructed along U.S. Route 34, just blocks from campus. Adjoining the park is LeSuer Nature Preserve, which serves as a biology field station and features a public nature trail. The college also maintains a valuable freshwater biology research station on the Mississippi River near Keithsburg.

Currently under construction, the 155,000-square-foot Huff Athletic Center will be the largest structure on campus, extending the 1925 gymnasium and the current Glennie Gymnasium more than half a block to the west. It is part of an extensive campus-wide improvement program that includes major renovations to Hewes Library, classroom facilities, the Stockdale Student Center, and the historic Dahl Chapel and Auditorium, Monmouth's oldest academic building.

Solidly financed with a growing endowment of $50 million, today's Monmouth College keeps pace with rapidly changing technology while offering generous financial assistance to its students. For a majority, the cost of attending this nationally ranked, private liberal arts college is comparable to that of most state universities.

Monmouth's tradition of individual attention is reflected in a student-faculty ratio of 14 to 1. The average class size is 19, and all classes are taught by members of the faculty. More than 90 percent of Monmouth's professors have earned the highest degrees in their disciplines. Nearly 85 percent of Monmouth students ranked in the top half of their high school graduating class.

Of the 2,325 four-year colleges and universities in the United States, Monmouth is one of only 218 institutions recognized by the Carnegie Foundation as a national liberal arts college, a highly selective group that awards at least half its degrees in liberal arts disciplines. Monmouth's innovative Four-Year Intentional Leadership Program, which helps students develop career goals that will assist them in employment or gaining entrance to graduate school, has been named one of the top 10

OPPOSITE PAGE
*Monmouth College's oldest academic building, Dahl Chapel and Auditorium, was extensively renovated in 2002.*

ABOVE *McMichael Residence Hall coeds (clockwise from top left) Corey McCann '04, Channon Corzatt '04, Tammy West '03, and Melinda Fry '03.*

*Former Fulton Hall residents and members of the Class of 2001 Jami Hamrick-Curl (left), Amber Kuhrts, and Nelena Brummett share a final moment together before graduation.*

exemplary programs in the nation by the respected National Association of Student Personnel Administration. Ninety-nine percent of graduates successfully enter the job market or continue their education within six months of graduation.

Each year Monmouth sends dozens of its graduates into teaching careers at elementary and high school classrooms throughout the Midwest. Preparing students for teaching has been a central mission of the college since its founding, and the education program is one of the most highly respected in the country. School superintendents in Illinois, Iowa, and Missouri regularly turn to Monmouth when seeking to fill teaching positions, assured that candidates will be well prepared.

In addition to education, Monmouth's most popular fields of study are business and accounting, science (chemistry, biology, and physics), and communications, including speech and public relations. In an era when study of the classics is often considered passé, Monmouth embraces the discipline, integrating Greek, Latin, and classical studies into the liberal arts program. Monmouth's curriculum itself continues to evolve to better prepare students for a changing world. As a special task force prepares to offer recommendations for change following a two-year comprehensive review of the curriculum, individual faculty members work to devise innovative courses and programs in their disciplines. Recent examples include an award-winning course titled Cosmology and Creation, the introduction of a graphic arts program, and the adoption of a public relations major.

Monmouth College has a strong tradition in the performing arts. Its drama organization, Crimson Masque, is open to all students, and any student may audition for a role in plays staged at the college's Wells Theater. The music department is a source of pride, featuring three choral groups and several instrumental ensembles. The acclaimed Monmouth Chorale, a 36-voice *a cappella* choir, annually tours the nation. In addition, Monmouth is one of the few colleges in the country to offer talent scholarships for the bagpipe.

A charter member of the prestigious Associated Colleges of the Midwest (ACM), Monmouth offers bachelor's degrees in 26 disciplines. Pre-professional courses prepare students for graduate work in 14 fields ranging from architecture to medicine. Through the auspices of the ACM, off-campus study opportunities are available in Africa, Asia, Europe, and Central America, while domestic study destinations include Washington, D.C., Argonne and Oak Ridge National Laboratories, and Chicago's Newberry Library. Monmouth also has exchange agreements with major universities in France, Greece, and Japan, allowing additional international study opportunities.

The Monmouth experience is more than academic studies. More than 60 clubs and organizations flourish on campus. Two of the first national women's fraternities, Pi Beta Phi and Kappa Kappa Gamma, were founded at Monmouth and still have active chapters here, along with another fraternity for women, Alpha Xi Delta. National

*At Monmouth, bagpipes lead the big parade.*

men's fraternities on campus are Alpha Tau Omega, Sigma Phi Epsilon, and Zeta Beta Tau. Student publications include the *Courier* newspaper and the *Coil* creative arts magazine, also available on the Web. Students operate a radio and television station, which are broadcast over a cable network and the Web.

Monmouth offers students opportunities to develop leadership and teamwork skills as well as a sense of responsibility in a wide variety of interests. Campus service organizations play an important role as students reach out to the community. During spring break, Monmouth students have traveled to Indian reservations, Appalachia, and the inner city, volunteering to help those in need.

OPPOSITE PAGE *Wells Theater at dusk.*

TOP *Art professor Marjorie Blackwell supervises a studio painting class.*

ABOVE LEFT *The String Ensemble, Monmouth College's newest musical group, was organized by professional cellist and music instructor Carolyn Suda (left).*

ABOVE *One of the spacious lounges in the new Bowers Residence Hall.*

Monmouth is proud of its Scottish heritage, sporting its own official tartan and playing traditional Highland games each spring during the Ceilidh festival. The college's sports teams are named the Fighting Scots, and the famed Monmouth College Pipe Band is featured at sporting events, in parades, and at other public venues.

During the last three decades, Monmouth athletes have won more than 50 titles in Midwest Conference competition. The Monmouth football team annually battles archrival Knox College for possession of the coveted Bronze Turkey in the second-oldest college rivalry west of the Allegheny Mountains. During the opening year of the 21st century, Monmouth and Knox met 17 times in head-to-head competition, and the Fighting Scots won every contest—in football, volleyball, baseball, softball, and men's and women's soccer and basketball. Monmouth's track and field program is perennially among the leaders in Division III, regularly turning out All-Americans.

Affiliated with the Presbyterian Church (U.S.A.), Monmouth honors the Christian principles of its founders while welcoming students and faculty members from all denominations and faiths. Students are encouraged to gain a broad understanding of the world's religious traditions—in the classroom, through various student organizations, and through programs sponsored by the chaplain.

Monmouth's 12,000 alumni take an active interest in their alma mater by serving on governing boards, recruiting new students, contributing financially, or offering their professional expertise. Graduates who are leaders in industry, education, science, and the arts often return to campus as lecturers and scholars in residence. Homecoming, Commencement, and Alumni Weekend are traditional occasions dear to the hearts of all Monmouth alumni, who annually flock back to campus to renew old acquaintances.

*Monmouth College's student improvisational comedy troupe, Scotch Tape.*

The philosophy and direction of Monmouth College on its 150th anniversary are accurately reflected in its sesquicentennial theme, "Toward a New Horizon." Ever embracing the strengths and traditions that have made it great, the college now pauses briefly to reflect on its storied past, while firmly focusing on the future. As the college hymn states, "O God, Thy blessing we implore on Monmouth College evermore. May all our effort ever be to honor Thee!"

*T. H. McMichael Residence Hall, built in 1914, stands near the center of campus, atop Dunlap Terrace.*

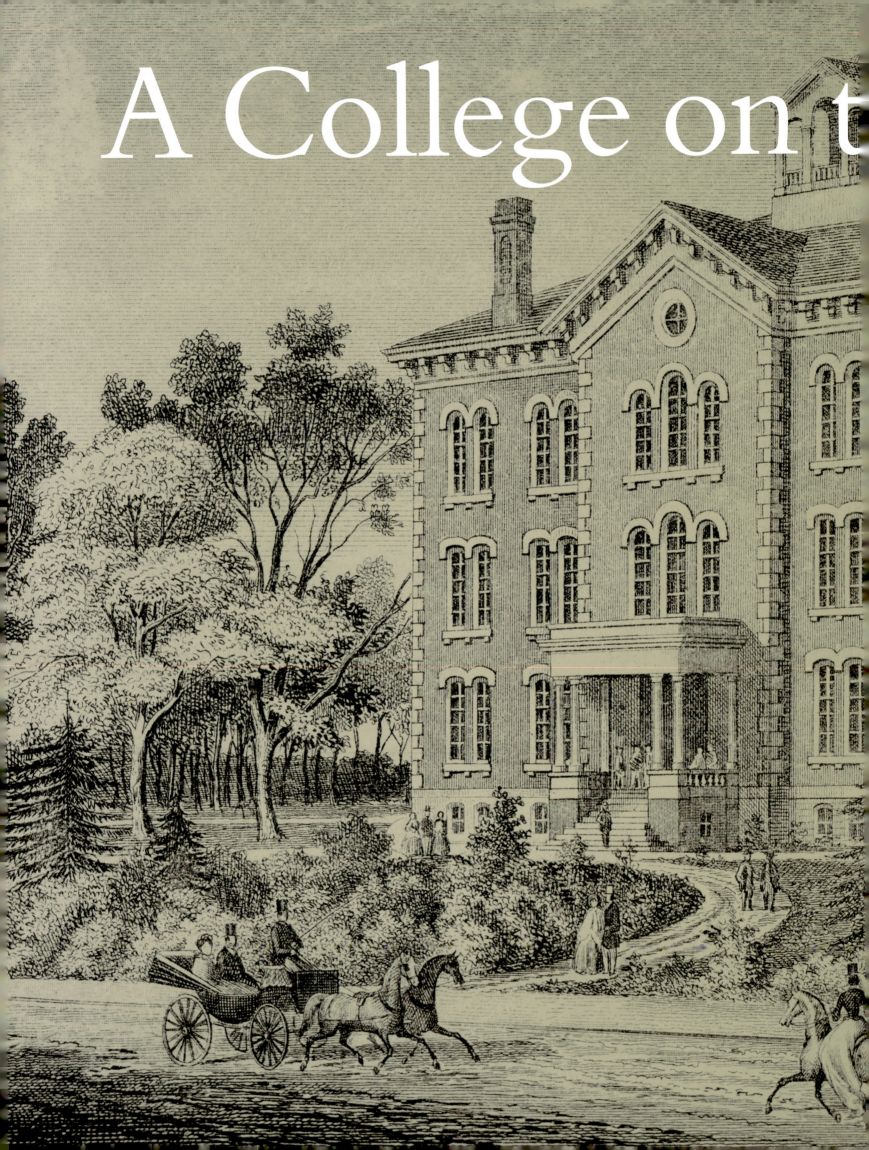
# A College on t

he Frontier 1853–1860

# Chapter 1

Founded in 1853 in the rapidly growing town of Monmouth on the midwestern frontier, Monmouth College embodied the ambitions and dreams of civic leaders and the denominational energies of Scotch-Irish Presbyterians who guided its development. Faith and economic prosperity, as well as educational need and religious spirit, combined to produce a new institution charged with meeting the demands of a diverse and changing society.

The promise and expectation of Monmouth College owed a great deal to the distinctive regional characteristics

PRECEDING PAGES
*An engraving of the proposed new Monmouth College recitation hall, from the 1857 catalog.*

OPPOSITE PAGE
*Although a Baptist by faith, Ivory Quinby was one of the strongest supporters of Monmouth's fledgling Presbyterian academy. A charter trustee, the industrialist and lawyer gave liberally of his money and expertise to the college until his death in 1869. This portrait of Quinby still hangs in the mansion he built, which is today the official residence of Monmouth College presidents.*

of western central Illinois in the early nineteenth century. Both the college and its town were the products of an unusually rich natural setting and the migration into the area of successive waves of native Americans, European explorers, military forces, land speculators, settlers, businessmen, and industrialists.

### Settling the Illinois Prairie

When European explorers first entered what would become the state of Illinois in 1673, they encountered an expansive sweep of open grassland. More than 60 percent of the area, approximately 22 million acres, was covered by prairie. The land was occupied largely by two Native American groups, the 12 tribes forming the Illiniwek (or Illinois) and the Miami. During the eighteenth and early nineteenth centuries, both the Illiniwek and the Miami lost territory as eastern tribes moved into the Illinois country.

In the early nineteenth century, a vanguard of white settlers from the east and south came into this mix of native groups. To encourage enlistments in the War of 1812, Congress had created a Military Tract, an area of 3.5 million acres between the Mississippi and Illinois Rivers. Every noncommissioned soldier who volunteered for service against the British was awarded a quarter section (160 acres) of land in this territory. As a result, after 1816, settlement moved up the Mississippi Valley from St. Louis as land speculators and settlers, whether they were veterans or not, poured into the area. In 1818, the population of the territory had increased sufficiently for Illinois to be admitted as the 21st state of the Union.

By 1829, there were already 30 or 40 families residing in what would become Warren, Henderson, and Mercer Counties, and a movement was already under way to organize Warren as a separate Illinois county. A petition was circulated to demonstrate that the area held sufficient population, and in June 1830 the county of Warren was organized.

The site selected for the town of Monmouth lay on the high open prairie about three miles south of Cedar Creek and 16 miles east of the Mississippi River. Local tradition would later maintain that the only trees to be found in the vicinity were two oaks with trunks only six inches in diameter. The survey of the town was accepted by the commissioners in June 1831, and the first residents were soon making their way across the prairie to claim their lots in the new county seat.

On November 29, 1836, the citizens of Monmouth voted to incorporate the town. It was still little more than a village. Judge William C. Rice of Oquawka recalled later in life that in the mid-1830s Monmouth could claim only 15 or 20 houses. The principal street through the town was the Big Road, now Broadway, which ran westward across Warren County toward the Lower Yellow Banks (later Oquawka) on the Mississippi. By 1834, the Big Road had become the route of a stagecoach line from Springfield to the Mississippi River.

Transportation was further enhanced in 1851, when construction began on Monmouth's first railroad, the Peoria and Oquawka. Completed in 1855 and absorbed by the Chicago, Burlington & Quincy, the rail line provided Monmouth with ready travel connections and routes for shipping products to both Springfield and Chicago. Monmouth's output of agricultural products was now joined by a range

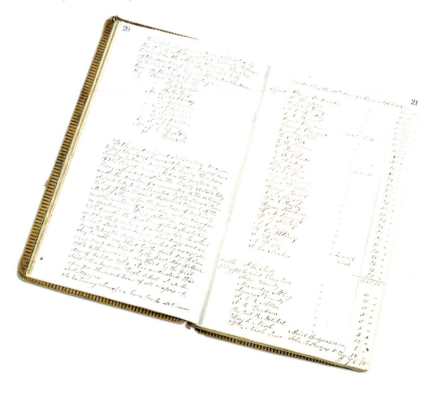

*The original leather-bound minutes of the Monmouth College Senate include a subscription list of $1,150 in pledges by local community leaders who were instrumental in Monmouth being selected as the site for a new Presbyterian academy.*

# The Real Birthplace of Monmouth College

THE OLD ACADEMY IS GONE—in 1902, it was converted to a soap factory, then torn down. And five years later, another beloved building, Old Main, succumbed to fire. Such was the fate of early frontier structures. But a Monmouth College shrine that predates both buildings continues to stand: an old one-room schoolhouse with a history of its own.

For a few weeks in the fall of 1856, after three years of existing as an academy in temporary facilities, Monmouth College still lacked a home. The new college building, which was being erected on a lot donated by trustee Abner Harding, did not yet have a roof. With classes scheduled to begin September 3, the board made arrangements to rent an old one-room district school located at the southeast corner of First Street and First Avenue.

According to the late college historian F. Garvin Davenport, it was in this schoolhouse that Monmouth Academy "became Monmouth College, consecrated by prayer, a song, and the faith of the founders." Davenport noted that while the building was only occupied for a brief period, its historical significance was great. "On Friday night of the first week of the first term," he wrote, "twelve young men called a special meeting in this makeshift college building and organized the first of the famous literary societies."

The two men who presided over these first classes, professors Marion Morrison and James Brown, would develop a sentimental attachment to the old building. Morrison later wrote of keeping a protective eye on the school as it was moved to a site near the present high school in 1857 and then to the corner of Archer Avenue and North B Street in 1860, where it remained as a dwelling for several decades.

About 1950, after standing vacant for many years, the state fire marshal declared the building a hazard and directed its removal. After a public sale, the house was moved to a new location at 816 North D Street, where the owner reportedly intended to tear it down and salvage the timbers. Try as he might, however, the ancient building proved too solid to dismantle.

Another 50 years have now passed, and while a number of Monmouth College buildings have since gone up or down, the college's very first building—once a public school, today a private home—remains steadfast.

*Dating from the 1840s, this former one-room schoolhouse has survived being moved three times and an attempted demolition. Within its walls, Monmouth's first classes met after the institution was elevated to a college in 1856.*

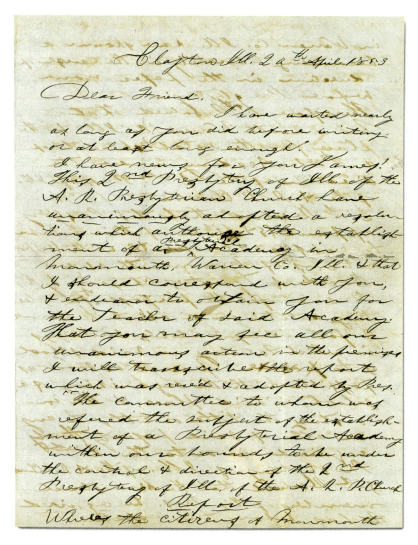

*Perhaps the earliest surviving document pertaining to the founding of Monmouth College, this letter was written on April 20, 1853, by the Reverend Samuel Millen, pastor of the Associate Reformed Church at Clayton, where the Presbytery had recently met to decide the location of the new academy. The letter is addressed to James Woodburn of Bloomington, Indiana, and offers him a teaching job at the school.*

of factory goods that would mark the beginning of the town's reputation as an industrial center. Cigars, plows, pottery, soap, and other products were all being manufactured in Monmouth, and the prosperity they brought to the community turned citizens' thoughts to social and cultural refinement and the need for expansion and improvement in all levels of education.

## The Presbyterian Mission in Illinois

As the frontier of pioneer settlement moved steadily westward, it was never far ahead of the missionary and educational work of the Protestant denominations. Baptists, Methodists, and other groups were all active on the western frontier, but the Presbyterians were frequently among the most influential. This was particularly true for the members of the Reformed Presbyterian and Associate Presbyterian churches. Presbyterian ministers were expected to be thoroughly familiar with English grammar, rhetoric, Greek, and Latin and to have a comprehensive knowledge of the Bible. A well-educated Presbyterian clergy helped to encourage broader literacy among the laity, and it also stimulated the continuing establishment of seminaries and other institutions of higher education to provide ministerial training.

From the late eighteenth century onward, Associated Reformed Presbyterians at the edge of settlement had created a succession of educational institutions in locations such as Service and New Wilmington, Pennsylvania, and Xenia and Oxford, Ohio. By the 1840s, Presbyterians were also becoming concerned about the need for additional schools and colleges in the rapidly expanding settlements of the Midwest.

The first representatives of the Associate Reformed Presbyterians to arrive in what are today Warren and Henderson Counties were the Clark and Jamieson families, who migrated from Indiana in 1829 to South Henderson Creek and established the frontier station of Jamieson Settlement. Within the next few years, more Presbyterian immigrants began to arrive from Associate Reformed communities in Ohio, Indiana, Kentucky, and the Carolinas. As a result, Warren County and Monmouth became a developing center for the Associate Reformed church and its mission activities on the Illinois prairie.

Monmouth-area Presbyterians interested in establishing educational institutions did not have to look farther than the next county to see the results of community initiative. In Knox County at Galesburg, immigrants from New York had founded Knox Manual Labor College in 1837, which was soon renamed Knox College. In 1852, Lombard College was also founded in Galesburg, and in 1853 an academy was opened in nearby Abingdon.

Warren County Presbyterians watching these developments in neighboring Galesburg were spurred to take steps of their own. They were led by two unusually capable Associate Reformed ministers, the Reverend James C. Porter of the Cedar Creek Church and the Reverend Robert

Ross of the South Henderson Church. At a meeting in South Henderson in October 1852, Porter called for the establishment of a Presbyterian high school. James G. Madden, a prominent Monmouth attorney, urged that the school be established in Monmouth rather than in one of the outlying towns such as Oquawka or Sparta. This school would eventually become Monmouth College.

In April 1853, Porter argued the case for Monmouth at a presbytery meeting, stressing that the county seat had a new railroad, occupied one of the most promising agricultural areas of the Midwest, and was safely distant from morally unsavory river ports like Oquawka, along the Mississippi. Porter's final point was the decisive one—a signed subscription list from James Madden and other community leaders pledging $1,150 for a school in Monmouth.

The Academy opened in November 1853 with the Reverend James R. Brown, a graduate of Miami University in Ohio, as its principal, and Maria Madden, sister of James Madden, as assistant principal. The initial student body numbered about 100, including pupils from Miss Madden's school and a private school that had recently closed. In curriculum and structure, the Academy was essentially a high school, providing a quality of education that was not available in the community's poorly run grammar schools.

The search for adequate space to hold classes until a proper building could be erected proved to be one of the Academy's greatest challenges. In 1853, the Academy rented space in the Christian Church at North Second Street and East Archer. Later, in the fall of 1854, classes were held in the basement of the Presbyterian Church in the 300 block of South Main. But financial solvency was also a critical issue. By 1855, so little income was being generated that James Brown relinquished his salary, in return for which the board of trustees paid his expenses, let him set up housekeeping in the classroom space, and allowed him to keep whatever tuition he was able to collect.

### Launching the College

As these challenges were surmounted and enrollment grew, plans were already being made to expand the institution into a full-fledged college. As was often the case in midwestern higher education, an academy or preparatory school was seen as a means to test the level of community support and prospects for an expanded program. The board of the Academy now felt that the time was ripe to create a college that would fully serve the needs of the western frontier.

In 1855, while preparing to petition the state legislature for a collegiate charter, the board stepped up its efforts to complete the new college building. A lot at what is now 506 North A Street had been donated in 1853 by Abner Clark Harding, the pioneer builder of the Burlington Railroad. Construction was begun on a substantial Federal-style brick edifice, simple in design, two stories tall, well lit with large windows on all sides, and holding eight classrooms and a chapel seating 300 people. But the institution's continuing financial difficulties threatened to bring construction to a halt. In 1855, with the building still lacking a roof, the board passed a

*The Reverend Robert Ross, pastor of the South Henderson Church, was a leading advocate for establishing Monmouth College. He also served as a trustee, a professor of Latin, and a financial agent for the college.*

*The Reverend James R. Brown served as the principal of the Monmouth Academy when it opened its doors in November 1853. When the academy was granted its collegiate charter, Brown was named professor of ancient languages.*

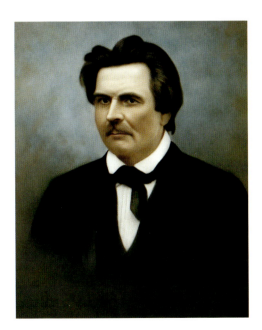

*One of the first Associate Reformed preachers to settle in what is now Warren County, the Reverend James C. Porter is credited with convincing the presbytery to select Monmouth as the location for its new academy. His impassioned plea, backed by a subscription sheet from Monmouth residents, turned the tide at a heated presbytery meeting in Clayton, Illinois, in the spring of 1853.*

## The Academy Building

SHORTLY AFTER THE ESTABLISHMENT of Monmouth Academy in 1853, local banker Abner C. Harding donated a lot on North A Street to be used for a permanent building. A building committee was convened, but it took nearly two years before enough funds were raised to begin construction on the two-story brick structure, which would be 40 by 80 feet in size.

Completion of the building became urgent in 1855 when the state legislature was petitioned to grant the academy a collegiate charter, but money was still needed to pay for a roof. To the rescue came the board of trustees, each of whom resolved to lend the college $50 so the building could be completed.

For seven years, the building would serve as the college's only home, but as early as 1859 it was clear that the growing school needed more room. A tract of land was donated on the east edge of town for a new campus, and in 1863 the college relocated to its new quarters. The old building still proved useful to the college, however, serving as its preparatory school for a number of years. It later housed a popular student boarding club and became known as "The Barracks."

In 1885 a Galesburg man purchased the building and converted it into a soap factory, manufacturing a product that would become nationally known as Maple City "Self-Washing" Soap. The old academy building was demolished in 1902 after the soap company moved to a larger facility.

*Although the land on which it was built had been acquired in 1853, Monmouth College's first permanent building was not completed until 1856. It continued to be used by the college as a preparatory school after the current campus was occupied in 1863.*

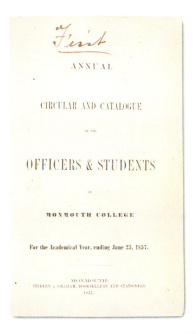
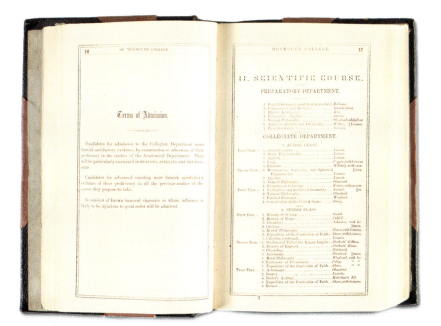

*The first annual catalog of Monmouth College was issued in 1857.*

resolution that each trustee would personally lend the college $50 to complete the building before winter.

The trustees were also moving to secure leadership and faculty for the new institution. The Reverend David Alexander Wallace, the former president of Muskingum College in Ohio, was elected the first president of the college. The Reverend Marion Morrison of Tranquility, Ohio, was appointed chair of mathematics and natural science, and James R. Brown, the principal of the Academy, was promoted to professor of ancient languages.

As September 1856 approached, it was evident that the delays in construction of the new building would keep it from being available for opening day. Determined that the college would open on time, the trustees decided to rent an old district schoolhouse, where on Wednesday, September 3, Monmouth College officially convened its first classes. By October, the brick college building on North A Street was finally completed, and faculty and students were able to move into the new structure. The three-year-old Academy became the Preparatory Department of the College and took its own place in the college building.

A few months later, on February 16, 1857, the state of Illinois granted a charter to "The Monmouth College" for "instruction of youth in the various branches of science and literature, the useful arts, and the learned and foreign languages." Control of the college was given to the Associate Reformed Synod of Illinois. The next year, the Associate Church and the Associate Reformed Church combined to form the United Presbyterian Church of North America, and legal control of the college was transferred by charter amendment to the United Presbyterian Synod of Illinois.

### Monmouth's Founding President

To lead the new institution, the board of trustees had selected a 30-year-old minister of the Associate Reformed Presbyterian Church in East

*A successful minister in Boston, David Alexander Wallace had been recommended for the Monmouth College presidency by an old friend, Matthew Bigger, a teacher at the Monmouth Academy. The two had met at Muskingum College, where Wallace was president before becoming school superintendent at Wheeling, West Virginia. When Wallace resigned the superintendent's post, he selected Bigger as his successor.*

**A College on the Frontier 1853–1860**

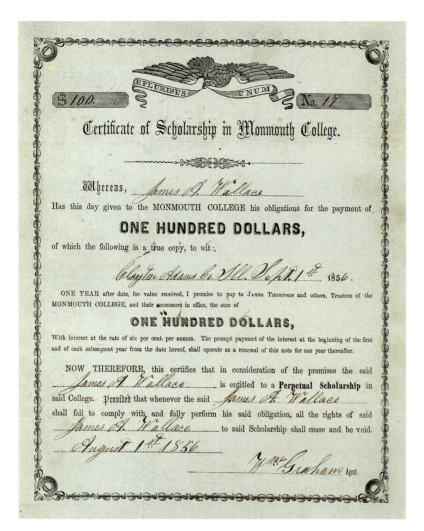

*The "perpetual scholarship" was a vehicle employed by several fledgling midwestern colleges to raise much-needed capital. At Monmouth, $100 notes were sold to the public, with the college providing scholarships to the noteholders in exchange for six percent interest—about one-fifth the actual cost of tuition. When David Wallace assumed the presidency, he immediately took steps to end this unprofitable enterprise.*

Boston, Massachusetts. The Reverend David Alexander Wallace was well known to the College trustees through the family of his wife, Martha Findley Wallace, some of whom had settled in Monmouth. But Wallace was equally attractive for his impressive academic record and his strong commitment to the ideals of Christian education.

Wallace was born in Fairview, Ohio, in 1826, the decendant of a long line of staunch Scotch-Irish Presbyterians. Exhibiting an early attraction to reading and study, he matriculated at Madison College in Antrim, Ohio, at the age of 12. After teaching school for several years as a teen-ager to support himself and his parents, Wallace entered the junior class of Miami University in Oxford, Ohio, in 1844. There he met Marion Morrison, who became his roommate and close friend. Wallace graduated in 1846 at the head of his class and, just a few months past the age of 20, moved on to become the president of Muskingum College in New Concord, Ohio.

Following three years as Muskingum College's president, Wallace resigned to assume an administrative post in the public school system of Wheeling, West Virginia. His true calling became evident, however, as he began private study and courses in theology at the Associate Reformed Presbyterian seminaries at Oxford, Ohio, and Allegheny, Pennsylvania. In 1851, Wallace was ordained by the Associate Reformed Presbytery of New York and assumed the pastorate of the Associate Reformed Presbyterian Church of Fall River, Massachusetts. In this ministry and in the one he subsequently assumed in 1854 at the Associate Reformed Mission Church in East Boston, Wallace developed into a persuasive preacher, skillful lecturer, and enthusiastic mission leader.

In choosing Wallace as its first president, Monmouth College found not only an effective teacher but an inspiring leader who could give substance to the ambitious dreams of the institution's founders. For Wallace, the presidency was particularly appealing because it fulfilled a long-held personal ambition. While still a student at Miami University, he and his friend Marion Morrison had talked often of devoting themselves to establishing a college. "Ten or 12 years before Monmouth College had an existence," Morrison later recalled, "when we were classmates and roommates in college, we often built our aircastles as to going west and building up a college, but Texas and not Monmouth was our contemplated point of operations." Now the midwestern prairie, not the Texas plains, was to be the focus of their energies, and the two friends were reunited as academic colleagues in shaping a new educational institution.

### Financial and Political Challenges

When David Wallace arrived in Monmouth in October 1856, the community bore little resemblance to the cultivated old New England towns he had left behind. Although Monmouth had received its city charter from the state in 1852, it lacked many municipal amenities. The streets were little more than muddy or dusty lanes, depending on the season. Sidewalks—

# The Theological Seminary of the West

IN ANTICIPATION OF THE PLANNED merger of the Associate Presbyterian and Associate Reformed Presbyterian churches in 1858, the Second Synod of the West directed that the theological seminary at Oxford, Ohio, be removed to Monmouth College. This was because the consolidation would have given the church four seminaries east of the state of Indiana and none in the promising western territory.

Charged with making the removal was the seminary's newly-elected professor of Hebrew and Greek exegesis, the Reverend Alexander Young. Young must have been skeptical when he first saw the little college building that would also house the seminary. At the time, its eight classrooms were stretched to capacity by 172 college students, but President David Wallace assured him that plans were already under way for a large new building just east of town. Besides, the number of seminarians Young would oversee that year totaled only eight. In addition to running the seminary, Young would also teach Greek and Hebrew at the college, and within four years would become co-pastor with David Wallace of the new college church, Second United Presbyterian. Known as the Theological Seminary of the Northwest, the institution welcomed members of all evangelical churches. Its three-year program was designed to make students familiar with the Bible by requiring them to read considerable portions in both Hebrew and Greek, and to prepare them for the ministry by delivering public sermons twice a year.

The Reverend John Scott, a native of Scotland and pastor of the nearby Henderson church, soon joined the faculty, teaching church history. The Reverend Andrew M. Black, a native of Ireland, also taught classes for a time, but low enrollments made further expansion unfeasible. By 1863, there were only 22 students, four of whom were serving in the Union Army.

After the Civil War, the seminary continued to function despite mounting financial problems. Finally, in 1874, it was brought back to Ohio and consolidated with the seminary at Xenia. Today, the Monmouth seminary is but a footnote in church history. Still, the handful of future ministers who trained there would later assist in the development of countless United Presbyterian congregations throughout the West.

*The Reverend Alexander Young, a professor of theology at Oxford, Ohio, accompanied the seminary when it moved to Monmouth in 1858. In addition to overseeing the seminary at Monmouth, he taught Bible and religion classes at Monmouth College and quickly became one of its most respected faculty members.*

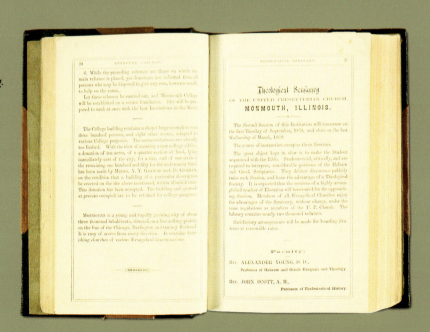

*Monmouth College first published an advertisement for the new theological seminary in its 1859 catalog. The United Presbyterian Church's efforts to recruit and educate clergy in the western territories proved less than successful, however, and low enrollments caused the seminary to be moved back to Ohio just 15 years later.*

*A College on the Frontier 1853–1860*

even plank ones—were rare, cows roamed at will, and prairie chickens could be seen flying over the public square.

For Wallace, however, the immediate future presented the challenge of finding sufficient financial support for the college. Funds were needed to hire additional faculty members, erect buildings, and purchase furniture, equipment, books, and supplies. Even more resources were needed to build the college endowment and assure economic stability for the future. The 1850s did not provide a promising environment for sustaining a new institution. In 1856, and again in 1857, farmers faced crop failures throughout the Mississippi River Valley. By 1857, the nation entered a severe financial recession with particularly harsh consequences for the Midwest.

The college's efforts to build an endowment in these conditions followed common fundraising practices of the time, however risky they would appear in hindsight. Before Wallace's arrival, the trustees had begun selling perpetual negotiable scholarships for $100 notes, each bearing six percent interest. In return, the college contracted to provide a year's tuition for a student—then about $30—for the $6 collected on the note. When this plan failed to generate sufficient income, the college modified it by offering the holders of the perpetual scholarships an opportunity to exchange them for 20-year scholarships paying 10 percent interest, an exchange most subscribers accepted. About 150 of the scholarships were sold before this plan was also abandoned.

Another fundraising plan involved the sale of scrip. For every $100 donated, the college issued $200 worth of scrip that could be exchanged for tuition. Many holders of the 20-year scholarships decided to exchange them for the scrip, while others gave up their scholarships without compensation in order to help the college with its financial problems. Unfortunately, most of the students attending Monmouth College were soon using the scrip, and the tuition that the college could have accrued was lost.

### The Growing National Crisis

Of equal if not greater concern in the late 1850s was the growing national political conflict centering on slavery and sectional division. The spirited 1858 contest for the U.S. Senate seat in Illinois pitted incumbent Stephen A. Douglas against Republican attorney Abraham Lincoln. Seven debates for the candidates were organized around the state, including one in Galesburg on October 7, when 10,000 to 20,000 people assembled in bitter, wet weather on the Knox College campus to hear Lincoln and Douglas speak. Four days later, after delivering a campaign speech in Monmouth, Lincoln entered the photographic studio of William J. Thomson and sat for one of his few known unbearded portraits.

While many Monmouth students were supporters of Lincoln and the Republicans, a significant number strongly favored Douglas and the Democrats. Douglas, who traveled as a circuit court judge, was well known to Monmouth residents. In 1841, he presided at Monmouth in a sensational hearing involving Mormon leader Joseph Smith. The town of Monmouth supported two actively partisan newspapers, the Whig-Republican antislavery *Atlas* and the Democratic antiabolitionist *Review*. When the election concluded in the fall of 1858, Lincoln had lost his bid for the Senate, but the moral and political issues of the campaign continued to resonate and grow more strident in the months that followed.

President Wallace supported the antislavery policy of the Associate Reformed Church, but he also realized that he could not give offense to partisans of either side if he hoped to secure widespread support for the college. Steering carefully between the growing political divisions of the day, Wallace sought to focus public attention on Christian education and to build a network of relationships across political and denominational boundaries that would secure the college's future.

# The "John Wayne" Connection

ON THE EVE OF MONMOUTH COLLEGE'S sesquicentennial (2002), the United States Postal Service announced plans to issue a stamp honoring John Wayne in its "Legends of Hollywood" series. Coincidentally, in the annals of Monmouth college history, an interesting connection with "The Duke" can be found.

John Wayne was a stage name. He was actually born Marion Robert Morrison—the third member of his family to bear the name "Marion." The first Marion, born in Ohio in 1821, was John Wayne's great-great uncle. He roomed with David Wallace in college and later became a colleague of Monmouth's first president, serving as professor of mathematics and natural philosophy.

When the Civil War broke out, the first Marion left the classroom to become Monmouth's financial agent, traveling widely to solicit funds for the struggling institution. In 1863, at the invitation of a former student, he visited the ninth Illinois Infantry camp in Tennessee, where he so impressed the officers of the regiment that they asked him to become their chaplain. Morrison accompanied the regiment (which suffered the heaviest loss of life of any Union regiment in the western theater) through the brutal Atlanta campaign, ministering to the soldiers' spiritual and physical needs.

The war took a physical toll on the first Marion Morrison, who spent a year recuperating in Monmouth before journeying to Lacon, Illinois, where he took charge of a United Presbyterian congregation. In 1870, he moved to Iowa, engaging in missionary work for eight years. He was then called to Mission Creek, Kansas, where he remained until 1890, building a tiny congregation into a thriving church.

Morrison's brother James, who had also emigrated to Monmouth from Ohio, greatly admired Marion and named a son in his honor. Marion Mitchell Morrison grew up in Monmouth and enlisted in Company B of the 83rd Illinois Infantry. During the Civil War, this Marion fought like a real-life John Wayne, surviving saber wounds to the chest and neck and bullet wounds to the head. After the war, he returned to Monmouth, where his son, Clyde, was born in 1884. Twenty-three years later, in Winterset, Iowa, Clyde became the father of the third Marion Morrison—the future John Wayne.

*Monmouth College's first professor of mathematics, Marion Morrison, was also a close confidant of President David Wallace. The two had been college roommates at Miami University in Ohio.*

*A College on the Frontier 1853–1860*

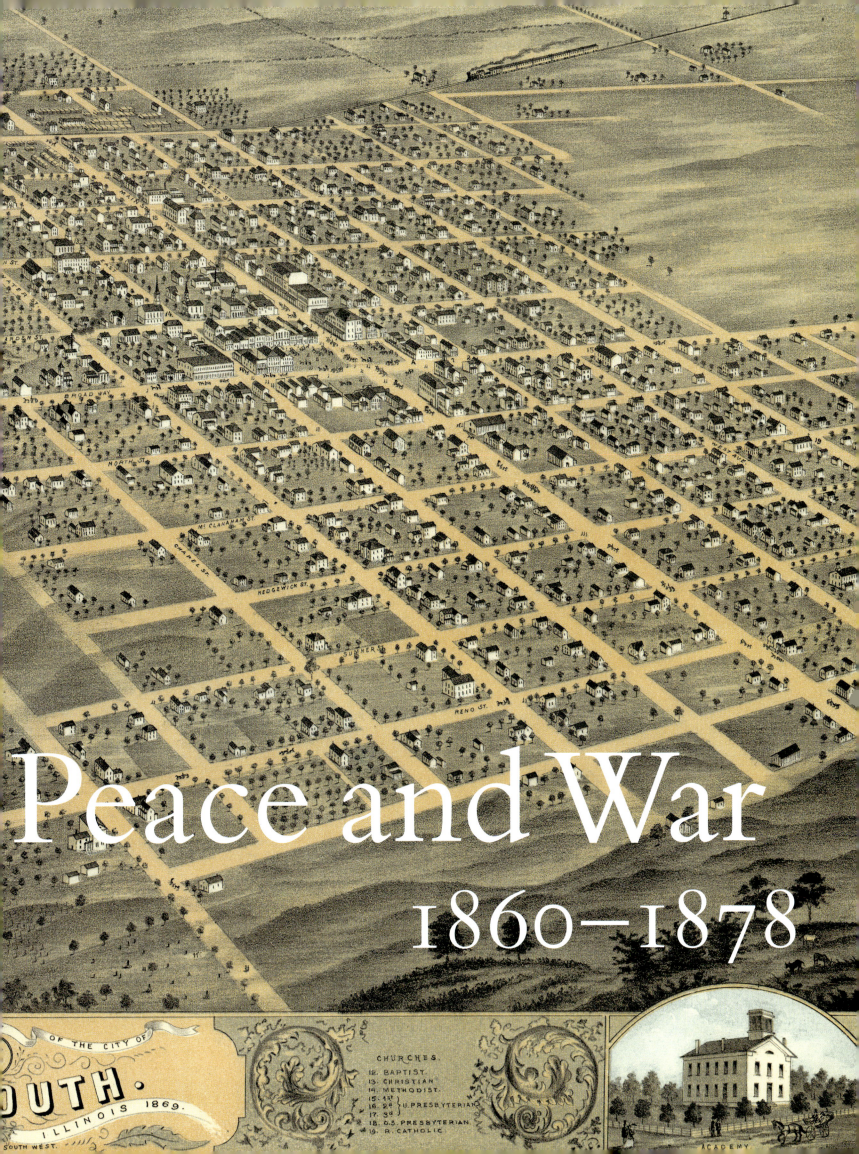

# Peace and War
## 1860–1878

# Chapter 2

The elevation of the Academy to Monmouth College in 1856 opened a period of intense activity in every aspect of the institution's work. The expansion of the faculty, the growth of student enrollment, the demand for additional space and equipment, and the need for an enlarged endowment all required careful attention and development. These concerns would have been absorbing in a time of peace, but the early years of the college were darkened by the Civil War and the impact of the national struggle on the still-fragile institution.

PRECEDING PAGES
*Detail from an 1869 panoramic map, with current and former Monmouth College buildings featured at the bottom.*

OPPOSITE PAGE
*Women practice surveying in an 1890s class.*

### Monmouth at War

The Civil War came suddenly to Monmouth College. The Confederate firing on Fort Sumter on April 12, 1861, and President Lincoln's call two days later for volunteers to meet the crisis later spurred an intense enlistment fever in towns and villages across the North. In Monmouth, a special public meeting was called in the courthouse on April 20, 1861, to form a military company to defend the Union. After 99 of the 100 men required for the company had enlisted, the chairman announced that he needed "but one more to complete the company." Josiah Moore, who had entered Monmouth College in September 1860, shouted out, "I am one Moore!" and rushed forward to sign the muster. "One Moore" was elected unanimously the captain of the new company.

Of the 100 men in the town of Monmouth who first offered their services to the military, 20 were students at the college. Before the war was over, the Monmouth student body, faculty, and trustees furnished one brigadier general, four majors, 17 captains, 13 lieutenants, one quartermaster, two adjutants, and three chaplains, for a total of 41 commissioned officers. In addition, the college furnished 48 noncommissioned officers and 143 privates to the Union army. A total of 232 Monmouth soldiers served in uniform, and of these one in eight lost his life and one in ten returned home wounded.

One company of the 83rd Regiment of Illinois Volunteer Infantry was composed primarily of Monmouth College students, all of whom enlisted and served in the field together in the pattern of Civil War recruitment. The company was led by John McClanahan, a college trustee and veteran of the War of 1812. The 83rd Regiment, of which the company was a part, was commanded by Monmouth businessman and college supporter Colonel Abner Clark Harding. McClanahan died in February 1863 at the Battle of Fort Donelson, where the 83rd Illinois repulsed attacks by a far stronger Confederate force led by Nathan Bedford Forrest. As a result of Harding's leadership of the 83rd in this crucial battle, he was promoted to the rank of general.

*Abner Clark Harding, an early trustee who gave Monmouth College $10,000 to endow a chair in English, also commanded the 83rd Illinois Infantry during the Civil War, a regiment composed of many Monmouth students. For his brilliant defense of Fort Donelson, a strategic post on the Cumberland River, Harding was immediately promoted and placed in command at Murfreesboro. On the shoulders of his dress uniform, which is still preserved, are single golden stars denoting his promotion to brigadier general.*

*Despite the heavy drain on enrollment and financial resources caused by the Civil War, President Wallace was determined that the college would remain open. His admonition that "We must educate whether there be peace or war," became a rallying cry and was even reproduced on college stationery.*

By the summer of 1862, so many students had enlisted and left for the front that Monmouth College appeared likely to close for the duration of the war. Faculty members and the remaining students were beginning to make alternate plans. At this juncture, President Wallace placed the following notice in the local newspapers:

> *The undersigned takes this method of stating that it is the full determination of the Faculty to resume the exercise of the College on the second day of next September. It is expected that every member of the faculty be at his post at the opening of the session.*
>
> *We must educate, whether there be peace or war.*
>
> David A. Wallace
> President of Monmouth College

Wallace's firm declaration not only served as a rallying point for those who wanted the mission of education to continue during the war, but it also set a high standard of commitment to education that Monmouth would maintain in all future times of war.

President Wallace increased his popularity by traveling to Fort Donelson, Tennessee, to visit Monmouth student troops on the front. Carrying letters and personal messages to the young men and to General Harding, Wallace journeyed by boat to Fort Henry on the Tennessee River, and then, with a squad of cavalry as an escort, rode cross-country in a four-mule-team army wagon to Fort Donelson.

# Monmouth's Civil War Medals of Honor

**James K. L. Duncan, U.S. Navy**

James K. L. Duncan served as an "Ordinary Seaman" in a little-known campaign of the Civil War, but his heroism under fire was so remarkable that it won him the first Congressional Medal of Honor awarded to a Monmouth student.

Duncan had been a student in Monmouth's preparatory department for little more than six months when he enlisted in the U.S. Navy in the spring of 1863. The 18-year-old Duncan was assigned to duty on the U.S.S. *Fort Hindman*, one of the Union's fleet of refitted ironclad steamboats operating on the western rivers. In early 1864, the *Fort Hindman* joined the Union's campaign in Louisiana's Red River Valley, a joint Army-Navy expedition intended to separate Texas from the Confederacy and capture stockpiled cotton for use in northern mills.

On March 2, 1864, while conducting operations on the Black River near Harrisonburg, Louisiana, Duncan's ironclad came under intense fire from Confederate artillery and sharpshooters. Onboard the *Fort Hindman*, a Confederate shell burst on deck, setting fire to the cloth tie on an artillery cartridge and threatening to produce a disastrous explosion. Acting instinctively, Seaman Duncan seized the flaming cartridge and threw it clear of the *Fort Hindman*, saving his boat and crew but shattering his right eardrum in the concussion of the exploding cartridge. Duncan's remarkable action was praised publicly by Admiral David Porter, and the U.S. Secretary of the Navy presented Duncan with the Medal of Honor.

**George H. Palmer, First Illinois Cavalry**

Only 20 years old when he enlisted as a bugler in his father's cavalry unit, Monmouth student George H. Palmer made his military reputation by leading a charge none of his fellow soldiers would undertake.

When the Civil War broke out, Palmer quickly enlisted as a musician in the First Illinois Cavalry, a local Monmouth company organized by his father. Just a few months later, on September 20, 1861, Palmer's cavalry was thrown into combat against Confederate forces in Lexington, Missouri. The Confederates had captured a house being used as a Union hospital and were using the building as blockhouse to direct deadly fire against Union troops. Two companies of Union infantry were sent to retake the hospital, and Palmer impulsively joined them. The lower floor of the building was easily seized, but none of the troops would follow their commander's order to charge up the stairway to the Confederate snipers above. At this point, Palmer wrote in his journal,

> *I ran forward and jumped onto the second step of the stairs and turned to the men and said, 'If you will follow me I will lead you! We must drive them out!' They cheered and came forward like dear brave men as they were. And on we went with a yell and a rush.*

With young cavalry bugler Palmer in the lead, the second floor of the hospital was soon retaken. Although Confederates captured the house once again and compelled the Union forces to surrender the next day, Palmer's heroism was not forgotten. In 1896, as a veteran of the western plains Indian wars and just three years before he retired from the U.S. Army as a major, Palmer was finally awarded the Congressional Medal of Honor on the basis of his selfless action on the staircase 35 years before.

*At the tender age of 20, Monmouth College student George H. Palmer led a fearless charge into a nest of Confederate gunmen, which would result in his receiving a Medal of Honor many years later.*

LEFT *In this period engraving, Monmouth College student James K. L. Duncan is depicted throwing a burning cartridge overboard the U.S.S. Fort Hindman after it was set afire by an exploding shell. He was awarded the Medal of Honor for heroism in the incident, which took place with a Confederate battery near Harrisonburg, Louisiana, in 1864.*

*Begun in 1861, Monmouth College's first substantial building was not occupied until 1863, when debt on the structure caused by numerous construction delays and the Civil War was finally liquidated. This view of Old Main, looking to the northwest, shows the three-story addition made to the rear of the building in 1876, which housed a larger chapel, library, and museum space.*

The troops greeted him eagerly, and he was cheered roundly when he returned to Monmouth and delivered his firsthand report to a crowd in the college chapel.

By late 1864, groups of returning soldiers began to appear on campus, and in June 1865 the remaining active troops came back to parade down the streets of Monmouth to the acclaim of the citizenry. By September 1865, many of the returning veterans, some of them permanently crippled on the battlefield, had resumed their college careers.

### Building a Campus

The tensions and losses of the war were not the only challenges faced by President Wallace and the Monmouth board of trustees. Within a few years of the college's opening, it was evident that growing enrollments and expanding programs would make it necessary to acquire more land and erect a larger academic building.

In 1860, brothers David and A. Y. Graham offered ten acres of farmland at the eastern edge of Monmouth to serve as the college campus. They also donated the proceeds of the sale of 25 additional acres of land, which came to be called the "College Addition" and supported a fund for erecting a new college building. The land and money were offered on the condition that a suitable brick or stone building should be started by September 1, 1861, and completed by September 1, 1864. On October 25, 1860, a committee was appointed to draw up plans for the proposed building and secure additional funds to support construction. President Wallace chaired the committee, which included a number of the college's strongest supporters, such as Ivory Quinby, James G. Madden, Abner C. Harding, Alexander Young, J. A. Young, and A. Y. Graham.

After consulting with the Chicago architectural firm of Carter and Bauer, trustee Ivory Quinby returned to Monmouth with plans for a three-story brick structure with a basement and attic. Construction began in 1861, but it was quickly interrupted when the builders gave up their contract and severed relations with the college. The building committee thereupon decided to direct the work itself and was surprised to find it was readily able to finish the job while saving $1,000 over the original contract price. The building was finally completed in August 1862, but substantial debt incurred during construction prevented the college from taking possession until the spring of 1863.

As the college continued to expand over the next decade, even this commodious structure required enlargement. In 1875, an addition to the original building provided a large chapel, library, more efficient science laboratories, natural history museum, and additional classroom and office space. The college grounds were also embellished with plantings and landscaping. Upon visiting the new campus, Marion Morrison expressed the feelings of pride that were shared by many at Monmouth:

> The campus is one of the most beautiful sites that could have been chosen, on the east and west sides little trickling rills run away toward the north and unite into one, as if to burlesque an Ohio or to strengthen one another on their long circuitous journey to the great Mississippi. From their banks the ground rises with a gentle slope till it meets the building [Old Main]. The lot is profusely adorned with forest trees of all varieties, both foreign and domestic, which are set out as nearly in imitation of nature as possible.

Buildings and land, however, were not sufficient to ensure the future of the college. To achieve this goal, a secure and growing endowment was still needed. Ivory Quinby made an important step in this direction in 1865 when he offered $5,000 toward the endowment on the condition that $45,000 in additional funds would be raised from other donors. Thanks to the energetic personal appeals of President Wallace and other college leaders, Quinby's challenge was met. By 1872, the Senate declared that an endowment of $100,000 was an absolute necessity. To advance this goal, the college issued 1,000 shares of $50 each, payable in five equal annual installments. This program was a valuable concept, but progress toward the ultimate goal of $100,000 was slow.

Still, by the late 1870s, a growing body of alumni was expressing loyalty to their alma mater with donations. More denominational support came with the attachment of the Iowa Presbyterian Synod to the Monmouth constituency in 1875. And equally important, the college appointed a treasurer to manage its business affairs, strengthening public and alumni confidence in the institution.

### Shaping Collegiate Education

From the time of its founding, the president and faculty of the college were committed to providing the best possible quality of education to their students. Speaking at his inauguration in September 1857, Wallace defined the three principal aims of a Monmouth College education: the communication of useful knowledge; the cultivation of intellectual powers; and the

*This clapper, from the Old Main cupola bell, called students to class for three decades. Currently in the college archives, it had been stolen in 1893 and was discovered between the walls in the ruins of the building after it was destroyed by fire in 1907. The bell itself, which by then had a new clapper installed, fell through to the basement during the fire and broke into pieces, which became prized souvenirs.*

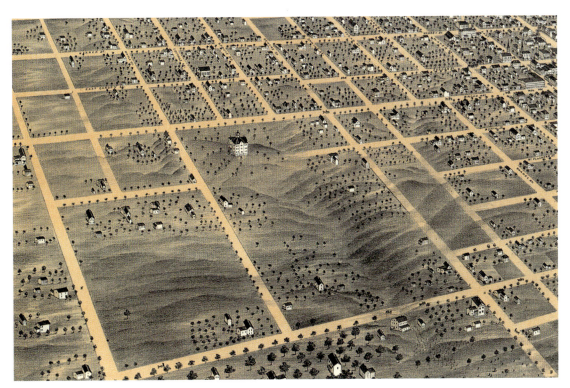

*A panoramic map of Monmouth, lithographed in 1869, shows the new college building at left center. The handful of houses in the vicinity were built within the "College Addition" to the city, land that was sold at auction to help finance the building of what would later be called Old Main.*

# Monmouth's Coeducational Tradition

AS EARLY AS THE 1860S, the Monmouth College catalog proudly proclaimed that women would be admitted "on an equal footing with men." It was a noble idea, but did early female students truly enjoy equality? A sampling of reminiscences suggests that their achievements often resulted from their own determined displays of independence.

Elizabeth Madden McClaughry, an 1859 graduate, recalled the formation of the first women's literary society—*Amateurs des Belles Lettres*—in the fall of 1857. Some had misgivings about creating an exclusively female academic society, she remembered, for in those days "any evidence of being 'strong-minded' was to be deplored in a woman."

The A.B.L. founders showed the courage of their convictions, though, when it came to appropriating a hall for their new society. Since the original college building had room only for the two men's societies, the A.B.L. women waited quietly until plans for the new college building were announced, then surprised the building committee and faculty by appearing before them and demanding their own meeting space. They stated that "if one was *not* furnished them they would no longer take part in the public exercises of the College."

Amy Rogers, Class of 1882 and a member of the Aletheorian Society, wrote that during the first years of the college, President Wallace insisted that women read their orations at public exhibitions, considering it unseemly for them to speak extemporaneously. Members of the society obliged this rule for several years, Rogers admitted, but by the time she was a student, the first evening of every term consisted of extemporaneous speeches by all Aletheorian members.

President Wallace's conservative nature also provoked the ire of Pi Beta Phi co-founder Ada C. Bruen, an 1869 graduate who would later become the mother of College President James Harper Grier. Wallace lectured women students against the custom of "permanent" gentlemen escorts, suggesting it would be better to "be independent and with lantern in hand go alone" than to be chaperoned by a particular male student. Taking him at his word, Bruen organized a company of lantern-equipped women who resolutely marched to and from the college building at night. This act of independence, it has been suggested, may have later inspired Bruen and her friends to organize the first national secret society for women.

Similarly, historians for the other national women's fraternity founded at Monmouth, Kappa Kappa Gamma, point to an 1869 lecture in Monmouth by noted social reformer Elizabeth Cady Stanton as a possible inspiration for the six young women who gathered to found Kappa the following year.

*The regulation that "ladies and gentlemen are admitted to all the privileges of the college on the same footing" meant that course requirements were identical for both sexes. Men and women enrolled in the Scientific Course during the late nineteenth century were both required to learn surveying. Taught by Thomas S. McClanahan, professor of practical surveying and engineering from 1873 to 1897 (shown standing in this 1888 photo), the skill was considered important during a largely agrarian era.*

*Lincoln's call for volunteers in April 1861 started an exodus of male students from Monmouth College that within two years would be virtually complete. In 1865, ten women comprised the entire senior class enrolled in the Scientific Course, seven of whom are pictured here. From left: Jane Graham of Wyoming, Wisconsin; Catharine McLaughry of Fountain Green, Illinois; Christiana Smiley of Monmouth; Rachel Walker of Spring Grove, Illinois; Ellen Anderson of LaPorte, Indiana; Margaret McCartney of Jacksonville, Illinois; and Harriet Paine of Monmouth.*

formation of elevated moral character. Each of these was to be supported by the highest Christian principles. "Whether we aim at communicating knowledge, training the intellect, or forming an elevated moral character," President Wallace declared, "we must use the Bible as a text book."

At the beginning of the college's work, the curriculum was experimental and limited in scope. The only core courses were the study of the Bible and related topics such as natural theology, evidences of Christianity, moral philosophy, and the principles of the Gospel. It should be noted that although the college was denominational in management, it was nonsectarian in its teaching, and students of all evangelical faiths were welcomed. This openness was reflected on the board of trustees as well. Ivory Quinby, one of the college's strongest supporters, was a devout Baptist.

In the fall of 1857, the curriculum was expanded into two courses of instruction, the Classical Course and the Scientific Course. Each in turn was divided into a preparatory department and a collegiate department. Freshmen and sophomores studied Latin and Greek and pressed their way through algebra, geometry, composition, and rhetoric. Classical Course juniors and seniors read Tacitus, Plato, and Cicero, as well as English literature, philosophy, theology, economics, and history. Scientific Course students concentrated on the sciences and higher mathematics, but their classes also included subjects such as history, English, philosophy, and rhetoric. In 1868 President Wallace introduced an Honors Course for particularly gifted students. In addition to the general baccalaureate programs, the college also developed a teacher's training course, and a special teacher's diploma was issued to the students who completed this work.

In time, a department of music and art was added, which was for the most part self-sustaining. Music courses in this department included piano, violin, and guitar. Qualified students could study vocal music and were given an opportunity for practical experience by performing before the various musical associations

*One of Monmouth's longest-tenured faculty members, John H. Wilson was hired as a Latin professor and librarian in 1861. He then chaired the mathematics department for ten years before becoming professor of Greek in 1875. In 1901, after 40 years on the faculty, he moved to Colorado, where he died in 1912.*

in the Monmouth community. The art courses included pencil sketching, pastels, and oil painting. In these and other curricular options, President Wallace and the faculty sought to recognize the diverse talents of individual students and provide opportunities for work in the fields for which they were most clearly suited.

### Creating a Student Community

One of the reasons for Monmouth's growing popularity stemmed from the fact that, from the beginning, it was a coeducational institution. The very first circular of November 1856 stated that male and female students would be admitted on the same terms. At that time, coeducation was still considered experimental, and even President Wallace was initially skeptical about its success. But Monmouth presented a progressive and western image that was in sharp contrast to the traditional all-male colleges common on the East Coast.

The organization of student life by the students themselves began as soon as the college opened its doors. On the first Friday night of the first week of the first term in 1856, while crowded into temporary academic quarters in the frame schoolhouse, 12 young men organized the first of Monmouth's famous literary societies, the Erodelphian Society, a name soon altered to Philadelphian and then shortened to Philo. At the suggestion of President Wallace, Philo was divided in January 1857, and the resulting new organization was given the name Eccritean. In the same year, women students at Monmouth organized the *Amateurs des Belles Lettres* (later known as A.B.L.). Five years later, in 1862, the second women's society was formed under the title of the Aletheorian. In addition to their social activities, the literaries promoted debate and public speaking. Monmouth was a charter member of the original Inter-State Oratorical Association formed in 1874; its purpose was to stress intellectual ability and eloquence rather than physical power and endurance.

Equally important in shaping an active student community on campus were the Greek-letter organizations that became a prominent feature at Monmouth. Monmouth lacked the resources to support fraternities in the 1850s, but veterans returning to campus after the Civil War brought an enthusiasm for adopting the Greek social system already spreading at other colleges. By 1866, Beta Theta Pi, Delta Tau Delta, and Phi Gamma Delta were established on the Monmouth campus. Within the next decade Phi Kappa Psi and Sigma Chi also established chapters at the college.

At a coeducational institution such as Monmouth, it was not long before female students began to discuss the need for social organizations of their own. The first step was

*By the late 1860s, programs and exhibitions by Monmouth College's literary societies had become popular entertainments. Pictured are a flyer for the 1868 Philadelphian or "Philo" exhibition and one for the 1869 contest between the two women's societies, Aletheorian and A.B.L. In the second flyer can be found the name of Ada C. Bruen, Pi Beta Phi founder and future mother of President James H. Grier.*

taken in the spring of 1867, when a group of Monmouth women gathered in a local home now known as Holt House to write a constitution, adopt symbols and pins, and emerge as the first American women's fraternity, I. C. Sorosis, a name later changed to Pi Beta Phi. The organization made its public debut at the chapel service on April 28, 1867, when the members paraded in as a group, each woman wearing a golden arrow in her hair as the symbol of the new organization.

The women of I. C. Sorosis were soon joined by a second secret women's organization, Kappa Kappa Gamma. While no surviving records indicate when the society was created, by April 1870 there were already six members, who met at the home of Mary Moore ("Minnie") Stewart. The group made its public debut by marching into the college chapel service on October 13, 1870, wearing the golden keys that would become the symbol of Kappa Kappa Gamma. The second member of the "Monmouth Duo" of pioneering women's fraternities may also have been the second such organization founded in the United States and the first to adopt Greek letters in its name. The only other contender for this honor, Kappa Alpha Theta at DePauw University, was founded almost simultaneously with Kappa Kappa Gamma in the spring of 1870.

The members of both I. C. Sorosis and Kappa Kappa Gamma began to contact women at other colleges to encourage the formation of chapters on their campuses. It was not long, however, before the nascent Greek movement at Monmouth was dealt a discouraging blow. In 1874, the college Senate outlawed all secret societies on the campus. The ban was prompted by the poor reputation Greek organizations had acquired at other colleges and the conviction that secret societies had no place in an institution committed to the principles of Christian education.

At first, the college did not enforce the ban on secret organizations very strictly. During this period, in fact, Elizabeth Wallace, the daughter of the president (who had belonged to a fraternity himself), was initiated into the Alpha chapter of Kappa. By 1877, however, the administration was more thoroughly enforcing the ban, and all open fraternity and sorority activities were brought to an end. Yet despite the policy against secret organizations imposed at Monmouth and many other colleges, the Greek-letter movement had played an important part in enlivening the life of students on campus and given them a sense of shared camaraderie and purpose.

ABOVE *An example of the first I. C. Sorosis pin, worn by the founders as they marched into chapel on April 28, 1867.*

LEFT *Pi Beta Phi founders Libbie Brook (left) and Ada C. Bruen (right), who shared the room at Holt House in which the women's fraternity was organized in 1867, pose with one of the Holt daughters in a period photograph.*

ABOVE *The Kappa Kappa Gamma key design was suggested by the mother of Alpha chapter founder Anna Willits, who said a key is usually associated with secrets.*

BELOW *An early set of portraits of the Kappa Kappa Gamma founders is on prominent display in Stewart House. From left are Anna Elizabeth Willits, Susan Burley Walker, Mary Moore Stewart, Hanna Boyd, Mary Louise Bennett, and Martha Louisa Stevenson.*

*During the decades that Greek organizations were banned from campus, local fraternities continued to operate in town. Kappa Alpha Sigma and Zeta Epsilon Chi, the pins of which are pictured above, were the sub-rosa incarnations of Kappa Kappa Gamma and Pi Beta Phi, respectively.*

### End of the Wallace Era

By 1875, President Wallace was showing the effects of nearly 20 years in office. From the first, Wallace had been closely involved with every aspect of the college's operations. As late as 1868, the president was still maintaining all of the academic and financial records of the institution himself.

Wallace's energies were also diverted by several lengthy pastorates in Monmouth churches. Immediately after arriving in Monmouth in 1856, Wallace agreed to become pastor of what would become the First United Presbyterian Church. He relinquished the position in 1860, but three years later he became co-pastor of Monmouth's Second United Presbyterian Church, a position he retained until December 1868. In 1873, the congregation of the Henderson church asked him to accept their vacant pastorate, and Wallace carried this responsibility until 1876. The recurring pastorates clearly offered deep satisfaction to Wallace, who remained in many ways a preacher as much as an administrator, but they also intruded on his time and contributed to his progressive physical decline.

Experiencing increasing exhaustion, Wallace submitted his resignation to the board of trustees in February 1876 but was persuaded instead to take six months' vacation. Wallace returned to Monmouth apparently reinvigorated, but by late 1877 he was again facing collapse and submitted his resignation once more. This time, the trustees reluctantly accepted his decision. Wallace left Monmouth in late December 1877 to return to the Presbyterian ministry full-time in Wooster, Ohio, where he died six years later at the age of 57.

Fittingly, Wallace's body was brought back to Monmouth for memorial honors and burial. Devoted though he was to every aspect of the ministry, his greatest and most enduring legacy was the thriving educational institution he had done so much to shape. As Monmouth's founding president and its first transforming educational leader, David Wallace remains one of the most significant figures in the college's history.

*When David Wallace assumed the Monmouth presidency in 1856, part of his salary came from the First United Presbyterian Church, where he served as pastor for four years before being asked to devote his full attention to the college. Located on the corner of West Broadway and North B Street, this wooden house of worship stood from 1856 until the 1890s.*

# The Canopus Stone

IN THE 1950S, a custodian showed Biblical archaeology professor Charles Speel chunks of plaster inscribed with Greek letters that he found under the basement stairs at Sunnyside, now Austin Hall. After taking the fragments to his classroom, where students helped piece them together, Speel noticed Egyptian hieroglyphics on the relics. He contacted Harold Ralston of the classics department, and together they found a notation in an 1882 *Monmouth Collegian* that indicated a cast of the Stone of Canopus had been presented to Monmouth College in 1872.

An article in an 1873 *Scribner's Magazine* told the story. Created in 238 B.C. by Egyptian high priests, the stone was a decree that told in three languages of a decision to correct the Egyptian calendar by tying it to the annual heliacal rising of the star Sirius. Carved in Greek, hieroglyphics, and demotic script, the stone was discovered in 1866 on a temple wall at the ancient city of Tanis by a German archaeological team. With inscriptions superior to those on the celebrated Rosetta Stone, the Canopus Stone became the real key to unlocking the mysterious hieroglyphic alphabet.

The original Canopus Stone was retained by the Egyptian Museum of Antiquities, but casts of it were made for the Royal Museum of Berlin, the British Museum, and Monmouth College. The latter cast was made at the request of the Reverend Gulian Lansing, an American Presbyterian missionary who was a member of the archaeological expedition. A year before the discovery, Lansing had been presented with an honorary degree from Monmouth. Before arriving at Monmouth, the stone made a stop at the Smithsonian Institution, where a mold was created so that future casts could be made if necessary. Monmouth's copy was displayed in the museum on the third floor of Old Main.

When Old Main burned in 1907, the plaster slab fell three stories to the basement and shattered. These were the pieces found in the 1950s.

With the assistance of President DeBow Freed and Professors Bill Urban and Tom Sienkewicz, a display case was created to house the pieces in Speel's classroom. In 1997, the case was moved to Hewes Library, where in 2001 a previously unidentified piece of the Canopus Stone was also discovered. A missing upper section containing most of the hieroglyphics has yet to be located.

*This illustration from* The Decrees of Memphis and Canopus *was published in 1904 and shows the original Canopus Stone, a slab inscribed in three languages that stood more than seven feet tall and was more than a foot thick. Discovered in Egypt in 1866, it proved to be more valuable in unlocking the mysteries of hieroglyphics than even the famed Rosetta Stone.*

mouth
1878–1903

# Chapter 3

American colleges in the late nineteenth century faced a host of challenges. At a time when the number of colleges frequently exceeded the pool of available financial resources and the supply of well-qualified teachers, every educational institution confronted difficult choices among competing demands. Monmouth College met the challenge of the late Victorian years with a fresh understanding of the ideals of Christian education. Under new leadership and with the steadfast energies of its faculty and students, Monmouth made its way into a new age.

PRECEDING PAGES *At the turn of the 20th century, Monmouth College's academic buildings consisted of Old Main and the Auditorium. This view was taken between 1896 and 1901 from the back yard of what is today Marshall Hall.*

OPPOSITE PAGE *Members of the 1904 women's basketball team.*

## The Jackson McMichael Era

A young institution's transition from its founding leader to his successor is often a crucial one. With David Wallace's resignation, Monmouth had lost its charismatic head, but the trustees acted quickly to fill the position with Jackson Burgess McMichael, a 45-year-old professor of church history at Xenia Seminary in Ohio.

When McMichael came to Monmouth in 1878 as the college's second president, he had the advantages of pastoral and teaching experience. In contrast to David Wallace's dynamic and inspirational personality, McMichael was decidedly more reserved and restrained, but his administrative skills over the next two decades proved sound and consistent, and his leadership qualities won him the respect of faculty, students, and supporters of the college.

Recognizing the principal issues that would shape his presidency, McMichael saw that while the college needed to continue to serve the needs of the United Presbyterian Church, it also had to broaden its appeal to students who were not intending to enter the ministry or take up missionary work.

McMichael was born in Poland, Ohio, in 1833 and grew up on his family's farm. After several years of independent study and tutoring, he graduated in 1859 from Westminster College in New Wilmington, Pennsylvania. Upon completing work at Xenia Seminary three years later, he was ordained and accepted the pastorate of the United Presbyterian Church in Sugar Creek, Ohio. The same year he married Mary N. Hanna. In 1872, he was appointed to the chair of church history at Xenia, but he arranged to continue his ministerial work at Sugar Creek while teaching at the seminary.

Monmouth, McMichael believed, played a crucial role in the mission of the church and the creation of an educated ministry and laity. But he also recognized that the college needed to adapt prudently to changing times by expanding its endowment, implementing modern administrative practices, and responding to the new educational and career needs of its students. If the college did not take these steps to solidify its position, McMichael wrote in 1891, people would turn away from Monmouth "like a flock of sheep from a juiceless rick of straw in early spring to pastures green."

## Modernizing the Curriculum

Jackson McMichael's most distinctive contributions to Monmouth's development came in curricular reform. While establishing new academic departments in speech and music, McMichael also placed greater emphasis on courses in history and created offerings in fields that were then considered quite novel, such as sociology, civics, economics, and psychology. In addition, with the growing popularity of all kinds of sports for both men and women, new programs were begun in athletics and physical culture.

In making these changes, McMichael and the Monmouth administration were responding to the newly emerging private and state-supported

*Jackson Burgess McMichael was not only Monmouth's second president, but he was the father of its fourth president and the grandfather of a future business manager. He started out as an apprentice carriagemaker, but his aspirations to the ministry eventually led him to the college presidency, which he assumed at the age of 45.*

universities, many of which had large sources of donor and public funding. Monmouth also faced competition from other midwestern church-based colleges, and it even found that it had to complete within its own United Presbyterian community.

Curricular change in the biological and physical sciences began to take effect in the 1890s, and by 1900 all science courses were reorganized into two departments: biology and physical sciences. Students working toward a degree in the biology department or preparing for admission to medical school took courses in invertebrate zoology and comparative anatomy, followed by courses in embryology and experimental biology. Perhaps the greatest controversy McMichael encountered was over the science curriculum. He kept Monmouth contemporary with courses reflecting Darwinism, thus setting the table for Monmouth College's science education fame in the next century.

In July 1897, Monmouth College launched the innovative Summer School of Biology on the banks of the Mississippi at Keithsburg, about 25 miles west of the campus. Founded by professor of biology Samuel Steen Maxwell, who had received his doctorate from the University of Chicago, the Monmouth Summer School of Biology and the University of Illinois research station at Havana were the only two freshwater facilities of their kind in the state.

Physical science also received renewed attention from the McMichael administration. By 1897, the physical science department was offering four courses in chemistry and one in physics. While a major in chemistry was not yet available, all sophomore students were required to take a general chemistry course, and more advanced courses in quantitative and organic chemistry were offered in the senior year.

*The chemical laboratory on the third floor of Old Main (1893).*

*When Monmouth College was founded, the town's public square was nothing more than a muddy plaza surrounded by a few rustic buildings. By the 1890s, the college had matured into a respected institution, while the square had acquired a formal park surrounded by an iron hitching rail, paved streets, and substantial examples of Victorian architecture.*

*An 1890s view looking southwest from the cupola of Old Main shows a growing number of fine homes and a skyline dotted by church spires and factory smokestacks.*

As with the sciences, the arts were also the focus of expanded offerings in the McMichael years. In both speech and music, Monmouth made its first efforts to bring students the benefits of modern technical training in the arts.

The college first engaged in intercollegiate oratorical contests beginning in 1873 and was a charter member of the Inter-Collegiate Oratorical Association, but it was not until the 1890s that a formal speech department was organized. The McMichael administration responded to student demand by adding elocution to one professor's duties and then another's, until the outlines of a speech program slowly began to develop. The elocution curriculum in place by the turn of the century called for "free gymnastics" and breathing exercises to strengthen the chest; after studying selections in English literature, the speech student moved on to master facial expression and gestures, with special attention given to classical literature and individual performance. At the end of the program, the students appeared on the public platform to receive the critiques of classmates and the instructor.

Monmouth's emphasis on oratorical and debating skills paid rich dividends in intercollegiate competitions. In 1880, James E. Erskine

*During the era when secret organizations were banned, most student social gatherings were the province of the literary societies, as was this outdoor "roast" sponsored by the Philadelphian Society. This image is from the scrapbook of Clara Kongable '15, herself a member of the Aletheorian Society.*

# Early Campus Social Life and the Literary Society

FOR MANY YEARS, student-run literary societies formed the core of campus social life, promoting student interest in debate and public speaking while stressing intellectual ability and eloquence.

Meetings of the four literaries—Philo, Eccritean, A.B.L., Aletheorian—typically opened with a debate on a leading issue of the day, followed by oratory, recitation, and what was called "sentimental" debate, when all members joined in discussing a single question. Led by the society's vice president, members critiqued performances, usually in a lighthearted vein. The evening concluded with a business meeting and the acceptance and initiation of new members by oath. Over time, the societies began to introduce variations to the program, including performances by musical quartets or visiting bands.

Rivalries between literary societies were intense. While competition focused on attracting and holding members or harmless pranks and practical jokes, it sometimes produced vandalism and fistfights. Literary societies also helped create unity. When debates were held in Galesburg or another nearby city, Monmouth students rented an excursion car or two from the Burlington Railroad and rode into declamatory battle as a group, their journey lightened by the music of a thumping brass band.

Around these basic rituals other traditions developed. One of the most strongly entrenched was Peanut Night. After Philo and Eccritean elected orators for the annual Philo–Eccritean contest, students bought large quantities of peanuts and treated other members of the clubs. Over the years, oranges, bananas, and apples were added, and students began the custom of marching around town to faculty homes, where peanuts and fruit were given to professors. Societies later added a marching band and speeches. By 1915, Peanut Night had become a full-blown annual banquet held downtown at the Colonial Hotel. The variety and size of dishes was invariably immense, but the lowly peanut always reigned.

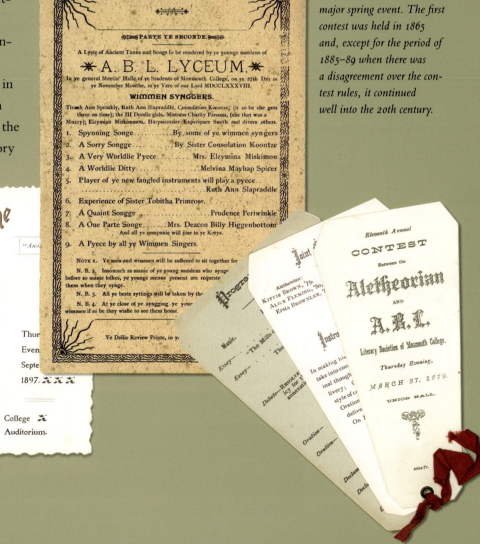

*The annual contest between literary societies was a major spring event. The first contest was held in 1865 and, except for the period of 1885–89 when there was a disagreement over the contest rules, it continued well into the 20th century.*

**Victorian Monmouth 1878-1903**

*Located near the southeast corner of Broadway and Eleventh Street, Monmouth College's original athletic grounds were a popular destination for outings to watch football, track, and baseball. During the 1890s, the baseball diamond was also home to a professional club, which occasionally played traveling Major League teams. The land was sold in the 1920s, when playing fields were constructed on campus.*

of Monmouth defeated two young competitors, William Jennings Bryan of Illinois College and Jane Addams of the Rockford Female Seminary, in the state intercollegiate oratory competition. During the years from 1873 to 1900, Monmouth College won five state firsts and six state seconds.

Music instruction followed the same pattern of a slowly developing program that improved substantially by the end of the century. Students had always been free to secure private instruction, but individual lessons were expensive, and not all students could afford them. As late as 1883, Monmouth College did not even own a piano. This situation began to change in the 1890s, when E. C. Zartman and J. B. Herbert developed a systematic program of music instruction. The aim of the new department was to teach music not just as an ornamental art but as "a part of a complete education, a higher culture." Within a few years, courses were being taught in piano, guitar, and organ, and a full four-year curriculum leading to a diploma was available for students of the piano.

The prestige of the music department was enhanced considerably in March 1897, when Monmouth opened the College Auditorium, its new space for chapel services, assemblies, and musical performances. The Auditorium was the first of several buildings designed for the college by Dan Everett Waid '87, an architect in Chicago who would later practice in New York. The Auditorium provided the college with a much-needed main hall that seated more than 800, as well as a smaller public hall and a music conservatory with practice studios. The Auditorium marked the culmination of the first sustained effort to enrich the cultural life of Monmouth's campus community.

### The Rise of College Sports

Few trends in American society of the 1890s drew more enthusiasm than the new fascination with physical fitness and competitive sports. Benefiting from growing amounts of leisure time and drawn to the ideal of vigorous health, middle-class Americans turned to bicycling,

*One of four society rooms in Old Main, the Philadelphian or "Philo" Room was the meeting place of a society founded during the first week of the college's existence. Philo was later divided into two separate societies at the urging of President Wallace to encourage a healthy rivalry. When Old Main was built, the Philos "bribed" their Eccritean rivals with $45 for the choice of a meeting room in the new building.*

gymnastics, tennis, and team sports in growing numbers. American colleges were strongly influenced by these developments, and intercollegiate competition on the playing field soon became a prominent fixture of campus life.

Team sports at Monmouth had their beginning after the Civil War, when Union veterans returning to the college began playing intramural rounds of baseball, a game they learned from fellow soldiers in the military camps. In 1891, another sport was introduced when Monmouth played its first official football game against Knox College. This game inaugurated the second-oldest college rivalry west of the Alleghenies. Monmouth was crowned the "college champion of Illinois" in 1905 and repeated in 1906 when the team recorded its first perfect season with an 8–0 record.

The college responded to the obvious interest of Monmouth students in 1894 by acquiring its first athletic field, a ten-acre tract of land on the southeast corner of Eleventh Street and East Broadway. Easily accessible by the Broadway streetcar, which ran past campus, the "11th Street Ball Park" was soon developed into a multisport complex, with a baseball diamond, a football gridiron, and a running track.

Monmouth's leaders also realized the need to incorporate athletics into the pattern of college education. In 1893, the first physical culture class was added to the curriculum. The college also arranged for male athletes to use the local YMCA

*The basketball team of 1902–03 did not have a winning record, but it created so much enthusiasm for the new sport that a spectator gallery was built overlooking the court. The gymnasium was so tiny that there was no room for bleachers at ground level.*

Victorian Monmouth 1878–1903

PRECEDING PAGES
*In 1891, tennis became an intercollegiate sport for Monmouth men. The coeducational Lawn Tennis Association had about 40 members, and permanent courts were erected near what is now Stockdale Center.*

LEFT *The class of 1887 wasn't large, but it dressed to the hilt for this senior photo, taken on the front steps of Old Main in the spring. Seated near the front right with his hat on his lap is Dan Everett Waid, who would become a noted New York architect and who would influence much of the architectural landscape of Monmouth College.*

OPPOSITE PAGE
*Because there was no space in the gymnasium for locker rooms, the women's basketball team (pictured here in 1904) had to dress in the Auditorium and walk next door to play their games. Despite the fact that women wore knee socks, President McMichael issued an edict that college men were to stay clear of the gymnasium door, lest they catch a glimpse of a young lady's ankle.*

gymnasium for their workouts and basketball games.

Men, however, were not alone in their obsession with the new competitive athletic contests. As Monmouth women students became more independent, they wanted to gain the same equal access to sports that they already enjoyed in the classroom. The YMCA might have been an agreeable makeshift home for male student athletes, but women could not use the facilities. Monmouth women began to agitate for the college to build its own gymnasium, and they were joined by male athletes, alumni, and even some of the faculty. Relenting to these demands, the Monmouth College administration began to draft plans for a gymnasium in 1897. The building, though, was not completed until 1902, and it was manifestly intended to be "temporary." Nonetheless, with a basketball court and subsequent addition of a perimeter running track, the gymnasium provided Monmouth's students with their first all-season home for physical culture and athletics.

But the women athletes of Monmouth were not satisfied. In 1900, a group of 14 women signed a declaration of athletic independence that read in part:

> *When in the course of college events it becomes necessary for the girls of M.C. to play Basket Ball in order to more completely develop their physical natures and to assume among the colleges of the land as great fame in athletics as the boys have long since acquired, a decent respect for the opinion of the public requires that they should declare the cause which impels them to do so.*
>
> *We hold these truths to be self-evident, that man and woman are created equal; that they are endowed by their Creator with certain inalienable rights, that among these are life, liberty, and the pursuit of happiness, that it is the right of the students to alter or abolish any custom not conducive to these ends.... Heretofore the exercise of the girls has been limited to cycling, tennis, Indian clubs, "skittering," and strolls—exercises good in themselves, but insufficient for the total development of their physical powers, which make the women of the nineteenth century loved and respected.*

Victorian Monmouth 1878–1903

*For more than four decades a stream ran through the middle of the Monmouth campus and was traversed by a long wooden bridge where it crossed Ninth Street. A popular trysting spot, the bridge also had historical significance. It was on this bridge that "two girls one day held a schoolgirls' conversation out of which grew the Kappa Kappa Gamma sorority." It was near the bridge that as a child John F. Wallace, Class of 1872, built his first dam. Wallace became the first chief engineer for the Panama Canal.*

*We, therefore, members of the first and third teams, as representatives of the Girls' Basket Ball Association of Monmouth College, do, in the name and by the authority of the good girls of the college, solemnly publish and declare that the girls of the college shall play basket ball.*

For both the women and men of Monmouth, athletic competition was not a mere diversion for leisure hours, it was a key element in their personal development and a point of pride in their college.

### A Testing of Limits

In 1897, after 19 years in office, President Jackson McMichael submitted his resignation. As he stepped down, McMichael could look back with satisfaction on his considerable achievements in expanding the curriculum and increasing the College endowment to $100,000. Yet much remained to be done, and a range of pressing issues would now devolve upon his successor.

Samuel Ross Lyons, the third president of Monmouth College, arrived in June 1898 and was the first alumnus to hold the position. He had served as a drummer boy in the Union army during the Civil War and graduated from Monmouth as a nontraditional student at the age of 28. Now, after a pastorate at a United Presbyterian Church in Indiana, he was called back to his alma mater. The opportunities before him were great, but so were the challenges. Monmouth College faced the continuing need to strengthen its financial resources while developing new curricular offerings and expanding the recruitment of new students.

Soon after he assumed the presidency, it was apparent that Lyons did not offer the best fit for

*One of only two Monmouth graduates to assume the presidency, Samuel Ross Lyons had a troubled administration and eventually resigned in 1901 over a disagreement with the faculty and Senate. Ironically, Lyons had previously been an influential member of the Senate before accepting the Monmouth presidency.*

# Monmouth's Old Mill Stream

CEDAR CREEK, a small, meandering stream located about five miles north of Monmouth, is undistinguished as creeks go, but its connections to Monmouth College run deep. It was on the banks of the Cedar in 1828 that Adam Ritchie built one of the first cabins in Warren County. Nearby, the Associate Reformed Presbyterians established the Cedar Creek Church, and welcomed their first pastor, the Reverend James C. Porter, in 1840. The church soon split into two congregations, with the Reverend Robert Ross pastoring at the new South Henderson Church. In 1852, Porter and Ross together would lead a successful campaign to establish a Presbyterian academy at Monmouth—the forerunner of Monmouth College.

Meanwhile, in 1834, Aniel Rogers had bought property along Cedar Creek from Adam Ritchie and built a sawmill. Shortly thereafter, the mill was sold to Silas Olmstead, who converted it to a gristmill. The picturesque setting, which included a manmade dam and waterfall, in time became a favorite leisure spot for Monmouth residents. Monmouth College students were no exception, holding class and club picnics there on a regular basis. By the turn of the century, Olmstead's Mill had ceased operation, but the popularity of the picnic grounds would remain undiminished for decades.

Today's Monmouth College students probably could not locate Cedar Creek on a map, but its legacy is still part of the college landscape. Dotting the lawn in front of Wallace Hall are large, white-painted limestone boulders. They were dragged from the bed of Cedar Creek through brute force and transported to campus by horse-drawn wagon. They stand today as memorials, each inscribed with the graduating year of the class that erected it. Another campus landmark is the famous Civil War cannon, intended as a gift from the Class of 1903 but stolen by the Class of 1904, which deposited it in the muddy waters of Cedar Creek, where it lay hidden for half a century.

*The most popular picnic spot for college men and women in the 1890s was near the former Olmstead's Mill on Cedar Creek, north of the city. Although the attire of these women does not seem well-suited for "roughing it," it was probably the most casual clothing they owned. Close inspection reveals they may have been out for some target shooting.*

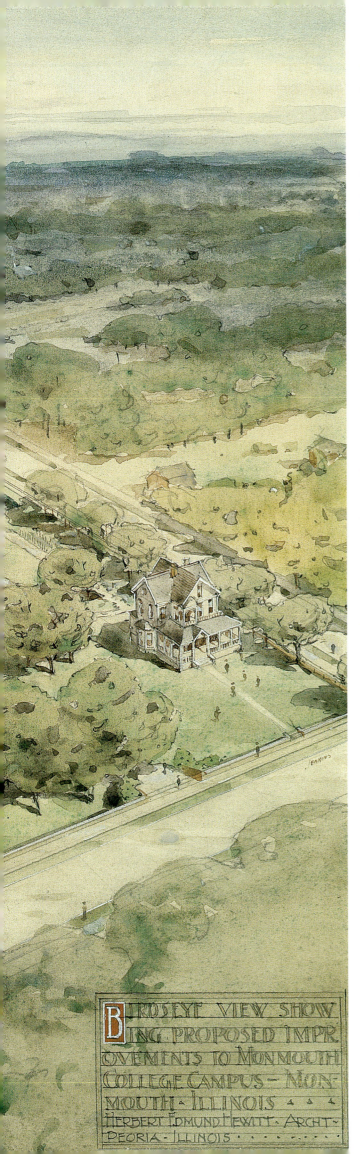

the expectations of the institution or its faculty. Seeking to reduce expenditures, Lyons asked several senior faculty members with higher salaries to retire. This inflamed not only the affected faculty but also those who felt loyal to their older colleagues. Lyons also believed that as president he should have the authority to hire and dismiss faculty members on his own initiative. When Lyons submitted his arguments to the annual meeting of the Senate in June 1900, his case was rejected on the grounds that it did not conform to the history and traditions of the institution or the college's state charter.

The stresses of the Lyons administration appeared likely to cause further disruptions to the campus community, but they were brought to an early end in the spring of 1901. With the unexpected death of Mrs. Lyons, President Lyons submitted his resignation and left the post he had held for only three years. Despite the circumstances, Lyons was to remain a loyal supporter of Monmouth for the rest of his life. Monmouth College entered an uneasy interim, its leadership in doubt and its prospects for the future temporarily clouded.

However, before he left, President Lyons did advance the careers of several key teachers who would become some of Monmouth's most important faculty members. He established the college's first independent department of history and installed Florabel Patterson at its head. He also added Luther Emerson Robinson to the faculty as professor of English.

Perhaps most notable was Lyons's appointment of Alice Winbigler to head the department of mathematics. The 1877 Monmouth graduate had begun teaching at her alma mater in 1879 and was made an associate professor of mathematics in 1894. The following year, after a summer at the University of Chicago, she became professor of mathematics and astronomy, and when her mentor (and former professor) John Rogers decided to retire, he asked that Winbigler be his successor. President Lyons concurred, appointing Winbigler to the position she would hold until her retirement after 50 years of teaching and administrating.

*At the turn of the twentieth century, a master plan was devised for the eventual construction of a modern college campus. This bird's-eye view, prepared by the Peoria architecture firm of Herbert Hewitt, never materialized exactly, although much of the general layout was followed. Pictured counter-clockwise from bottom left are the Auditorium, the president's manse, the science hall, the ladies' dormitory, the heating plant, an unknown building, the library, and the gymnasium. In the center is Old Main, which burned in 1907. The mystery structure may have been a memorial to David Wallace, which was being planned at the time. Its purpose is uncertain, but there was talk of the literary societies erecting their own hall so that the rooms they occupied in Old Main could be converted into classrooms and offices.*

Victorian Monmouth 1878–1903

omes of Age
1903–1920

# Chapter 4

The turn of the century brought Monmouth College into years of great uncertainty and challenge. The viability of the college, the nature of its leadership, and the prospects for its future growth all seemed open to question. But just at this crucial juncture a new leader was found, and in his confident and assured manner the trustees, faculty, and students found renewed hope and cause for expectation.

The sudden resignation of Samuel Lyons in June 1901 left Monmouth College in an uneasy interregnum. In the absence of a president, three faculty members assumed

PRECEDING PAGES *The faculty in 1907. Front row, from left: Alice Jeanette Tinker '05, mathematics and history; Russell Graham '70, vice president of the college and professor of social science; President T. H. McMichael '86; Alice Winbigler '77, mathematics and astronomy; and Albert Fulton Stewart '08, Latin. Middle row: Andrew Graham Reid, director of athletics; John Henry McMillan, Latin; Florabel Patterson, history; George Herbert Bretnall, biology; Luther Emerson Robinson, English; Thomas Beveridge Glass '92, Greek; and Isabelle Rankin Irwin '03, English. Back row: G. Edgar Turner, oratory; and John Nesbit Swan, chemistry and physics.*

OPPOSITE PAGE *Thomas Hanna McMichael was the epitome of vigor and youth when he accepted the Monmouth presidency in 1903.*

*October 27, 1903, was a banner day for Monmouth College, as it inaugurated its second President McMichael. The college classes led the inaugural procession from Old Main to the president's manse on its way to the Auditorium, where ceremonies would be held. The classes were followed by dignitaries (from right): J. C. Hutchinson, professor emeritus; President-Elect McMichael; Thomas McCracken, student representative; Joseph Kyle, Senate representative; H. F. Wallace, brother of the first Monmouth president; J. Ross Hanna, chairman of the board; and J. R. Thompson, representative from Tarkio College.*

responsibility for leading the institution. John Henry McMillan, the vice president under President Jackson McMichael, took on the role of acting president. Russell Graham, professor of history and sociology, and John Nesbit Swan, professor of chemistry and physics, assisted McMillan in managing the college. While Monmouth's trustees searched for a successor over the next two years, the college remained in stasis. By the spring of 1903, only 143 students were enrolled in regular courses, and serious financial problems loomed.

Into this breach stepped one of the most dynamic figures in Monmouth's history. Thomas Hanna McMichael, the son of Jackson McMichael, was born in Ohio and came to Monmouth when his father assumed the presidency in 1878. Young Tom finished his pre-collegiate training in the Monmouth public schools and entered Monmouth College in 1882 at the age of 19. The first years of his collegiate career were famously erratic. After breaking up a meeting of the Christian Union and behaving in a disorderly fashion in chapel, Tom was expelled from college at the request of the faculty and with the concurrence of his father, the first President McMichael. As with most misbehaving students who were suspended during this era, Tom was readmitted within a few weeks, and he returned to classes sobered if not entirely chastened.

Despite this reverse, in his last two years of college Tom McMichael showed welcome signs of a growing maturity. His abundant natural talents as a writer and public speaker became steadily more apparent. He also won acclaim for his prowess as a star pitcher on the Monmouth baseball team, once winning both games of a doubleheader over the University of Illinois. Most surprising, following his graduation in 1886, Tom McMichael chose to follow in the footsteps of his father by entering the ministry. He graduated from the United Presbyterian seminary in Xenia, Ohio, in 1890, married his college sweetheart the same year, and assumed successive pastorates in Indiana and Ohio. He was in the seventh year of his career, serving as minister at the First United Presbyterian Church of Cleveland, when the Monmouth trustees called on him to take on his father's mantle and accept the college presidency.

McMichael's inauguration on October 27, 1903, brought an immediate change in the campus mood. Handsome, gregarious, and persuasive, the young President McMichael radiated confidence in the future, and his enthusiasm was soon shared by trustees, faculty, students, and friends of Monmouth College. Within three years, the local Monmouth *Atlas* was praising McMichael as a sterling educator, scholar, businessman, diplomat, and executive. While improving town-gown relations, McMichael also raised the college's profile within the United Presbyterian Church and led the college to greater influence within the denomination than ever before in its history.

### Trial by Fire

T. H. McMichael nurtured great ambitions for Monmouth College, but he knew his dreams would not be realized without substantial physical improvements to the campus. In 1903, the college grounds were occupied by Old Main, the Auditorium, the president's house, the janitor's house, and the small, temporary frame gymnasium—a physical plant valued at only $90,000. Drawing on his skills as an advocate, McMichael was able to persuade the college's trustees and friends to support a dramatic effort to reshape Monmouth's physical environment.

In 1906, industrialist and philanthropist Andrew Carnegie offered the college $30,000 for the construction of a library on the condition that Monmouth match the gift with a $30,000 maintenance fund. In the face of discouraging economic conditions, President McMichael launched an energetic fundraising campaign and within one year secured the necessary funds. By commencement in the spring of 1907, the cornerstone of the library was laid, and construction

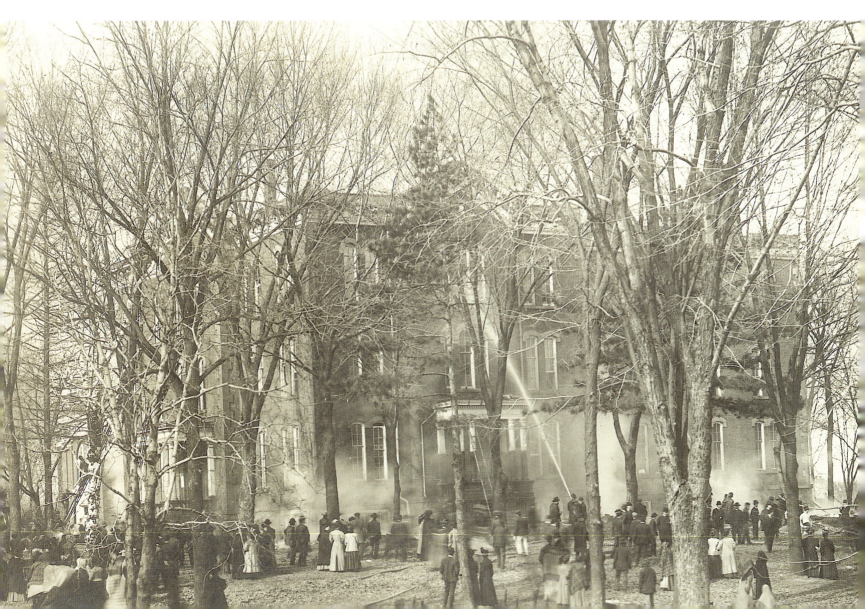

*In vain, firefighters train water on the east entrance of Old Main as students and townspeople look on.*

*By the evening of November 14, 1907, all that remained of Monmouth's once-proud academic building was an empty shell.*

*OPPOSITE: Within months of the devastating fire that destroyed Old Main, construction was well under way for the new academic hall, named in memory of Monmouth's first president. Selected by architect and alumnus Dan Everett Waid, the Georgian-style design for the edifice would influence the architecture of the college campus to the present day.*

was begun on a central heating plant to replace the separate furnaces and boilers in individual buildings.

On the morning of November 14, 1907, all of Monmouth's newfound optimism was suddenly imperiled. Sparked by a defective attic chimney, fire broke out in the rafters of Old Main, and flames were soon pouring through the ceiling of the third-floor biology lecture room. As Old Main began to fill with smoke, faculty and students interrupted their classes and evacuated the building in orderly fashion. The eaves of Old Main were enveloped in flame, and by the time firemen arrived, the entire roof was burning fiercely. Faculty, students, and townspeople threw themselves into a desperate effort to save as much as possible of the college's furniture, books, and laboratory equipment. The roaring fire continued to burn throughout the day, destroying the roof, setting off an explosion in the chemistry lab, collapsing the floors, and buckling all but the front walls of the building into the basement. By evening, Monmouth's proudest symbol and strongest link to its past was a smoking ruin.

President McMichael faced the greatest test of his young presidency. With diligent assistance from the faculty, classes were shifted to the Second United Presbyterian Church, the Auditorium, the Gymnasium, and the homes of professors. Construction of the Carnegie Library was rushed to completion, and it was soon serving as the college's principal classroom building. While many courses in arts and literature were able to resume in short order, courses in the sciences had no adequate laboratory space, little equipment, and few supplies and materials that had not been consumed in the fire.

### Enhancing the Campus

Faced with these needs, Monmouth's president and trustees committed themselves to a $150,000 campaign to replace Old Main and construct two additional campus buildings, a scientific laboratory and a residence hall. The new "Old Main," to be named after President Wallace, was planned first. The college opened a competition for architectural designs, and the seven best plans were referred to alumnus architect Dan Everett Waid for his judgment. Waid selected the plans of Herbert E. Hewitt of Peoria, and the cornerstone for the new structure was laid on June 10, 1908. By late in the year, Wallace Hall, with its impressive entrance pillars, was nearing completion, and on February 8, 1909, with

*The chemistry laboratory on the top floor of McMichael Hall was one of 13 laboratories in the building. The tabletops, wood floors, and table shelving on the chemistry floor required 28 tons of Alberene soapstone.*

*A thoroughly modern building for its day, the new science hall was named in memory of President J. B. McMichael and was designed largely by chemistry and physics professor J. N. Swan, who had visited many of the leading laboratories on the East Coast to gather ideas for the architects.*

work on upper floors still continuing, the first classes were convened on the building's first floor. On February 22, 1909, the completion of Wallace Hall was formally celebrated with class banquets at noon and a large town and gown evening dinner in the building's basement.

Attention next turned to the needs of science. Working with architects Whitefield and King of New York, John Nesbit Swan, professor of chemistry and physics, developed specifications for Monmouth's new Jackson B. McMichael Science Hall, completed in 1910. The first floor was devoted to laboratories for biology, histology, botany, and zoology, along with a dissecting room and darkroom. The second floor held space for chemistry, with laboratories in quantitative, qualitative, organic, and general chemistry.

The crowning achievement of Thomas McMichael's ambitious building campaign was one that held a special place in his heart. The president felt strongly that it was essential for Monmouth College to create a supportive residential environment for its women students, an enhancement that he called a "ladies' home." The cost of Wallace Hall and McMichael Science Hall had proven greater than anticipated, and the construction of a dormitory for women was postponed for a time. With the president's persistent expression of interest, however, architect Dan Everett Waid was persuaded to offer his services once more and draw up plans for a building of impressive scale. Rising three stories above ground level with a basement and subbasement, McMichael Home (later McMichael Residence Hall) provided living quarters for 85 women students, a dining hall and kitchen, recreational rooms, and an infirmary. McMichael Home opened in September 1914, offering a comfortable and capacious residence appropriate for modern women at a rising educational institution.

The completion of Carnegie Library, Wallace Hall, and McMichael Science Hall, which all

# The Architect of Monmouth College: Dan Everett Waid

OVER THE PAST 150 YEARS many Monmouth College graduates have gone on to fame and fortune, but few have given back to their alma mater to the extent of architect Dan Everett Waid.

Waid, who moved to Monmouth at the age of 14, was a member of the Class of 1887 and a college chum of future president T. H. McMichael. The pair's fathers, Andrew Jackson Waid, a prominent local dentist, and J. B. McMichael, the president of Monmouth College, were also close friends.

As a teenager, Dan Waid spent hours in the workshop behind the family home on North Third Street creating beautiful wooden objects with a scroll saw. Recognizing his potential, Waid's father encouraged him to pursue a career as an architect. Upon earning his bachelor's degree, Waid found a job as a bookkeeper at the construction site of a large grain elevator at Dubuque, Iowa, where he gained knowledge of practical construction methods. He then moved to Chicago, securing a position as draftsman in the office of prominent architects Jenney & Mundie, where he rose to the position of head draftsman. In 1894, after taking a course at the Art Institute of Chicago, he decided to become an independent architect.

Waid's early commissions were modest, but his career took off when he was commissioned to draw the plans and specifications for the Silver Cross Hospital in Joliet, Illinois. Then in 1896 he embarked on what would be a lifelong relationship with Monmouth College, designing its Auditorium, an Old English-style chapel seating 900.

In 1898 Waid and an associate submitted the winning design for the Long Island College Hospital in Brooklyn, New York. Working as their own draftsmen and specification writers, they moved to Brooklyn and toiled day and night until the job was completed. Waid then opened a small office on Fifth Avenue in New York and shortly thereafter was appointed architect for the Board of Foreign Missions of the Presbyterian Church. Over the years, the board would call on Waid to design hospitals in Puerto Rico and Alaska and school buildings in Cuba and the western United States.

Waid's career reached its pinnacle when he became chief architect for the Metropolitan Life Insurance Company and moved his offices to the Metropolitan Tower at One Madison Avenue. His initial job was rating and valuing buildings offered as security for loans, but soon he was designing buildings for the company, the most notable of which was the new Home Office Building at 11 Madison Avenue, designed with his friend Harvey Wiley Corbett. Originally planned to be the tallest building in the world at 100 stories, it was a victim of the Depression and was capped off at 29 floors in 1933.

While Waid's stature as an architect grew, he never forgot his Monmouth roots or his friendship with the McMichael family. When Monmouth College's Old Main burned in 1907, he personally supervised the selection of architects for the new Wallace Hall. He helped in the planning of the McMichael Science Hall and designed and supervised construction of the college's first dormitory, McMichael Home. He also designed the gymnasium and gave the $10,000 necessary to install its swimming pool. When Waid's wife and college sweetheart, Eva, died in 1929, he endowed a fine arts department at Monmouth College in her memory.

Waid's death came ten years later, in 1939, but his influence at Monmouth College continued for years to come. His associate, Arthur O. Angilly, designed Grier Hall (1940), Winbigler Hall (1946), and Fulton Hall (1951).

*Dan Everett Waid had aspirations of becoming an architect when he graduated from Monmouth College in 1887. Nine years later he designed the college Auditorium, the first in a long series of projects for his alma mater. As a prominent New York City architect, he not only directed the shape of the modern campus but became one of the college's most generous benefactors.*

*Built largely without the aid of modern machinery, McMichael Home, a spacious new women's residence hall, rises on the east side of campus in 1913. President McMichael's determined efforts to raise money for a women's dormitory during difficult financial times caused the trustees to name the building in his honor.*

occurred within three years, brought 50,000 square feet of new floor space, classrooms, offices, laboratories, and library stacks to the Monmouth campus. To this was now added the living space of McMichael Home, a building that alone cost $120,000, or the equivalent of more than $2 million in today's currency. By the standards of any other college of the time, T. H. McMichael had built expansively, and Monmouth would benefit from his vision and its donors' generosity for years to come.

*Although pictured here as a member of the 1917–18 men's basketball team, F. L. "Jug" Earp '21 (back row, second from right) would achieve fame as a football player, playing center for the Green Bay Packers from 1922 to 1932 and winning three championship rings. Related distantly to the legendary Wyatt Earp, the colorful athlete earned his nickname from the discarded stoneware he would bring home from the Monmouth pottery where he worked.*

### The Rise of Monmouth Athletics

Baseball had been played enthusiastically since the Civil War, and for some years it seemed to be the only sport many Monmouth students cared about. The turn of the century, however, brought new games to Monmouth and other college campuses, and they would begin to redefine the meaning of college spirit.

The first official basketball games took place in 1900, when Monmouth played Lombard College of Galesburg three times and the YMCA team of Galesburg once. Managed by Roland Hamilton, the first team on the court included captain Frank Gainer, W. M. Clarke, John Cusack, John Wallace, and Bert Marshall, whose son Dr. James Marshall would later serve as the college's team physician for more than 40 years. The record compiled by the earliest Monmouth basketball teams was uneven at best. Sometimes Monmouth finished with a winning record, but in other years the basketball team struggled far below the .500 mark.

The football teams did far better. The first informal football games at Monmouth were played sometime in the 1880s, but it was not until 1893 that the college hired its first football coach, J. A. McGaughey, who in the custom of the time both coached and played left tackle.

McGaughey was the first of a long string of gridiron leaders; between 1893 and 1925, Monmouth had no fewer than 33 different coaches.

In the 1890s, Monmouth often played against such larger rivals as the University of Chicago, Illinois State University, and Drake University. This demanding competition seems to have been beneficial, for by the 1906 season under coach C. Clifford Bell, Monmouth developed its first great football team. In that year, Monmouth beat all of its opponents, outscoring them 217 to 9, and decisively defeated Beloit, the champion of both Wisconsin and Michigan, in the final game. From 1906 to 1910, coach A. G. Reed introduced the forward pass to Monmouth, and the college continued to sustain its fearsome reputation.

In 1912, the Athletic Conference of the Middle West was established, also known as the Little Five. Monmouth joined along with Knox, Beloit, Millikin, and Lake Forest Colleges. Monmouth was also considered part of the Little Nineteen conference, which was composed of all the colleges in Illinois and which determined the state championship.

Monmouth produced another legendary football team in 1914 under coach Harry K. Ghormley. With Chester Smith, a veteran of the 1906 team, and his brother Glenn Smith as assistants, the 1914 football team won the Little Five conference championship, outscored its opponents 260 to 42, lost only one game, to Coe College, and went on to claim the Illinois state football championship. In 1915, under coach Hermann J. Stegeman, Monmouth tied its great rival, Knox, for the Little Five championship, and it went on to win the Little Five title outright in 1916.

The great string of Monmouth victories in the Little Five conference was beginning to raise doubts about the competitive strength of its

BELOW *The Night Shirt Parade, or "Nighty-Night," featured freshmen and sophomore boys parading the streets in their sleeping attire. Their adolescent antics sometimes got out of hand — on one occasion they managed to breach the fortifications of the women's dormitory and were promptly arrested on the orders of President McMichael.*

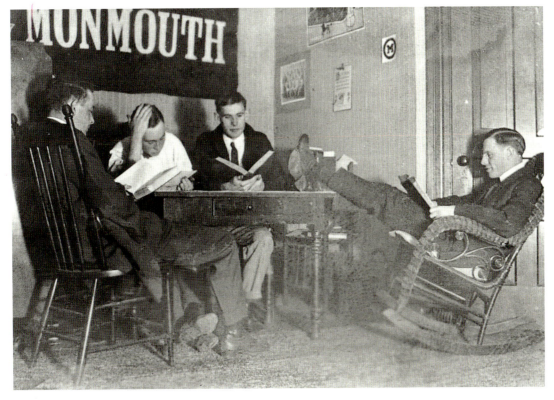

*In the days before men's dormitories, male students generally roomed off-campus while taking their meals at private boarding clubs. In this 1912 photograph, Scott Findley '13 (in rocking chair) and his roommates strike a studious pose.*

Monmouth Comes of Age 1903-1920

PRECEDING PAGES
*Legendary coach Harry Ghormley (back row, left) led his 1914 football team to an 8–1 record, winning the Little Five Conference and state championship. During the season, Monmouth outscored its opponents 260–42.*

RIGHT *In their heyday, the YMCA and YWCA were among the most active student groups on campus. The annual conference at Lake Geneva, Wisconsin, in late August was a highlight of the year. At right, Monmouth students are among the many delegates at the 1916 conference.*

*Members of the German Club sit for a photograph on the steps of Wallace Hall in 1917. Shortly thereafter, the club would be disbanded, as German was removed from the curriculum in response to America's entry into World War I.*

opponents. Monmouth football players were looking forward to the possibility of new intercollegiate triumphs in the coming year. But events in Europe were about to bring a sharp interruption to many of Monmouth's most cherished traditions. When the Great War ensued, all athletic schedules for 1918 were cancelled, and Monmouth students found themselves once again marching off to distant lands.

### Over Here, Over There

While the brief Spanish-American War of 1898 had created barely a ripple on the Monmouth campus, the United States' entry into the Great War in 1917 immediately left its mark. Beginning in April of that year, 115 men left college to enlist in the military. Monmouth's total contribution to the war effort from members of the student body, and former students amounted to more than 400.

The rapid departure of male enlistees left the Monmouth campus starkly depleted of students. In response to this situation, President McMichael in 1918 invited the U.S. War Department to establish a unit of the Student Army Training Corps on the Monmouth campus. The purpose of the SATC units was to give college men military training while they continued their education. Officer candidates were selected from the various corps on the basis of their military aptitude and scholastic standing. Six men from Monmouth were sent to Fort Sheridan, Illinois, for training, and they returned to campus to assist the commanding officer in establishing the SATC unit on October 1, 1918. Woodbine, a house that served as the residence of Monmouth presidents beginning with T. H. McMichael, was converted into a dormitory for 60 of the SATC soldiers. A remodeled barn behind Woodbine was converted into housing for 20 more SATC men. The SATC unit went to classes each morning and from 1 p.m. to 2 p.m.

# May Fete: The Rites of Spring

EACH SPRING, as green leaves and bright flowers returned to campus, Monmouth College was graced by an elegantly conceived outdoor dramatic performance. In the natural wooded swale that lay between McMichael Science Hall and McMichael Home, the women students of Monmouth produced the annual May Fete.

Sponsored by the YWCA, the May Fete was overseen for many years by professor Alice Winbigler. As Monmouth's dean of women from 1910 to 1914, Winbigler maintained firm control over the social lives of women on campus. As YWCA adviser, she supervised the May Fete and was primarily concerned about preserving the decorum of the event and setting appropriate lengths for the dresses of the dancers.

However, Winbigler's requirements did nothing to diminish enthusiasm for the Fete. Attired in elaborate and fanciful costumes, students danced and swayed in allegorical depictions of fairies, maidens, and nymphs. Before them, on a raised stage decorated with colorful bouquets and budding boughs, a wreath-crowned May Queen presided in royal splendor.

Faculty members, students, and townspeople crowded the shady slopes to watch the performances.

The annual festival continued into the 1950s, when the location was moved to the south lawn of the gymnasium, with the May Queen and her chancellor processing down the Wallace Hall hill. The coronation was followed by an exhibition of modern dance by Orchesis Club and always concluded with the traditional winding of the May Pole.

ABOVE *1923's May Fete featured holiday dances representing Valentine's Day, the Fourth of July, Halloween, and Christmas. Seated on the stage are Chancellor Roderic Smith and May Queen Lucile Douglass.*

LEFT *Originated in 1896, the May Fete soon blossomed into a popular spring spectacle, complete with royal court, elaborate choreography, and exotic costumes. In this 1912 photograph, the newly crowned May Queen, Helen McCorkle, poses in front of Wallace Hall.*

ABOVE *The 1917 May Fete was the first to be held in the Valley Beautiful, the natural amphitheater south of McMichael Hall. Here, a group of women perform the Rainbow Dance. From left: Clara Schrenk '20, Ruth Creswell '19, Mary McClellan '18, Martha Glass '19, Mary Watt '18, Zelpha Brook '19, Margery Armsby '20, Florence Megchelsen '18, Roberta Craig '18, Mildred White '20, Evelyn McCain '18, and Beth Craine '19.*

BELOW *In the waning days of World War I, Monmouth College was one of 256 institutions nationwide selected to host a Student Army Training Corps unit. On October 1, 1918, approximately 100 cadets took up quarters in Woodbine Cottage, in the residence's remodeled barn, and in the gymnasium. The dining room of McMichael Home became the mess hall, while the basement of the library housed the supply room. Training was soon hampered, however, by an outbreak of Spanish influenza. Despite the signing of the armistice in November, the corps remained on campus until Christmas, when the last flu victims were released from sick bay.*

each afternoon. Thereafter, they performed two hours of drill and devoted two hours each evening to study. SATC men went to the Monmouth YMCA for recreation, where they found books, magazines, games, and special foods prepared and served by the president's wife, Minnie MacDill McMichael.

The SATC training had hardly begun before it was threatened by the national outbreak of the Spanish influenza epidemic. In October 1918, the college was put under strict quarantine and closed to all nonmilitary students, mostly women, until January 1919. The SATC soldiers were moved across East Broadway into Wallace Hall, and the Gymnasium and the Woodbine residence became influenza infirmaries. The SATC men were ordered to wear flu masks at all times except at mess. A total of 27 flu cases appeared among the SATC soldiers, but fortunately most of them were not serious.

### Heroes Remembered

On December 19, 1918, with the end of the war in Europe and after little more than two months in uniform, the Monmouth College SATC unit was demobilized. Early in 1919, with the influenza epidemic brought under control, the college was once again opened to students.

America's involvement in the First World War, while comparatively brief, brought a heavy measure of grief to those who had lost husbands, sons, brothers, and friends. Resuming the tradition of the graduating class gift, the Monmouth class chose to use its funds to commemorate the heroism of the college's soldiers who had died in the Great War. A bronze tablet presented by the Class of 1919 was placed at the entrance of the Carnegie Library, and on it were inscribed the names of the nine Monmouth men who had given their lives. For every student entering the library in the coming years, the tablet was a tangible reminder of Monmouth's proud tradition of service and sacrifice.

*Known as Woodbine Cottage, after the Woods family that originally owned it, this stately Queen Anne home directly across from the campus became the presidential manse in 1912. Except for a brief interlude when it housed cadets during World War I, it was home to Monmouth presidents until 1949, when President Grier moved to the Manor two blocks west. Later, the house was used for academic and administrative purposes before being converted into a fraternity house for Zeta Beta Tau in 1975. Structural problems led to its demolition in 1984.*

# The College
## 1920–1936

## Chapter 5

The end of the European war and the return of veterans to campus signaled a remarkable period of growth in American higher education. Spurred by educational opportunities and the expansion of the American economy, students arrived on college campuses in unprecedented numbers. At Monmouth, the strong record of President Thomas McMichael's visionary leadership continued into the postwar years. Monmouth entered the Roaring Twenties with optimism and confidence, and within a few years the character of the college and its community was decisively transformed.

PRECEDING PAGES *The look of the buildings along the front of campus has changed very little since this photograph was taken in 1922, but the look of the faculty and students is certainly different. Standing at front center is President T. H. McMichael.*

OPPOSITE PAGE *Known to generations of students as "Robbie," Luther Emerson Robinson was a brilliant scholar who not only headed the English Department for 37 years but took an enormous interest in community affairs. He was an alderman, served as superintendent of the Warren County Library, and almost single-handedly established a city park board. He was also the author of both a seminal book on Abraham Lincoln's literary style and an ambitious history of Monmouth and Warren County.*

### The Resurgence of Fraternities

In the late nineteenth and early twentieth centuries, life at the college drew much of its strength and appeal from the active personal involvement of its students and faculty. As a small and tightly knit community in a modestly sized midwestern town, the college relied on its own resources for entertainment and enlightenment.

The most significant counterweights to the absence of fraternities on campus following the 1874 ban had been Monmouth's literary societies. By the time of World War I, however, the great era of the literary societies was drawing to a close. Aletheorian and *Amateurs des Belles Lettres* (A.B.L.), the two women's literary societies, decided to disband in the fall of 1925. Their fate was mirrored shortly thereafter by the men's literary societies. Philo and Eccritean continued to hold meetings, but recruiting new members proved difficult, and traditional declamation programs met with increasing disinterest from the college community. In 1932, Eccritean finally came to an end, and the next year Philo also ceased to exist.

The predominant force that displaced the literaries was the Greek movement, now sprung back to public life after decades of underground existence. In 1922, the Monmouth faculty and administration relented to increasing alumni and student pressure by deciding that Greek-letter organizations could once again be accepted on campus as long as they were willing to abide by the college's rules and regulations. In 1928, the McMichael administration took the additional step of allowing Monmouth's fraternities and sororities to resume national affiliation. The women's organizations had been the most tenacious in maintaining a covert existence during the long years of the administrative ban, and they now took the lead in resuming open activities. Zeta Epsilon Chi had been operating on and off campus since 1899, secretly sponsored by local Pi Beta Phis who saw it as the nucleus of a reinstated Alpha chapter. With the help of the women of Zeta and the support of some of the original founders and President and Mrs. McMichael, the national convention re-established the Monmouth Alpha of Pi Beta Phi, which was formally installed in May 1928.

The Pi Phis were not alone in their loyalty to Monmouth's Greek tradition. A local fraternity for women, Kappa Alpha Sigma, had been organized in 1900 with the aim of reinstating the Alpha chapter of Kappa Kappa Gamma. Support came from prominent Kappas nationwide, and in 1934, with the approval of the national organization, the Alpha chapter of Kappa Kappa Gamma was officially reborn at Monmouth. Two more women's organizations soon joined the reinstated "Monmouth Duo." Alpha Xi Delta was installed in 1932 and soon became known for its strong support of the social and academic life of the campus. In 1930, Theta Chi Mu was formed, and in 1936, it was accepted as the Beta Gamma chapter of the national Kappa Delta sorority.

Within a few years of the 1922 decision welcoming Greek organizations, a number of

*Once college regulations against dancing were rescinded in 1930, dance cards became cherished mementos for women who attended fraternity dances. These colorful cards, which came in a dizzying variety of shapes and sizes, remained popular through the 1950s.*

# EXTRY!
## ON WITH THE DANCE!!

This is the story of the end that came to five otherwise innocent little girls who, knowing not what they did, attended one of those disgraceful knee-rubs, commonly called a DANCE.

From out the Bastile on the eve of April 22nd issued forth five well-escorted coeds. Turnkey Morton had, out of the benevolence of her heart, granted permission to these fair ladies to attend that Mecca of all pleasure seekers, the Bijou. Approaching this paradise of pleasure, the erring ones heard issuing from that "den of iniquity," the Armory, the plaintive whine of saxophones and the twinging twang of the banjos.

Just as Ulysses of old was unable to resist the lure of the sirens, so the victims of the U. P. inquisition succumbed to the forces of evil. They entered this hall of vice and there indulged in pastimes that would make all U. P.'s and other decent folks shudder with horror.

But was this crime so heinous when viewed in the light of comparative morality? Consider, if you will, that most barbarous exhibition of feminine anatomy held under the very shadow of the Bastile and called "The Maypole Dance." Viewed by the church people themselves, this array of scantily clad maidens is as greedily enjoyed as the devouring of Christians by savage lions was enjoyed by the Romans. This most infamous debauch will attract more attention than Earl Carroll's wine bath party.

When one considers this coming event of immorality, is the sin of these five misunderstood and well-meaning girls unpardonable?

We would therefore beseech Tom, "The Silver Haired Warden of the Bastile," to reconsider the punishment he has meted out to these innocents. Just as the Master in Galilee said of His persecutors, "Father, forgive them, for they know not what they do," even so may Tom be moved to compassion.

Even now the stool pigeons of the "Forces of Right" are on the trail of the writer as the bloodhounds of Harriet Beecher Stowe chased the footsore and shivering Eliza across the icy river.

R. E. Acheson   W. A. McClanahan

*Robert Acheson '28 and some of his Phi Sigma Alpha brothers had this flyer printed in protest of President McMichael's edict against student dances.*

*This freshman cap belonged to Dr. James Marshall '36, the college's longtime physician. He didn't have to wear it long, because shortly after the start of the 1932 school year his class defeated the sophomores in the Pole Scrap. Only a handful of times during the five decades the scrap was held did a freshman manage to climb a telephone pole and replace the sophomore colors with those of his own class, thus earning the right to discard the beanie.*

ABOVE *Kappa Kappa Gammas from Monmouth and across the nation crowd the Wallace Hall steps during the reinstallation of Monmouth's Alpha chapter on October 3, 1934.*

men's fraternities were also operating on campus once more. A local, Xi Gamma Delta, affiliated with the national Beta Kappa in 1926, and when the national merged with Theta Chi, the local became Beta Phi of Theta Chi. The local chapter of Tau Kappa Epsilon was chartered in 1928, an outgrowth of an earlier local, Phi Sigma Alpha, that was founded in 1908. All the fraternities were soon occupying their own houses adjacent to campus.

The reinstated women's fraternities, while quickly resuming an active role as social organizations, did not maintain their own residential houses, but they did eventually have their own chapter rooms in Marshall Hall, a former nineteenth-century residence.

### Conference Athletics

As Greek organizations re-established their position on campus in the 1920s and 1930s, Monmouth's athletic program also experienced a new surge of interest. In 1921 the new Midwest Collegiate Athletic Conference was formed at Coe College, and in 1924 Monmouth became a member.

Monmouth's entry into the Midwest Conference was marked by another significant addition to the physical campus: the construction of a new gymnasium. Completed in 1925, the gymnasium was built at a cost of $250,000 and was designed by architect Dan Everett Waid. The gymnasium contained a main floor of 120 by 80 feet with balconies on three sides. Within the basement level was

ABOVE LEFT *Pi Beta Phi founders Margaret Campbell (left), Clara Hutchinson, and Emma Kilgore pose with Grand President Amy Onken (right) outside Woodbine Cottage during a weekend of re-installation activities for Monmouth's Alpha chapter in May 1928.*

**The College Community 1920–1936**

## Holt House and Stewart House: Birthplaces of a Movement

*Still stately after more than 150 years, Holt House is known internationally as the birthplace of Pi Beta Phi. In the upstairs bedroom on the left, which was shared by two of the founders, the first national secret organization for women was founded on April 28, 1867, originally known as I. C. Sorosis.*

KNOWN THROUGHOUT THE WORLD as the birthplace of Pi Beta Phi and Kappa Kappa Gamma, Monmouth, Illinois, is also home to the two historic houses where those organizations—and the women's fraternity movement—were born.

In April 1867, a group of 12 female Monmouth College students decided the time had come to organize a national secret society for women, similar to the ones enjoyed by their male counterparts at the college. Meeting in a bedroom of the house owned by Major Jacob Holt on East First Avenue where two of the women boarded, they wrote the constitution for a society that they called I. C. Sorosis. (The word "sorority" had not yet been coined, and to this day the organization is still known as a fraternity.)

True to their design to "establish it in as many chartered institutions as possible," the members of I. C. Sorosis immediately began working to establish chapters at other colleges. Within 20 years, more than 30 chapters had been established, and at the national convention in 1888, it was voted to change the name to Pi Beta Phi—the first letters of three Greek words that were traditionally spoken in accompaniment with the fraternity handshake.

At their Pasadena Convention in 1940, the Pi Phis voted to restore the home of Major Holt, where the fraternity was first conceived.

Dilapidated and abandoned, Holt House was purchased at a delinquent tax auction for $1,100, and a nationwide fund drive was started to refurbish it. Now more than a century and a half old, the white frame house still stands majestically as a living tribute to the founders.

A few blocks to the northeast, just across the street from the college campus, stands another white frame house with an equally proud history. In the spring of 1870, another group of young women gathered at the home of Mary Moore ("Minnie") Stewart and signed the charter for Kappa Kappa Gamma, the second national Greek-letter fraternity for women.

Built around 1865 by Minnie's father, James, a prominent attorney who drew up the charter for the fraternity, the house was owned by the Stewarts and their descendants until 1988. Realizing its historic significance, a group of Monmouth-area Kappa alumnae formed the Minnie Stewart Foundation and purchased Stewart House in September 1989. In 1992, the foundation completed a Historic Structures Report, and plans were made for the home's restoration. Six years later, the project got a significant boost when the Minnie Stewart Foundation merged with the national Kappa Kappa Gamma Foundation.

Today, restoration of the National Register property continues with great care extended toward achieving authenticity.

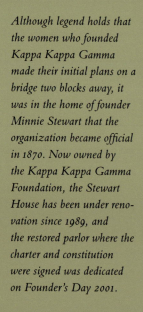

*Although legend holds that the women who founded Kappa Kappa Gamma made their initial plans on a bridge two blocks away, it was in the home of founder Minnie Stewart that the organization became official in 1870. Now owned by the Kappa Kappa Gamma Foundation, the Stewart House has been under renovation since 1989, and the restored parlor where the charter and constitution were signed was dedicated on Founder's Day 2001.*

*Organized in 1926, the Pi chapter of Beta Kappa grew out of a local fraternity, Xi Gamma Delta, and was the first Monmouth fraternity to affiliate nationally after the ban on fraternities was lifted in 1922. In 1942, following a national merger, it became Theta Chi. Chapter members in this 1932 photograph are (front row, from left): Leroy Dew, Leland Johnson, Leo McLoskey, James Heath, Lorance Evers, Clarence Patterson, James Regan, Everett McKeown, and Morton Hickman. Second row: Bob Dew, Durbin Ranney, Gordon Winbigler, Robert McConnell, housemother Mrs. Martin, John Winbigler, Malcolm Reid, Edwin Davis, and Robert Dickey. Third row: Robert Jones, Stanley Kyle, Kenneth Sanderson, Jack Sanders, Charles Frazer, Clyde McDaniel, Wallace Hamly, Eugene Beste, and Clyde Wilson. Fourth row: Frank Gibson, Vincent Upton, Sterling Shrauger, Neal Terrey, Lloyd Wilson, Thomas Robinson, Harold Hubbard, Howard Stevenson, and Robert Hickman.*

housed a 100-yard cinder track for indoor training in inclement weather. Architect Waid and his wife further embellished the building with the Waid Pool, a swimming pool that was considered one of the finest then available at any college in the state.

Adjacent to the site of the new gymnasium, the college had been developing an athletic field capable of hosting intercollegiate events. Beginning in 1906, successive lots were purchased, resulting in a ten-acre expanse. The grading of the field started in 1921 and required moving more than 70,000 cubic yards of earth.

In 1924, Herbert L. Hart was appointed to the post of physical director, and Monmouth entered a period of encouraging athletic success in men's sports. Swimming, boxing, and wrestling were added to the curriculum, and in 1925 the baseball and football teams were both conference champions, a feat repeated by the baseball team in 1926. Track and field men were also winning honors, with Jack McIntosh gaining national recognition when he won first place in the all-around championship meet at the University of Illinois.

The basketball team shared much of the glory. Beginning in the 1929–30 season, Monmouth put together four straight winning seasons. The key to victory was provided by two athletes from Murphysboro, Illinois,

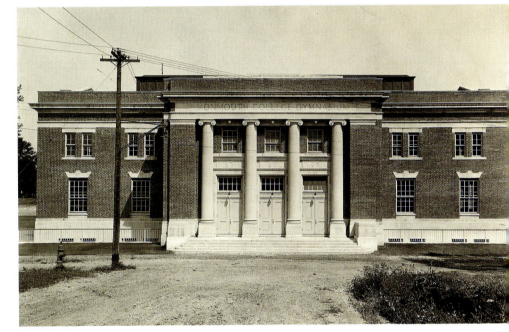

Robert G. "Bobby" Woll and Jack Ozburn. Woll, who stood only five feet four inches and weighed just 126 pounds, played forward. Ozburn was the team's center and highest scorer. Other notable players from this period of Monmouth basketball included Robert Smiley, Edgar Saville, and Glenn "Jelly" Robinson, all of whom, like Woll, went on to coach the game.

Monmouth was also quick to establish its conference reputation in football. In 1925, its first year against its new Midwest Conference rivals, Monmouth went undefeated and won co-champion honors with a record of 7–0–2. Monmouth was the conference football

*Completed in 1925, Monmouth's first substantial gymnasium was designed by alumnus Dan Everett Waid and included a swimming pool given by Waid and his wife. The auditorium, which could seat 2,000 people, included not only a basketball court but a stage for concerts and a movie projection booth.*

**The College Community 1920–1936**

RIGHT *Doris Holt, a Monmouth College student who twice won the Illinois collegiate tennis singles championship, was also the niece of famed illusionist The Great Nicola. In 1928, she took a two-year leave from college to accompany him on a trip to the Far East. There, Holt's tennis skills so impressed a maharaja that he presented her with a baby elephant.*

BELOW *The Fighting Scots opened their 1932 football season at the University of Chicago's Stagg Field. Despite an impressive performance by 129-pound quarterback Bobby Woll, Monmouth was outmatched and lost 41–0. When Woll left the game in the fourth quarter, the partisan crowd of 15,000 gave him a resounding ovation.*

*Harold Hermann '27, who became Monmouth's first alumni secretary following graduation, is credited with creating the college's Scottish theme. Not only did he name the Fighting Scots, but he also made first use of the Menzies tartan and brought the first bagpiper to campus.*

champion again in 1931, 1932, and 1934, all under the coaching of Herbert Hart. Bobby Woll made his name on the gridiron as well as on the basketball court, and he emerged as the star of the Monmouth teams from 1931 to 1933. The most heralded of these championships was in 1931, when Monmouth produced a record of 9–0–1 as the only undefeated team in the state and reigned as champions of the Little Nineteen as well as the Midwest Conference.

The age of Monmouth's great athletic triumphs was also notable for the creation of two enduring college traditions. In 1928, two local newspapers, the Monmouth *Review Atlas* and the Galesburg *Register-Mail*, decided to enhance the traditional Monmouth-Knox Thanksgiving football game with an unusual trophy. A large bronze turkey was purchased from a Chicago trophy wholesale house and established as the prize for the annual gridiron rivalry. Since 1928, the Bronze Turkey game has been the emotional focus of the Monmouth football season, symbolized by the brazen bird that carries the college's tradition and the marks of many legendary on- and off-field adventures.

Equally important for Monmouth's athletic identity was the imaginative contribution of Harold Hermann, who became Monmouth's first alumni secretary, following his graduation from Monmouth in 1927. Moved by the rich Scottish background of the United Presbyterian Church and the Scottish lineage of many alumni, Hermann determined that the name for the Monmouth teams would be the Fighting Scots, and he titled the biographical section of the alumni magazine "Clan News." Aided by Mrs. Harry Lightner, who later became Bobby Woll's mother-in-law, Hermann chose the Menzies clan's hunting plaid as the college's tartan and replaced green freshman caps with Scottish plaid caps brandishing the college tartan. To top off his creation, Hermann brought the first bagpiper to campus from Chicago in support of the new Fighting Scots tradition.

### Theater and the Arts

As sports flourished at Monmouth during the 1920s and 1930s, so too did the cultural arts. In 1901, T. Merrill Austin was appointed to direct the college's Conservatory of Music, and a formal vocal and instrumental music program began to take shape. Under Austin's direction, new choirs were created, orchestras were formed, and additional music courses were added to the conservatory curriculum. By the time Austin retired in 1936, he had become one of the country's most significant college choir conductors and vocal music teachers.

In the 1920s, Austin's musical program was extended by the addition of new faculty members. Grace Gawthrop Peterson graduated from the conservatory and joined the Monmouth faculty in 1922, and Glenn Shaver arrived in 1925. While teaching at the college, Peterson served as the choir director at the Second United Presbyterian Church and Shaver as choir director at the First United Presbyterian Church. Monmouth's vocal music program was soon one of the strongest in the region. The college could claim a Choral Society, a Concert Choir, a Chorale, and a Men's Glee Club, which under Shaver's direction claimed the title of the best in Illinois in 1931.

Monmouth's musical growth was matched by important new ventures in the theatrical arts. When Northwestern University graduate Ruth Williams first came to Monmouth's speech department in 1923, the catalog listed only a single course in theater, and the campus offered no drama organizations or facilities. Undaunted, Williams determined to create a presence for the stage at Monmouth. On November 4, 1925, under Williams's leadership, 60 students formed the Crimson Masque. The charter members of the organization immediately turned their efforts to remodeling the old gymnasium into the Little Theater, and they went on to found a chapter of the National Collegiate Players in 1929.

At first, the Crimson Masque produced comedies and simple dramas, but with increasing experience the organization was soon able to present Monmouth audiences with works of Ibsen, Molière, Shakespeare, Shaw, and Wilde. Launched auspiciously and led by an inspired director, the Crimson Masque contributed substantially to the enrichment of Monmouth's cultural life.

### A Notable Faculty

During the T. H. McMichael presidency, as Monmouth strengthened its social life, athletic competitiveness, and participation in the arts, the college also grew academically. Some of Monmouth's legendary teachers joined the faculty during the McMichael era, and their influence was to be felt for years to come.

Luther Emerson Robinson arrived at Monmouth in 1900 and assumed the Harding Professorship of English Language and Literature, heading the department until his retirement in 1937. A graduate of Drury College who had also done graduate work at the University of Chicago, Robinson taught literature as his principal specialty. He focused on Browning, Milton, Shakespeare, and the Romantic poets while creating an additional expertise as a historian of Illinois and the career of Abraham Lincoln.

In 1917, Edna Browning Riggs joined the faculty as a teacher of piano in the conservatory of music. She was a decisive influence on the career of Grace Gawthrop Peterson, who collaborated for many years with Riggs in annual twin-piano concerts. Peterson was to become best known as the director of annual musical revues, which were staged at Monmouth's town motion picture theater with scores of students participating.

T. Merrill Austin, after whom the current music building is named, was the first director of the Conservatory of Music and is credited with legitimizing the vocal program at Monmouth. At his retirement in 1936, he was one of the country's most significant college choir conductors.

BELOW LEFT Seven legendary players and coaches who would later be inducted into the M Club Hall of Fame were part of the undefeated 1931 Fighting Scots football team. The future Hall of Famers were: Gene Tinker (front row, second from left), Leino Corgnati (holding the football), Bobby Woll (front row, right), Glenn "Jelly" Robinson (next to Woll), Coach Warren Taylor (second row, left), Virgil Boucher (behind Corgnati's left shoulder), and Coach Herb Hart (back row, left).

# The Monmouth Chautauqua

"CHAUTAUQUA IS THE MOST American thing in America!" So stated Teddy Roosevelt, himself a frequent speaker at the phenomenon that swept the United States at the turn of the twentieth century. Originating on the shores of Chautauqua Lake in southwestern New York State, the Chautauqua Lake Sunday School Assembly program began in 1874 as a religious program. But it quickly became a nationwide movement that has been described as a "lecture series, community concert series, camp meeting and lyceum combined in the atmosphere of a tent circus." In 1904 the movement reached Monmouth College, where for the next two decades it would become a summer fixture on the campus.

The Monmouth Chautauqua Association was organized by a group of leading citizens—the college's T. H. McMichael was its first president—and brought an endless parade of orators and preachers, bands and orchestras, and other cultural attractions to the people of western Illinois. A tent city would be erected in "Valley Beautiful," the wooded vale at the base of Wallace Hall hill, and for ten days in August families would camp out in rented tents or commute in their Model Ts to hear the likes of William Jennings Bryan and Robert LaFollette, the Progressive governor of Wisconsin. Reserved seats were ten cents; children under ten were free; and an automobile pass could be had for $1.50. The average yearly attendance was 2,500 to 3,000 people.

Also popular were the Junior Chautauquas, in which area children—including future Monmouth College piano instructor Grace Gawthrop Peterson—performed musical selections, usually based on popular hymns and Bible stories.

The last Monmouth Chautauqua was held in 1924. By that time, the event that had entertained and informed the public for an entire generation fell victim to a new type of diversion—the motion picture.

*From 1904 until 1924, Chautauquas were an annual summer event on the Monmouth College campus. President T. H. McMichael (center), a principal supporter of the popular event, served as the Monmouth Chautauqua Association's first president.*

Eva Hanna arrived at the college in 1923 as a graduate of Washington State University, joining Professor Robinson in the English department, and the two became an effective teaching team. Hanna added courses in modern poetry, modern prose, and creative writing to the curriculum, enriching Monmouth's literary offerings.

Another of President McMichael's strong additions to the faculty was Monmouth alumnus Samuel Martin Thompson. The son of a Presbyterian minister who was also a Monmouth graduate, Thompson received his master's degree from Princeton University and his doctorate from Yale University. Thompson began his 46-year teaching career at Monmouth in 1926.

No two members of the faculty better represented the growing academic stature of Monmouth College than William S. Haldeman and Garrett Thiessen. Haldeman began teaching chemistry at Monmouth in 1917; he was a graduate of the University of Pennsylvania and the successor to Professor John N. Swan, who had drawn up the plans for McMichael Science Hall. In 1918, Haldeman received his master's degree from Harvard University, yet he always regretted not earning a doctorate. His legendary motto, preached to hundreds of chemistry majors, was: "The bachelor's degree is not enough." Haldeman's teaching was strengthened in 1930, when Garrett Thiessen joined Monmouth's chemistry faculty. Like Haldeman, Thiessen had a strong academic record. He had graduated Phi Beta Kappa from Cornell College in Iowa and had gone on to earn a master's degree and doctorate in chemistry from the University of Iowa. Thiessen joined Haldeman in building Monmouth's chemistry department into one of the strongest liberal arts college programs of its kind in the country.

In biology, professors Arthur Gerhart and Donald McMullen worked diligently to solidify a department that had earlier generated controversy over the teaching of evolution. Like his father before him, President McMichael stood firm in his support of the faculty, and Darwinism stayed.

### Commendations and Celebrations

As McMichael's administration entered its last years, the college passed some memorable milestones. Commencement week of 1929 was dedicated to Alice Winbigler on the occasion of her retirement after 50 years of teaching. The Winbigler Commencement culminated in a gala banquet held in the gymnasium, with hundreds of the students she had taught and influenced in attendance.

The following year, the gymnasium was the site of another milestone, the first college-approved dance. Watching from the sidelines,

*Ruth Williams was the mother of Monmouth's long and successful theater tradition. In 1925, she convinced the administration to turn the old gymnasium into a playhouse and founded the Crimson Masque. Four years later, she established a chapter of the National Collegiate Players.*

BELOW *Glenn Shaver (right), who joined the faculty in 1925, was one of the college's most popular and successful choral directors. His Men's Glee Club was named best in Illinois in 1931. Shaver also introduced the annual college production of* Messiah.

*From its earliest days, Monmouth College prepared scores of graduates to be Presbyterian missionaries, many of whom were later based in Egypt. In the fall of 1933, nine of Monmouth's students had been born in Egypt, the children of alumni missionaries. Pictured from left are: Paul McClanahan (later president of Assiut College and a Monmouth chaplain), Jeanette Baird, William Baird, Jane Hoyman, Charles Owen, Earla Hoyman, Kenneth Baird, Mary McClanahan, and John Owen.*

*Monmouth faculty have long been fond of mixing education with pleasure. The Campus Club Christmas party of 1935 had a Dickens theme. Among those pictured are Mr. and Mrs. Lyle Finely, Mr. and Mrs. J. Dales Buchanan, Emma Gibson, Louis Givens, and David McMichael.*

PRECEDING PAGES
*President McMichael (standing, center) and his wife, Minnie (seated), share a happy moment in 1926 as they host their former classmates for their 40th college reunion. Mrs. McMichael holds their class memorial. Standing from left are: Col. S. H. Finley, Margaret Evans Duff, Emma Roberts Hubble, Nellie Higgins Johnson, McMichael, Katherine Oliver McCoy, Alice Patterson, and Nelle Shields. Seated from left are: the Reverend J. F. Jamieson, Lindy Simmons Daly, Mrs. McMichael, Clem D. McCoy, and the Reverend A. N. Porter.*

Eva Hanna was heard to proclaim, "We are seeing history made tonight."

The college again kicked up its heels in 1931, when the 75th Anniversary Diamond Jubilee was held. It was calculated that since 1853 no fewer than 2,454 men and women had graduated with Monmouth degrees. The climax of Monmouth's 75th anniversary celebration came at the annual alumni banquet in the gymnasium on Wednesday evening, and it concluded on Thursday with the 75th anniversary commencement exercises. (Monmouth would later establish 1853 as its official founding date.)

These celebrations came just as Monmouth was entering the most severe years of the Depression. Under the college's business manager and the president's son, David McMichael, the faculty for a time had to be paid in promissory notes. In 1934, as the college's deficit grew, the regular faculty and staff went out to recruit students, resulting in a larger class the next year.

The college would survive the Depression, as it had always survived such challenges before. When T. H. McMichael stepped down as president in 1936, he could look back on an impressive record of achievement. During his administration, a struggling school with three buildings and only $200,000 in endowment had become a full-fledged educational institution with a modern physical plant and an endowment of more than $2 million. Monmouth had more than 40 faculty members, and in the 33 years of the McMichael administration the size of the student body had grown from 160 students to more than 500. Monmouth had claimed a position of distinction among its academic peers, and it was poised to meet the challenges of a new age.

*Eva Hanna's natural vivacity and enthusiasm turned the study of English literature into a pleasure for four decades. Later in life, she married the widowed dean John S. Cleland. In 1966, the year of her retirement, the college named a new residence hall in the Clelands' honor.*

*The son of a Presbyterian minister who had graduated from Monmouth, Samuel Thompson served 46 years on the faculty. Today, Thompson is legendary among hundreds of successful lawyers, ministers, and teachers who took his demanding but thought-provoking classes.*

*Possibly the most versatile faculty member in Monmouth's history, Alice Winbigler '77 taught mathematics, astronomy, Latin, history, English, and rhetoric. She also served as dean of women.*

# Hawcock's Cafe—"The Place to Eat"

THE MERE MENTION of Hawcock's Cafe to anyone who attended Monmouth College in the first half of the twentieth century brings back a smorgasbord of memories.

Opened in 1911 by Ernie Hawcock and his wife, Jennie, the cafe grew to be the fourth largest restaurant in the United States in a community of under 10,000, serving an average of 800 customers a day. For scores of Monmouth College students, Hawcock's provided a welcome source of employment with the added benefit of free meals—an important perk during the Depression.

Even during lean times, Hawcock's employed a staff of 40 and offered a menu that was far from lean—a cut of meat with gravy, potatoes, vegetable, salad, and a drink was standard fare and sold for just 35 cents. With its slogan "The Place to Eat," the East First Avenue restaurant was also the place to be…after dances, movies, and football games, and for the famous Sunday dinner, which consisted of whole sides of beef and ham, platters full of chicken, and mounds of fresh vegetables and homemade bread. Its banquet room was the site of many a gala college event, from class dinners to club socials.

While Ernie and Jennie Hawcock devoted themselves to running a sound establishment, it was their son Emory who developed a passion for the restaurant business and was responsible for many improvements. By the 1940s, under Emory's direction, the cafe boasted a delicatessen, a bakery, a soda fountain, and a full line of salads and desserts. A former Monmouth College student whose education had been interrupted by World War I, Emory eventually studied domestic science at Iowa State University and became the restaurant's chief cook, but he always regretted not finishing his bachelor's degree at Monmouth. Later, he befriended Monmouth College chemistry professor Garrett Thiessen (they were both crack rifle shots), who persuaded him to re-enroll at Monmouth, and he finally graduated in 1959.

By that time, Ernie had died, and Emory had sold the business to pursue a career as a dietician. The restaurant lived on for a few years as the Marine Room, but it was not successful and closed in 1955. The building was demolished in 1970 and replaced by a parking lot.

*A dinner plate from Hawcock's Cafe.*

# An Era of Cha[nge]
## Depression an[d ...]
### 1936–1952

## Chapter 6

Monmouth College was still feeling the many constraints of the Depression when the college and the nation were confronted with the even greater challenge of mobilizing for a second world war, this one fought on a truly global scale. As the country and higher education underwent dramatic social and cultural changes, Monmouth grappled with the need to remain true to its heritage while building academic programs that would prepare its students for the demands of mid-twentieth-century life.

    T. H. McMichael's lengthy tenure and strong institutional vision had made him the

*PRECEDING PAGES: Mail call was the highlight of the day for the Navy men in training on campus during World War II.*

*OPPOSITE PAGE: Crowds descend on Monmouth's Rivoli Theatre for one of Gracie Peterson's popular stage shows.*

OPPOSITE PAGE *In the spring of 1940, these student leaders could not have guessed that life on the Monmouth College campus would soon be drastically altered by the specter of war. In the back row from left are Student Council president Howard Jamieson '40, YMCA president Wiley Prugh '41, senior class president Dwight Russell '40, junior class president Robert Cleland '41, and sophomore class president John Fidler '46. In the middle row from left are Oracle editor Scott Hoyman '41, freshman class president Robert Barnes '45, and Ravelings editor Robert Black '41. In front is Margaret Jean Hutchison '40, president of the YWCA.*

virtual personification of Monmouth, both in the Presbyterian denomination and in the national liberal arts college community. Monmouth's next president, the college trustees realized, would confront the dual challenges of succeeding a widely respected figure while working to maintain and extend the college's enhanced academic reputation.

After evaluating many candidates, in 1936 the trustees turned to a familiar figure, 54-year-old James Harper Grier, the popular minister of the Second United Presbyterian Church of Monmouth. Grier had distinctive family ties to the college. Both his father, James Alexander Grier, and mother, Ada Bruen Grier, had graduated from Monmouth, and his mother was one of the founders of Pi Beta Phi. In James Grier's youth, his father became a professor of theology at Allegheny Theological Seminary, later the Pittsburgh-Xenia Theological Seminary, and later served as the seminary's president.

*Following in the footsteps of T. H. McMichael as Monmouth College president was no easy task, but James Harper Grier seemed ideally suited to the job. The son of two prominent Monmouth College alumni (his father had been president of Allegheny Theological Seminary), Grier had taught at Assiut College in Egypt, Westminster College and Pittsburgh Theological Seminary. At the time of his election to the Monmouth College presidency, he was serving in his sixth pastorate, at Monmouth's Second United Presbyterian Church.*

James Grier graduated from Westminster College in 1902 and spent the next three years teaching chemistry and English to students at Assiut College in Egypt. Upon returning to the United States, Grier graduated in 1909 from Pittsburgh Theological Seminary and served successively as a pastor at churches in Buffalo, New York, and Pittsburgh and Cannonsburg, Pennsylvania. His ministry was interrupted during World War I, when he served with the YMCA in France. He survived a perilous experience on the return voyage, when a submarine sank his ship in the Irish Sea 125 miles from land. In 1922, Grier returned to the seminary to teach Old Testament languages and literature, and in 1930 he resumed his ministry in Pittsburgh and at Second Church in Monmouth.

Grier recognized the significance of the advances in scholarly standards achieved during the Thomas McMichael years, and he believed it was essential to continue to emphasize high academic goals for both professors and students. More than this, however, he believed that scholarship at its best could not be divorced from the beliefs and ideals of Christian faith. Grier encouraged tolerance of differing religious traditions and sought to integrate the values of faith and ethics into the Monmouth educational experience.

To strengthen the campus community, President Grier also continued the physical expansion undertaken by his predecessor, T. H. McMichael. In 1940, a new three-story women's residence hall, James Harper Grier Hall, was completed. In 1947, Alice Winbigler Hall, a two-story residence hall named for the former professor of mathematics, provided additional housing for women. In 1951, accommodations were further enhanced by the completion of Fulton Hall, a three-story men's residence hall. Named for Samuel A. Fulton, a prominent Presbyterian layman who led the fundraising efforts for the building, Fulton Hall was the most expensive structure on campus when it was completed. In total, the three new residence halls were valued at nearly $1 million. The Grier administration also met a longstanding

ABOVE *Completed in 1940 under the Grier administration and named in Grier's honor, Monmouth's third residence hall offered young women many of the amenities of home. The first men's residence would not be built for another decade.*

ABOVE RIGHT *Welcoming the returning servicemen in the fall of 1947 was a new student union in the basement of Wallace Hall, complete with tartan-topped tables and wall murals depicting the seals of Midwest Conference schools.*

campus social need by creating Monmouth's first student union, a center that opened in the basement of Wallace Hall in September 1947. The union provided a lounge, dance hall, snack bar, and lunch room. The walls of the union were decorated with murals and the official seals of the colleges of the Midwest Conference, all painted by student artists.

### Reshaping Athletics

Monmouth's athletic program, like those at other colleges, was significantly affected by the Depression. Many Americans in the 1930s found college games to be one of the few affordable forms of entertainment, while colleges saw athletics as an important way to gain publicity and attract students. At Monmouth, as elsewhere, collegiate sports took on an enhanced financial significance that prompted renewed questions about their role in education.

Monmouth was forced to confront these issues through a controversy surrounding one of its athletic directors. For some years, an executive of the Illinois Bankers' Life Insurance Company headquartered in Monmouth had offered jobs to students who otherwise could not afford to enroll in the college. As many as 40 students were employed by the company, and a substantial number of these students were typically star members of the Monmouth football team. When Monmouth's athletic director Herbert Hart resigned in 1938, the Bankers'

Life Insurance executive pressed the college to replace him with Ivan Cahoon, a professional football player. Cahoon came with the recommendation of Francis Louis "Jug" Earp, who was the public relations director for the Green Bay Packers and a former member of Monmouth's football team. When Cahoon was appointed athletic director in 1938, he arrived on campus with a group of new players he had recruited for the team, all of them notable for their physical size. After a series of overmatched contests with conference opponents in 1938 and 1939, President Grier decided that the academic integrity of Monmouth's athletic teams was being undermined by Cahoon's professional approach to sports, and he dismissed the athletic director from his position.

Grier took his dramatic action against a background of increased concern within the Midwest Conference that athletic teams were being recruited and fielded without sufficient attention given to academic values and classroom education. In a key resolution on the subject, the conference had declared that "physical education in our respective Mid-west colleges should be considered definitely an academic program…[in contrast to] the attitudes of certain universities and colleges that make intercollegiate competition of pre-eminent importance…."

In response to President Grier's action, Bankers' Life Insurance informed the college that football players would no longer be allowed on its payroll. As a consequence, basketball coach Bobby Woll, who was appointed athletic director and football coach after Cahoon's firing, played the 1940 season with 20 lettermen sitting in the stands, since the players could not afford to give up their jobs to take the field. In 1941, Woll brought in his teammate and lifelong friend Glenn E. "Jelly" Robinson to coach Monmouth football. The situation had been stabilized with new leadership, but it would be years before the football program fully recovered.

In the meantime, Monmouth basketball entered a period of legendary triumphs. Bobby Woll had assumed the position of basketball coach in 1936, and under his direction teams were shaped by disciplined drills, frequent intrasquad scrimmages, and a methodical reliance on a few set plays. In 1937–38, Monmouth won its first Midwest Conference championship in basketball. The Monmouth community was so proud of this accomplishment that it purchased miniature golden basketballs for everyone on the team.

Bobby Woll's Monmouth squad came back to win the Midwest Conference championship for the second time in 1941–42, but the season was a grueling one in many ways. Star player LeRoy King was lost to appendicitis after just two games, and the Fighting Scots were barely able to top Coe College when George Trotter hit a game winning lay-up—the ball hit

COACH WOLL · WILLIAMS · THOMSON · PLUNKETT · MANNEN · JAMIESON · BROUSE · VEST · ATH. DIR. HART
MGR. ADAIR · DEW · SCHANTZ · LUSK · BOLON · MOODY · GIVENS · DICKY HART
1938 · MONMOUTH COLLEGE · MID-WEST BASKETBALL CHAMPS · 1938
M·C· 26 — CORNELL 24   M·C· 34 — CORNELL 30   M·C· 40 — LAWRENCE 28   M·C· 33 — COE 32
M·C· 38 — KNOX 36   M·C· 44 — CARLETON 26   M·C· 43 — COE 24   M·C· 48 — BELOIT 40
M·C· 36 — RIPON 22   M·C· 39 — KNOX 37

ABOVE *The Monmouth community got together and purchased miniature gold basketballs for the first college team to win the Midwest Conference, the 1937–38 squad, coached by Bobby Woll (white shirt, far left).*

LEFT *The 1941–42 basketball Scots were undefeated in conference play, earning Coach Woll his second championship in six years. The team included six future Hall of Famers—George Bersted, Gordy Huber, LeRoy King, Glen Rankin, George Trotter, and Buck Worley.*

An Era of Challenge 1936–1952

the rim, held motionless for a moment, then fell through the net. Still, Monmouth finished the season with an 11–1 record, and the dual Midwest championships were welcome evidence that Monmouth would remain a formidable and competitive athletic force.

### Broadening the Curriculum

The fundamental aim of Monmouth's educational curriculum continued to be broad exposure to the liberal arts. General degree requirements included a reading knowledge of one foreign language; one year of a laboratory science, and either another year of general science or a year of mathematics; five hours of Bible and religion; two hours of speech; six hours of English; and four semesters of social studies. During the Grier administration, this basic set of requirements was enhanced with a range of new offerings. Rigorous courses were offered for premedical, predental, and preministerial students. Teacher training was also increasingly popular, leading to the expansion of the education department and the development of courses in elementary education. An accounting laboratory was established with business and accounting machines, and noncredit courses were provided in typewriting, shorthand, and office practice. Separate departments were developed for home economics and sociology.

Beginning in the late 1940s, several affiliation programs were also developed in nursing, occupational therapy, and engineering. These gave students the opportunity to spend two or three years at Monmouth and then transfer to an approved hospital or technical school. In engineering, an option called the Binary Program let a student complete three years of liberal arts courses at Monmouth followed by two years of engineering at Case Institute of Technology in Cleveland. At the end of this five-year curriculum, the student was awarded a degree from both Monmouth and Case.

Prompted by the college's expanding curriculum, Professor Samuel M. Thompson, chair of the philosophy department, proposed a new structure for articulated studies known as the Thompson Plan or the Senior College Program of Study. Thompson suggested that instead of restricting juniors and seniors to courses in one or two departments, they should have the opportunity to draw on all the resources of the college. Calling for broad interdepartmental cooperation, the Thompson Plan recommended the creation of integrated courses that could be taught by members of one department or a combination of instructors from several departments. Although Thompson's ideas were never formally adopted, one new interdepartmental seminar was created for senior majors in history, English, and sociology. Courses and polices were evaluated, revealing that some elements of the plan were already in operation, among them a number of interdisciplinary offerings such as the history of American culture.

Of all the sciences, chemistry remained the strongest feature of the Monmouth curriculum. Professor William S. Haldeman's commitment to chemical education was reinforced by the teaching of Garrett Thiessen and Benjamin Shawver. In 1946, Monmouth's academic program in chemistry won approval for professional certification from the American Chemical Society. The Steelman Report on

*A former high school principal, Frank Phillips was appointed Monmouth College's first academic dean in 1922 to relieve some of the burdens on President McMichael. The president, however, was too set in his ways to share much authority, prompting Phillips to return to the public school system after three years. Phillips would later return for a second tour of duty at Monmouth, serving as dean of men from 1946 to 1956.*

*Although he taught English his entire career, Charles A. Owen's passion was for Arabic studies. A 1907 Monmouth graduate, he was head of the English department at Assiut College in Upper Egypt from 1913 to 1937. During that period, he earned a doctorate in Arabic from Yale University. Owen joined the Monmouth College English department in 1937, becoming one of its most popular professors until his death in 1951.*

# Haldy's Boys

WILLIAM S. HALDEMAN did not have the type of formal education that is usually associated with a college professor, but he devoted his career to making sure that his students would. After learning about their chemistry professor's personal hardships—which included arduous self-teaching to pass a state teaching college entrance exam as well as attending school during summers and on weekends to finally earn a bachelor's degree at age 33—many of his students were inspired to pursue advanced degrees and careers in chemistry.

It's remarkable that Haldeman, who taught at Monmouth from 1918 to 1952, even managed to become a Monmouth professor after initially only completing grammar school, but what truly distinguished him as an educator was the significant number of successful chemists who came out of his classroom (88 of his 343 chemistry graduates received a PhD).

Haldeman had two key beliefs about education. First, he constantly reminded his protégés that "the bachelor's degree is not enough," stressing the need for aspiring chemists to continue their education in graduate school. Second, he put his money where his mouth was, dispensing more than $20,000 in loans to graduates so that they could do just that. Haldeman claimed that every penny in his revolving loan fund was eventually repaid.

"He teams up with [his students] for the duration, with possible financial aid in early days; with counsel in later days; and with friendship, always," said a *Christian Herald* article chronicling Haldeman's career.

The slight professor devoted his career to his students. He didn't marry until after his retirement, and he lived a Spartan life, forgoing owning a home or even an automobile. "My boys are my family, and there are too many of them for me to ever be lonely," he once said.

Haldeman's reputation was built upon his ability to bring out the very best in his students, who were popularly known as "Haldy's boys."

They include a significant number of men—and women—who went on to be leaders in the chemistry field. Haldeman, who tracked all of his chemistry graduates through an annual self-published directory, noted that Clair Boruff '23, Charles Owen Jr. '36, and David Turnbull '36 had each published at least 70 scholarly articles, and that Eugene Moffett '29 and Frank McMillan '34 had a combined 64 patents to their names. Betty Weiss Oberstar '43, retired director of international development for the Clairol, Inc., and a patentee, was a "Haldy's girl."

Though extremely modest, Haldeman could not escape the spotlight when the St. Louis section of the American Chemical Society chose him in 1950 as the recipient of its Midwest Award, the first educator to be so honored. Haldeman's inspirational story appeared in *Time* magazine and newspapers from coast to coast.

"It is the intimate contact with students that distinguishes the opportunities of the small college teacher and those of his university colleague," said Haldeman in his Midwest Award acceptance speech.

*Standing before a display containing the names of hundreds of his former students, celebrated chemistry professor William S. Haldeman poses with some of those students at a retirement tea in Carnegie Library during the 1952 commencement weekend.*

# Gracie's Shows

*Gracie Peterson '22 began teaching piano in the Conservatory of Music before her graduation, beginning a tenure of 50 years on the music faculty. During her long tenure, she developed a remarkable rapport with students, directing a glee club, a church choir, and a series of enormously popular musical revues.*

BELOW *A medley of songs about spring rain was a highlight of Gracie Peterson's 1949 show, "Hits and Misses."*

IN THE SPRING OF 1942, Grace Gawthrop Peterson, Monmouth College's popular and energetic young music instructor, had an idea. In the 20 years since joining her alma mater's music department, she had achieved considerable success directing the girls' glee club, performing two-piano recitals with her mentor, Edna Browning Riggs, and producing an ambitious annual candlelight Christmas service. Her great love, however, was the show tune—à la Gershwin, Berlin and Porter. Having recently formed a male chorus, she saw an opportunity to bring this type of music to the masses.

Gracie Peterson and her Collegians, a group of 45 young men singing religious, barbershop, college and patriotic songs, were soon performing for such audiences as the American Legion Auxiliary Convention in Chicago. On a weekend in May 1942, in conjunction with a showing of *Blondie Goes to College*, "Musical Moods" premiered at Monmouth's Rivoli Theatre, the first in a long line of revues, which would eventually bump the feature film and play to sold-out houses, with two shows Friday and three on Saturday.

The following fall, with the war in full gear, Peterson decided to go patriotic and formed the "Yankee Doodle Boys." By the spring of 1943, most of the men on campus had enlisted in the service, causing her to switch strategies and form an all-girl chorus in conjunction with the YWCA. Based on a popular radio program, she presented "The Hour of Charm" with 64 coeds performing such favorites as *Smoke Gets In Your Eyes* and *Heart and Soul*.

Another radio program, *Girl of the Year*, provided the inspiration for the 1944 spring production, which featured a girl and a song for each month. The show proved especially popular when it went on the road to Camp Ellis and was viewed by 2,000 enthusiastic soldiers.

With the return of the G.I.s, the spring 1947 show for the first time featured men and women. "This Is It" was a colorful spectacle with elaborate sets and amazing variety, including tap dancing, a violin number directed by Professor Hal Loya, oriental and South American costume pieces, a Spike Jones comedy routine, and the introduction of the college beauty queen.

The annual event, which had by now become an institution, continued to grow. In 1948, "Spree-For-All" introduced a revolving platform and giant magazine covers to frame the lovely women. The following year, "Hits and Misses" was the first show to make use of black light and luminescent scenery. The 1950 entry was perhaps the pinnacle of the series, as 4,500 people watched "Scots 'N Skits," and $1,000 was raised for the new dormitory fund.

The curtain went down on the last Rivoli show—"Up 'N Atom"—in 1951. Not long after that production, the Rivoli was modernizing with a new screen, and stage shows were no longer possible. Just in time for the college's centennial in 1953, the new Lincoln Elementary School opened, and its commodious stage was put to use for "Town Topics," an extravaganza that concluded with a coronation number, "Through the Years with Monmouth College."

On February 28, 2002, at Galesburg's Orpheum Theatre, an audience that included many of the past performers from her Rivoli shows gathered to pay tribute to Gracie Peterson in a gala 100th birthday celebration. The guest of honor was given a standing ovation when she sat down at the grand piano and effortlessly played a medley of the Rivoli tunes that had made her famous a half century before.

Manpower for Research stated that from 1936 to 1945, Monmouth and four other small colleges together had "produced more candidates for the doctor's degree in chemistry than Johns Hopkins, Fordham, Columbia, Tulane, and Syracuse Universities combined." In 1950, Haldeman received the Midwest Award of the American Chemical Society, the first recipient chosen for contributions to education rather than pure research.

Success in science was balanced by achievement in other areas of the curriculum, including music. In 1936, Heimo "Hal" Loya arrived at Monmouth as the new instructor in string instruments and director of the college orchestra. Three years later, Loya was asked to assume direction of the college band. For the first time in the college's history, Monmouth College band members were provided with uniforms, sharp outfits consisting of black pants decorated with plaid stripes and red jackets. In the late 1940s, two new members of the band, David and Floyd Hershberger, introduced the bagpipe tradition, and several majorettes and dancers joined the band's outdoor performances.

Loya's influence was also felt in the orchestra, choirs, recitals, and College Concert Series. Music was a key element of chapel services and vespers, and the choir and orchestra organized popular tour programs. Music at Monmouth during these years included the Monmouth Choral Society, the College Concert Choir, the Chorale or Chapel Choir, the Concert Band, the College Orchestra, Pi Alpha Nu fraternity, and many productions of operas, operettas, and popular musicals. The musical arts, like the chemical sciences, flourished as never before on the Monmouth campus.

### Transformed by War

At Monmouth, as on other American campuses, the experience of World War I had led many to support international efforts to address the causes of war. Monmouth's understanding of conflict in world affairs was sharpened by the work of one of its alumni, Takashi Komatsu '10, who was the official translator for the Japanese delegation at the Washington Disarmament conference of 1921. Early the next year, Komatsu visited Monmouth, emphasizing the need for mutual understanding, the reduction of standing armies and navies, and the significance of his Monmouth Christian education on shaping his interest in peace. In 1940, Komatsu was awarded an honorary degree by Monmouth for his work on behalf of international accord.

Other voices were also being raised on campus that same year. In December 1940, at the invitation of President Grier, socialist Norman Thomas spoke to a capacity crowd in the Auditorium on "America's Role in World Affairs." Unreserved support of Great Britain would revive and strengthen the forces of colonialism and capitalism, Thomas said; America should use its power and influence to begin shaping plans for a more just postwar world.

These concerns were put in sharp relief by the attack on Pearl Harbor on December 7, 1941. Monmouth's enrollment began an immediate and precipitous decline as all able-bodied men left campus to join the armed forces and women

*One of several Monmouth professors who received their first teaching experience at the Assiut Mission School in Egypt, Ben Shawver joined the Monmouth chemistry faculty in 1946. He later became a professor of education, chairing that department from 1965 until his retirement in 1974, after which he taught part-time in the chemistry department until 1985.*

*An accomplished violinist and music educator, Heimo "Hal" Loya had been director of the well-known Sibelius Male Chorus of Chicago when he joined the Monmouth faculty in 1936. Over the next 37 years, he would bring the college orchestra to regional prominence, organize a marching band, chair an expanding music department, and originate the Liberal Arts Festival.*

*A third-generation administrator for Monmouth College, David McMichael (right) served as business manager—and eventually as vice president—between 1929 and 1953. The grandson of President J. B. McMichael, he briefly shared an office suite in Carnegie Library with his father, President T. H. McMichael, as seen in this 1933 photograph.*

# World War II Military Training Programs

IN NOVEMBER 1942, President Grier and business manager David McMichael went to Washington, D.C., to offer the college campus to the U.S. Navy as a training facility. Within a month, Monmouth was designated as a site for a Naval Flight Preparatory School. The first group of aviation cadets arrived on January 7, 1943, and by March 1943 there were 600 naval cadets on campus.

The presence of the Flight Preparatory School was evident from the U.S. Navy NP-1 biplane on the lawn in front of Grier Hall, the just-completed women's residence hall that had been converted into military housing and a cadet sick bay. Cadets were also housed in East Hall (Austin Hall) and McMichael Hall, which served as the cadet mess hall. Women students displaced from Grier and McMichael moved into Monmouth's now-empty fraternity houses. The cadets acknowledged the presence of Monmouth's coeds by giving a series of well-received formal dances.

Monmouth's professors—not naval officers—taught the cadets navigation, mathematics, code communication, and recognition of planes and vessels. Due in large part to the teaching abilities of these men and women, Monmouth cadets outscored all others across the country in their final exams, and Monmouth's program was judged the best of its type in the nation.

By 1944, as the Navy redirected its operations to larger military airfields, Monmouth's Preflight School was replaced by a Navy Academic Refresher Unit (NARU), which prepared veterans and servicemen for officer training programs. NARU students were older and more experienced than the naval cadets who studied a more traditional liberal arts curriculum. After the war, many preflight and NARU men returned to campus to enroll as regular students and earn a Monmouth degree.

*A cadet regiment marches to afternoon classes in Wallace Hall.*

*Flown in from Glenview Naval Air Base, an NP-1 Spartan Trainer was installed in front of Grier Hall. Nicknamed the "Yellow Peril" by cadets, it was representative of the aircraft cadets would train on when they left Monmouth.*

PRECEDING PAGES *In January 1943, Monmouth's women began evacuating their dormitories to make way for incoming naval cadets, many moving their belongings by sled and writing their new telephone numbers on the walls for the benefit of the servicemen. For the duration of the war, women occupied Bruen Hall, Marshall Hall, Van Gundy Hall, and the fraternity houses, including the Theta Chi house, as seen here.*

*Harold "Red" Poling '49, who enrolled at Monmouth College after having attended the naval flight school during World War II, escorts May Queen Dorothy Kern '49 down the Wallace Hall hill during the annual May Fete. The following year, Poling joined Ford Motor Company as a college trainee and eventually was promoted to chairman and CEO of the corporation. He retired in 1994.*

enlisted in the WACS or WAVES or took jobs in war industries. A report to the Senate in 1944 said that from a high of 311 men on campus in 1940 the number had shrunk to 33. Even those who did not qualify for military service were working in defense plants or had postponed their college careers.

To meet both the national defense emergency and the college's enrollment crisis, Monmouth College in 1942 petioned to become a U.S. Navy training facility. After a naval inspector visited campus and approved the facilities in December 1942, Monmouth was notified that a Naval Flight Preparatory School would be established. Within four months, there were 600 naval cadets in training on campus. By 1944, the Navy was able to redirect its operations to larger airfields in the western and southwestern United States, and the Naval Flight Preparatory Schools were discontinued. In their place, however, Monmouth was designated as the site for a Navy Academic Refresher Unit (NARU) designed to prepare veterans and servicemen for officer training programs.

As the mobilization for World War II came to an end in late 1945 and the last of the Navy men left the campus, Monmouth received an official Mark of Commendation

*In 1944, 19-year-old Robert Meneilly (shown on the porch of the old "Teke" house) was preparing to enter Pittsburgh-Xenia Theological Seminary, following which he and his future wife, Shirley Dunlap '47, would become missionaries in China. The Communist revolution ended those plans, and instead the Meneillys went to Prairie Mission, Kansas, where they built a new church that rapidly grew into the second largest Presbyterian congregation in the country, with 6,000 members in 2002.*

from James Forrestal, Secretary of the Navy. Monmouth's connection with the military and its veterans was not at an end, however. Spurred by the G.I. Bill, many preflight and NARU men re-enrolled at Monmouth as regular college students, and they were joined by former Monmouth students who resumed interrupted educations. By 1947, no less than 45 percent of all students on campus held G.I. Bill scholarships, and by 1948 the total college enrollment swelled to more than 900 students.

### Post-War Adjustments

World War II had left one other important mark on student life. The military draft and the transformation of Monmouth into a military training camp had disrupted the normal cycle of activities for the Greek organizations. Monmouth's fraternities were deactivated during the war and were not re-instituted until the second semester of the 1945–46 school year. Once they reopened, fraternity houses were required to hire housemothers, provide evidence that the fraternity had abandoned all forms of physical hazing, and supply a list of eligible students who had placed bids and received invitations for membership from the fraternity.

These regulations were a clear indication that the college intended to exert firm control over fraternity life. Equally important was the sharply changed nature of the student body. Veterans returning to campus after the war were older and more mature than the students of 1940. They had experienced the rigors of warfare and had traveled to battlefields in Europe, Africa, and the Pacific. They were committed to completing their education, establishing families, and launching careers. Their values would shape the Monmouth College experience in the postwar era.

*Jean Liedman, a 1927 Monmouth graduate, returned to her alma mater in 1936 as an instructor in speech and served the college until her death in 1974, as both a professor and dean of women. Fondly known as "Dean Jean," she was honored in 1968 when a new dormitory for women was dedicated in her name.*

*Monmouth women barely had a chance to enjoy the elegant panelled living room of the new Grier Hall, when they were forced to relocate at the beginning of 1943 to make way for Naval cadets. Thirty-three months later, they were allowed to return.*

# The Monmouth College Cannon

DURING THE FIRST SEVERAL DECADES of the college's history, rivalries between the classes often reached battle pitch. Perhaps appropriately, one of the most celebrated of those rivalries—between the Classes of 1903 and 1904—involved a large piece of military ordnance.

On the eve of their graduation, members of the Class of 1903 managed to secure a Civil War cannon from the Rock Island Arsenal, which they planned to place in front of the flagpole on Broadway as a class gift. When certain juniors heard rumors that a sign—derogatory to their class—was to be erected near the cannon, they saw red and assembled to plot the cannon's abduction.

After delivery, the cannon stood unattended for several days on the platform of the C.B. & Q. freight depot, but eventually railroad officials deemed the cannon a nuisance and had it removed to a nearby dray yard, where it was stored in a barn. This was the opportunity that a group of nine young men—most from the Class of 1904—had been waiting for.

One night, after the last streetlight was extinguished, two horse-drawn wagons pulled up to the barn. The students hooked the cannon carriage to the back of one wagon, but when they tried to lift the 816-pound barrel onto the other wagon, it slipped into the mud, and they spent the next 90 minutes struggling to retrieve it.

By this time it was well after midnight, and the original plan—to dump the cannon in the Mississippi River—had to be abandoned. Instead, the young men tried to sink it in Cedar Creek, but the ground was too soft to allow them to get close enough to the water. Desperate, they burned the carriage, then took off for a nearby elevated bridge where they heaved the barrel into the muddy water. The next day, a farmer discovered the charred carriage remains, tipping off the seniors that their gift had been purloined. But despite an extensive search, the whereabouts of the cannon barrel and the identity of the perpetrators remained a mystery for nearly 50 years.

In 1950, Wallace Barnes, a newspaper publisher in Gallup, New Mexico, stepped forward to admit that he was the lead conspirator in the plot, revealing the story behind the theft and the location of the cannon barrel. A series of expeditions to find the barrel ensued, but because the stream had shifted course over the years, it was nowhere to be found.

Finally, Professor Garrett Thiessen, who had become obsessed with the hunt, enlisted the aid of the gas company, and a metal detector was brought to the scene. On October 9, 1952, the cannon was found. It was raised from the mud, brought to campus, and buried nose-down in a collar of concrete (to discourage potential thieves) just below Thiessen's office window in McMichael Science Hall.

The cannon was later moved across campus to make way for the new Wells Theater, but it retained its concrete collar. In 1996, one of Professor Bill Urban's history students mentioned that her father, a Civil War reenactor, thought the cannon could be restored. Shortly thereafter, the relic was exhumed and meticulously cleaned. Meanwhile, the family of the late Kenneth Mueller '60 donated a faithful reproduction of the original carriage in his memory. Today, the restored weapon resides in the lobby of Haldeman-Thiessen Science Center, where a heavy chain and padlock guard against future class hijinks.

*Neil Verigan '54 (left) was one of the lucky people present when the elusive barrel of the Class of 1903's cannon was finally located in October 1952, nearly 50 years after it had disappeared in Cedar Creek. Standing is education professor Albert Nicholas, who led the search party along with chemistry professor Garrett Thiessen and classics professor Harold Ralston.*

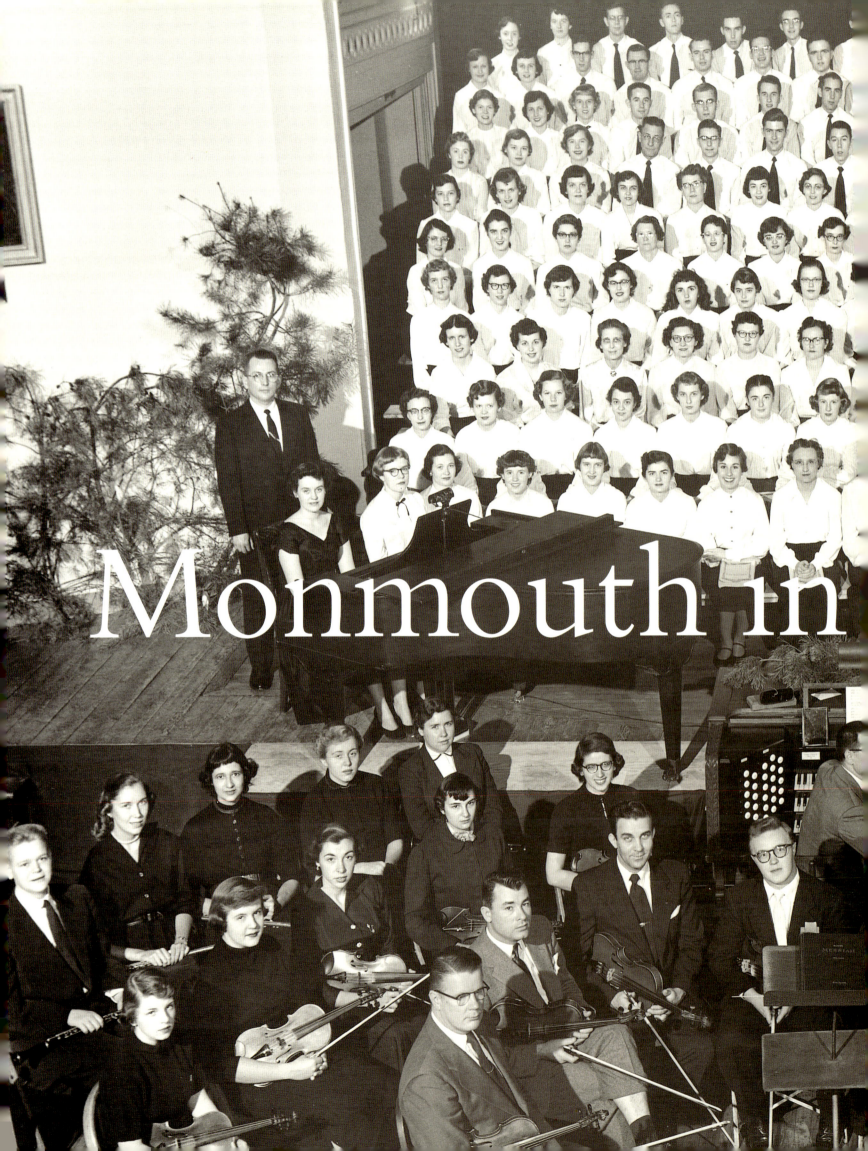

# Transition
## 1952–1964

## Chapter 7

For Monmouth, the 1950s and early 1960s were years of apparent calm and stability. Monmouth's strengths as a liberal arts college were effectively sustained, as were its traditionally close ties between faculty and students. Yet many aspects of American life were being affected by a widespread shift in values, a change that would impact Monmouth and all other institutions of higher education. Administrators and faculty at Monmouth recognized the scope of these developments and responded with new plans for the college's future.

PRECEDING PAGES
*A highlight of the school year during the 1950s was the annual performance of Handel's* Messiah *in the Auditorium. Students, faculty, and townspeople combined their talents, accompanied by piano, organ, and a full-fledged orchestra.*

OPPOSITE PAGE *In the fall of 1952, President Robert Wesson Gibson visits with freshmen sporting their special Centennial caps.*

### Religious Values

In the autumn of 1952, Robert Wesson Gibson arrived in Monmouth to assume the office of president. He followed five predecessors in the position who had also been ministers. Fifty-six years old and a native of Vermont, Gibson was a graduate of Muskingum College and Xenia Seminary. His career was marked by success as a pastor and as a church administrator in the role of general secretary of the Board of Christian Education. Gibson was especially concerned with maintaining the influence of the United Presbyterian Church in its affiliated colleges, and his leadership on this issue made him an appealing candidate to the Monmouth College search committee.

Monmouth College in the early 1950s was an institution still strongly shaped by its relationship to the United Presbyterian Church of North America and to denominational Protestantism. Nearly 25 percent of the college's alumni were United Presbyterians and another 50 percent were associated with other Protestant churches. While faculty members were not required to be members of a particular congregation, they were expected to support the college's relationship with the United Presbyterian Church and the ideal of education in a Christian tradition. Because the faculty was dedicated and loyal to Monmouth's mission, this assurance was freely given.

Religious organizations and activities played an important social and spiritual role on the campus. Gibson, as president and pastor, directed a monthly vesper service. Traditional daily chapel services continued to be held in the Auditorium, and attendance was required of all students. Chapel was a social event as much as a religious experience, a chance for the entire student body to come together to hear announcements and enjoy skits on Fridays. Many lasting friendships and romances developed between chapel seatmates. Chapel was also the scene of student pranks—flour that sifted down from a ceiling trap door onto the senior class, hundreds of marbles rolling down the floor during a solemn moment, and missing fraternity trophies found stuffed into organ pipes.

The College Choir, which performed in chapel services, also presented Handel's *Messiah* during the Christmas holidays and a cantata or other devotional piece during the Easter season. Student gospel teams met weekly and traveled to churches in Illinois and Iowa to conduct worship services. The Ichthus Club, a student Christian group, conducted a Sunday afternoon devotional hour and was responsible for one of the daily chapel services during the week.

Monmouth was also home to an active YMCA and YWCA movement. Students involved in the "Y" met a wide range of needs within the Monmouth community, such as providing food baskets for the needy, performing yard cleanups for the elderly, holding blood drives, tutoring underprivileged children, and coaching basketball games in the city's YMCA youth league. Many students involved in the "Y" were also active in the gospel teams and the Ichthus Club.

In 1958, the United Presbyterian Church of North America merged with the Presbyterian Church in the United States to form the United Presbyterian Church (USA). With this change, Monmouth came under the authority of the

*A Presbyterian minister and administrator, Robert Gibson came to the Monmouth presidency with an interest in strengthening church ties while promoting Christian values both in and out of the classroom.*

# Monmouth's Centennial

IN THE SPRING OF 1953, Monmouth celebrated its Centennial with a series of special programs and commemorations. Planning was already under way when President Gibson arrived on campus. "The previous administration had set the stage for the Centennial year," Gibson later wrote, "and immediately I found myself thrust into an important role in that drama." In honor of the anniversary, a Centennial version of the college seal appeared and was featured on the plaid caps worn by incoming freshmen.

President Gibson's inauguration on April 17, 1953, was one of the most impressive Centennial events. Representatives in academic dress from 200 colleges and universities gathered to march into the Auditorium with members of the Senate, the faculty, and the Centennial class of 1953. In a ceremony marked by congratulatory addresses and solemn hymns, President Grier formally installed President Gibson as his successor in office and presented him with the college seal. Honorary doctoral degrees were awarded to chemistry professor William Haldeman and Emma Jean Cherry, a nationally known hymnologist. Later President and Mrs. Gibson joined guests for a luncheon in McMichael dining hall and hosted a reception for visitors at the presidential residence, the Manor. Inauguration day also brought the official publication of *Monmouth College: The First Hundred Years, 1853–1953*, the Centennial history written by Professor F. Garvin Davenport.

The anniversary reached its culmination at the beginning of June. On June 7 and 8, the college honored returning alumni with a musicale of vesper music, an alumni-library tea, baccalaureate service, class reunion luncheons, and an alumni banquet in McMichael Residence with members of the 50-year class of 1903 as special guests. The next day, 95 seniors received their degrees in the Centennial commencement held outdoors in front of Wallace Hall. Six distinguished guests were presented with honorary doctorates, including commencement speaker Rudolph Nottleman, Assiut College lay missionary Milo McFeeters, and Mrs. Edith Reese Crabtree, national president of Kappa Kappa Gamma. As the alumni *Bulletin* reported, "the weather held," and Monmouth began its second century with warm memories and renewed commitment.

*The recently recovered Class of 1903 cannon was celebrated in the centennial homecoming parade with a float titled "Shooting Thru a Century."*

*The humiliations of the freshman year were somewhat lessened in the fall of 1952 as new students got to wear a special cap commemorating the centennial.*

Monmouth in Transition 1952–1964

newly established Synod of Illinois. The institutional governance of Monmouth College remained in the hands of the College Senate, a body of 40 members, 22 of which were chosen by the church judicatories, the synods, and the presbytery.

Monmouth also continued to benefit from financial support of the church, although the level of support began to wane by the end of the 1950s. Until the time of the Presbyterian merger in 1958, Monmouth had received $55,000 or more annually. In the first year after the union, church support was maintained at $55,000, but thereafter the annual amount declined until it reached $30,000 in 1962. As America's public and private colleges and universities expanded in the 1950s, the Presbyterian Church felt increasingly drawn to focus its work on the growing student populations at the largest state institutions. Other needs such as civil rights and Third World missions were also becoming more prominent. With the decline in formal church financial support and the rising costs of operating the college, Monmouth officials recognized that fiscal integrity would increasingly depend on a steady base of student enrollment and the continuing support of alumni and friends. This meant outreach beyond the traditional Presbyterian base.

In the next decade, further shifts in Monmouth's relationship to the Presbyterian Church occurred as traditional religious beliefs and practices on campus were eroded by the growing influence of secular values and the college's increasingly diverse population. The transition was seen in many aspects of the college's communal life, but perhaps no more prominently than in the steady decline in the required chapel service. From the scheduled daily service that had been maintained for more than a century, the chapel meetings were reduced to three a week in 1959, two a week in 1962, and then to one a week in 1963. By the beginning of the 1960s, changes in society and in the student body had also begun to have an effect on participation in religious organizations on campus. Interest in the gospel teams and the Ichthus Club had fallen, and traditional YMCA and YWCA programs experienced similar declines.

Through these transformations, President Gibson remained steadfast in his commitment to the importance of Christian values in undergraduate education. But he also understood that the times required a reassessment of the college's academic offerings and a reinvigoration of culture and the arts on campus. Advances toward these goals would become the hallmarks of his administration.

### New Ventures in Education

In the spring of 1954, the Illinois State Academy of Science held its annual meeting at Monmouth, bringing 2,000 participants and 500 exhibits to the campus. Hosted by Professors Garrett W. Thiessen and Lyle Finley, the event also received the strong support of President Gibson, who saw the gathering of scientists as an avenue for exploring Monmouth's academic needs in the next generation. From the Illinois Academy meeting came the beginnings of Monmouth's planning for two significant facilities, a new science center to replace McMichael Science Hall and a modern library to succeed the Carnegie Library. Although these plans would not be realized immediately, their development was an important focus of faculty and administrative energies.

*Students walking to chapel were a familiar morning sight during the Gibson years.*

Equally significant for Monmouth's academic expansion was the formation of the Associated Colleges of the Midwest in 1958. An outgrowth of the Midwest Athletic Conference, the ACM was established with a substantial grant from the Ford Foundation. This new consortium brought Monmouth into closer association with its private liberal arts peers and served as an incentive for further educational development. It also provided possibilities for an array of cooperative programs, including overseas study centers, urban studies, and collaborative development of library resources. For Monmouth, membership in the ACM helped support offerings such as the Washington Semester, its first off-campus program. Under the direction of Professor F. Garvin Davenport, this program enabled selected students to study in the nation's capital.

The renewal of liberal arts at Monmouth took many forms, but among the most satisfying to President Gibson was the successful launch of a studio program in art. Expanding on the art department's existing emphasis on art appreciation, Gibson recruited Harlow Blum in 1959 to head a program devoted to drawing, painting, and sculpting. Blum's successful program became an important keystone in Monmouth's new ventures in the arts.

In 1959, Gibson also launched the Liberal Arts Festival, an imaginative program bringing together important intellectuals, artists, and political figures to discuss issues of the day for the benefit of the college and the Monmouth community. The first festival in 1959 explored the role of the liberal arts in the modern world. It was followed by a second in 1961 on the past as prelude to the future, a third festival in 1963 devoted to the role of Asia in world affairs, and a fourth in 1967 examining Latin America. Each festival was enhanced by a week of concentrated studies on the main theme and a series of related programs throughout the academic year.

Like the Illinois Academy meeting, the Liberal Arts Festival generated an important new venture in education. In the months leading up to the second festival in 1961, a faculty committee explored ways to establish an East Asian Studies program. Consultants engaged by the college recommended that the program emphasize Japanese studies. As part of the Liberal Arts Festival that year, President Gibson announced the creation of the new academic program.

Significant steps were also taken to expand Monmouth's offerings in language studies. In an era when the role of the United States was expanding throughout the world and when competition with the Soviet Union was increasing, knowledge of foreign languages took on fresh importance. In May 1961, Professor Dorothy Donald concluded a four and one-half-year effort to establish a state-of-the-art language laboratory at Monmouth. Under Donald's influence, the ACM had made language study a major aspect of its cooperative programs, and she expanded on this base by successfully securing a grant provided by Title IV of the National

*A 1924 graduate of Monmouth College, Lyle Finley joined the faculty in 1931 as a mathematician. He directed the science division of the college's U.S. Naval program during World War II and later became chairman of the physics department.*

## A Classicist Turned Chemist

WHILE WILLIAM HALDEMAN receives due credit for laying the groundwork for Monmouth College's nationally known chemistry department of the mid-twentieth century, his endeavor was aided considerably by Garrett W. Thiessen, who joined the faculty in 1930. Forty years later, the two legendary professors were linked in perpetuity by the naming of the new Haldeman-Thiessen Science Center.

While Haldeman tenaciously focused his efforts on the training of chemists, Thiessen's fertile mind refused to be focused on any one subject for long.

Said one student, "He is probably the most well-rounded professor that Monmouth College ever had. He could teach any course in chemistry, math, and physics and took no back seat in languages and classics."

A Phi Beta Kappa graduate of Cornell College with majors in both classics and chemistry, Thiessen decided that chemistry was the more practical occupation, and he pursued his doctorate in that discipline from the University of Iowa. Coming to Monmouth, he rose through the ranks from instructor to full professor, embracing Haldeman's vision of Monmouth as an incubator of chemists. In 1952 he succeeded his colleague as chair of the department.

In 1957, the Manufacturing Chemists Association named Thiessen one of the nation's six outstanding teachers of undergraduate chemistry. Three years later, he was the first chemistry professor to receive an appointment to the faculty at Argonne National Laboratories in conjunction with the Associated Colleges of the Midwest's Argonne Semester Program.

There was life beyond science for Thiessen, though, including his commitment to service in the Second United Presbyterian Church, where he was a deacon, an elder, and a Sunday school teacher.

A lifetime member of the National Rifle Association, Thiessen convinced the college to establish a rifle team and served as its coach, producing two national individual champions and one championship team.

"Doc," as Thiessen was called, was also well known for his sense of humor. He composed a large number of limericks that he could recite endlessly, including the following example, entitled *Udder Confusion*:

> *There once was a farmer named Menser,*
> *Who installed an electrical fencer;*
> *But his favorite cow*
> *Got a shock on her prow*
> *And would not let him work her dispenser.*

*Wearing his glasses high on his forehead, Garrett Thiessen demonstrates a complex experiment. A trademark of the beloved chemistry professor was his habit of letting the glasses drop to the bridge of his nose when needed by raising his eyebrows.*

Thiessen was also known for finding and protecting the stolen Civil War cannon that was intended as a senior gift from the Class of 1903. When Thiessen's search party located the cannon in Cedar Creek in 1952, he had it placed outside in a large cement ring just to the south of McMichael Science Hall where he could see it every time he looked out his office window.

Sadly, Thiessen did not live to see the dedication of the new science building named in his honor. He died suddenly in 1967 while still a member of the faculty.

*Charter members of Monmouth's Tau Kappa Epsilon fraternity attend a 1953 homecoming banquet in honor of the chapter's 25th anniversary. Front row (from left): former national TKE president Harrold P. Flint (who installed the chapter in 1928), Robert Piggott '31, David Livingston '22, George Worcester '30, business manager Richard Petrie '29, philosophy professor Sam Thompson '24, and Benjamin Hill '20. Back row: Richard Homes '28, Harold Mekemson '31, "Gus" McClanahan '29, Robert Shauman '30, trustee Robert Acheson '28, and George Mekemson '31.*

Defense Education Act. With support from federal funds, the Eva Louise Barr Language Laboratory was created on the top floor of Wallace Hall. Featuring listening cubicles and a playback sound system, the laboratory became the center for a staff of 11 full-time instructors teaching courses in Spanish, German, French, Russian, and Japanese.

### Recasting Liberal Arts

These new initiatives aimed at expanding the educational programs prompted a systematic review of Monmouth's liberal arts curriculum. A special Faculty Long-Range Planning Committee was formed, with a broadly representative membership that included Ben Shawver, Mary Crow, Garvin Davenport, Dorothy Donald, James Herbsleb, John Ketterer, Heimo Loya, James McAllister, and Floyd Rawlings. The committee's final report, "Profile of Monmouth College, 1954–1974," was submitted in the spring of 1961, and its recommendations were formally implemented in 1962–63.

The profile affirmed that Monmouth would remain a residential, coeducational college offering a comprehensive liberal arts program of high quality to a selected student body. Reflecting forecasts of increasing national college enrollments, the report projected that Monmouth's student body would grow to a high of 1,600 and its faculty to 90. Students would be offered the new range of liberal arts courses then being developed—independent study, East Asian studies, audio-visual education, and overseas study programs. Equally important, the report introduced a new 3–3 curriculum, which divided the academic year into three 11-week terms, with each student taking three courses each term. The 3–3 curriculum permitted faculty to teach fewer courses while providing students with more focused, in-depth study and less distraction from competing courses.

In adopting the profile's recommendations, the college also took further steps to refine the focus of liberal arts education. The secretarial and home economics departments were discontinued, and the emphasis of economics and business instruction was shifted to economics, a subject that had stronger scholarly credentials and was more closely tied to the liberal arts. Students capable of mastering material in specified courses could take an advanced placement examination and move directly to upper-level work. In addition, all entering freshmen were now required to read a specified list of books before coming to campus. In their first week on campus, freshmen would meet with faculty to discuss the

*1954 homecoming queen Margaret Ramsdale and her attendants—Joan Bayliss, Martha Gadske, Rusty Nichols, and Sandra Mason—ride a float down Broadway.*

*Longtime English professor Adele Kennedy (center) is honored upon her retirement in 1977 by former colleagues Eva Cleland (left) and Dorothy Donald.*

PRECEDING PAGES
*An instructional innovation of the 1960s was the language lab, in which students could practice their pronunciation of foreign languages by listening to audio tapes of native speakers. Simultaneously, an instructor could listen to and interact with any given booth. Located on the third floor of Wallace Hall, Monmouth's lab was named in honor of alumna and longtime German and Spanish professor Eva Louise Barr.*

ABOVE RIGHT *Rod Lemon '64 lays out an issue of* The Oracle. *Today, Lemon is professor of political economy and commerce at Monmouth.*

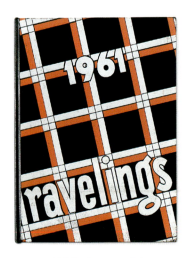

*While the cover of the student yearbook has changed regularly to reflect the times, it has retained the name* Ravelings *since its first issue in 1892.*

books, and later in the year they would be given an examination to test their comprehension of the material.

Following these dramatic curricular decisions, President Gibson began the expansion of the faculty recommended in the profile. In 1963, 17 new faculty members were hired, substantially increasing the size of the faculty and raising the number of faculty with PhDs to 64 percent. Accompanied by an increase in enrollment to 880 students, the new profile of liberal arts education at Monmouth was now beginning to take shape.

### Enhancing Student Life

Following a nationwide trend, Monmouth students of the 1950s found new outlets for their energies through an explosion of new clubs, activities, and athletic teams.

Student government elections reached a fever pitch, as electioneering included torchlight parades, taxi service, brass bands, portable loudspeakers, and even free cigarettes. In the days before an election, the lobby of Wallace Hall became a miniature Times Square, with flamboyant posters and banners hanging on walls, stairways, and ceilings. When the number of votes cast in one election exceeded the enrollment, the *Chicago Tribune* commented that perhaps the Chicago political machine could take lessons from the Fighting Scots. Such flagrant abuses led to the implementation of an electoral system in 1958, in which each class was given a percentage of votes based on how many of its members voted.

The postwar decade saw a surge of popularity in the sciences—including psychology and sociology and the myriad experiments associated with those disciplines. When preparing a paper about memory, one student switched the toothbrushes of the residents of Winbigler Hall. The finding was that about 60 percent of the women remembered the color of their toothbrush. Less than 25 percent remembered the brand, and nearly 100 percent did not appreciate the exercise.

In the 1950s, Greek-letter organizations remained a strong presence on campus and were the center of Monmouth social life. Each year, the eight fraternities and sororities pledged the maximum number allowed, but this still left many non-Greek students without much social life. Their needs were met by the formation of an independent organization open to both men and women, with "Indie" social events mirroring those of the fraternities and sororities.

At the outset of President Gibson's administration in 1952, there were 219 students in the entering freshman class, and Monmouth's total enrollment was 537 students. With enrollment growing to more than 800 and further expansion projected to as many as 1,600 students, the

# Crimson Masque and the Monmouth Theater

WHEN RUTH WILLIAMS, a graduate of the highly respected Northwestern University School of Speech, came to Monmouth College in 1923, she knew she faced an uphill battle. Not only was there no dramatic organization or facility for producing a play, but the Senate had passed a resolution just 15 years earlier stating, "Whereas the Modern Theatre is recognized by Christian People as an education in vice and a corrupter of morals…therefore Resolved that the Senate of Monmouth College recommend…that nothing will be given that is inconsistent with the Christian Character of the Student or the Christian influence of the College."

Through Williams's perseverance, however, the Crimson Masque was organized on November 4, 1925, with 60 charter members. She immediately convinced the administration to give the former gymnasium to the program, which was transformed into the Little Theatre. Over the next 65 years, it was home to dazzling productions of Shakespeare, Shaw, Ibsen, Williams, and Albee.

The theater was organized on a professional basis with house managers, a business manager, technicians, and a publicity manager. In 1929, Williams established a chapter of the National Collegiate Players.

When she left Monmouth in 1947 to accept a position at Mississippi State College for Women, Williams was succeeded by Ralph Fulsom, another product of Northwestern. Fulsom's genius for perfection brought the theater program to fruition with challenging productions of *Antigone* and *The Glass Menagerie*. Fulsom left in 1950 to continue graduate work and was replaced by Howard Gongwer, who directed the theater until 1956, the 30th anniversary of Crimson Masque. In that year, an ambitious production of *Hamlet* was staged, with Charles Chatfield '56 in the lead role and a supporting cast that included Aleece Reifinger '56, Ken Lister '56, John Niblock '58, Judy Reed '57, and Hal Sanford '56.

Taking over for Gongwer was a young man just out of graduate school, Parker Zellers. One of his first efforts was a highly successful production of *Brigadoon*. But his most memorable experience occurred during the Liberal Arts Festival of 1959, when actress Agnes Moorehead (best known for her role as Samantha Stevens's mother in the hit television series *Bewitched*) attended his production of Shaw's *Arms and the Man*. She was made an honorary member of Crimson Masque.

Brooks McNamera, who later became a respected theater historian at New York University, considered his brief tenure as theater director—from 1961 to 1963—a valuable education in stagecraft and the art of getting by with what you have. "To my dying day I'll never forget the experience of directing plays in the winter when cast, crew, and director were forced to be bundled up in overcoats during much of the rehearsal period," he wrote a few years later.

For the next four decades, the theater would be in the worthy hands of James De Young, a graduate of Beloit College who earned his PhD from the University of Minnesota. De Young presided over the maturation of the program, guiding it beyond the Little Theatre to the experimental Red Barn East in the former Carnegie Library, and finally in 1990 to its permanent home in the Wells Theater. Along the way, he gave students a first-hand look at the British stage through the ACM London Arts Program and independently organized trips abroad.

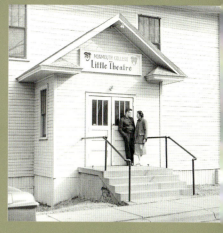

*Originally the college gymnasium, the Little Theatre was home to Crimson Masque productions for more than 60 years. The beloved structure was razed in 1990 to make way for additional parking when the new Wells Theater was completed.*

*Parker Zellers directed a memorable production of Lerner and Lowe's* Brigadoon *in 1958.*

Monmouth in Transition 1952–1964

*Students help clear fallen tree limbs from the front of Wallace Hall following a devastating windstorm that blew through campus on September 26, 1959.*

*Smartly dressed majorettes lead the Monmouth College marching band in a 1950s homecoming parade.*

college needed to improve conditions for student housing and activities.

President Gibson's first steps were to redecorate East Hall (later Austin Hall) and McMichael Residence Hall. Plans were initiated for a new student center so that Wallace Hall could be used exclusively for classrooms and faculty offices. In 1958, Gibson also moved the college's administrative offices from Carnegie Library to the former Fine Arts Building at Sixth and Broadway so that the library's space could be dedicated exclusively to the book collections.

In 1959, Monmouth erected its second men's residence hall, named Graham Hall for Professor Russell Graham, Class of 1870, former professor of social science, and his son Dr. Ralph Graham, Class of 1897, who had served as college physician and trustee. Graham Hall provided three stories of living quarters with spacious lounges and a guest apartment.

In 1963, the new Student Center opened in its own building at the foot of the slope north of Wallace Hall. The facility contained the college's main dining hall, and a basement snack bar later named The Styx in honor of the occasional flooding that occurred there. Other space in the building provided post office boxes, conference rooms, student publications, banquet halls, a game room, a bowling alley, a radio station, and a TV lounge. The college bookstore, which was managed by James Foster, Class of 1914, was also moved into the Student Center; the concentration of facilities made the center an immediate focus of college social life.

The Gibson administration took additional steps to enhance the experience of women on campus. All women students, except some "townies," lived in the dormitories. For years the freshman women's residence hall had both a housemother and upperclassmen who served as counselors. At the suggestion of the president, Dean Jean Liedman assigned dorm counselors into each of the women's residence halls. The counselors interacted with students on a less restrictive basis than the former housemothers, and they also assisted with the management of numerous clubs and organizations.

The situation of sororities was also improved. Unlike Monmouth's fraternities, the women's Greek organizations had never had residential houses; instead, the college provided meeting rooms. In 1951, Alpha Xi Delta, Kappa Delta, Kappa Kappa Gamma, and Pi Beta Phi vacated their chapter rooms in the Terrace, the former president's home at the corner of Ninth and Broadway, and moved into larger quarters in

*Joe Tait '59 (center) helped pioneer radio broadcasts of Fighting Scots sports. Today, he is the radio voice of the NBA Cleveland Cavaliers and a member of the Broadcasters Hall of Fame.*

*Led by the legendary "Three Macs"—Bob McLoskey, Bob McKee and Jerry McBride—the 1956–57 Fighting Scots compiled a record of 22–4 and reached the NCAA tournament before losing to the University of South Dakota 62–52. From left are Bob Yarde '58, Jim Rilott '58, Ken Mueller '60, Tom Reimers '58, McLoskey '58, McKee '58, and McBride '58.*

Marshall Hall. A former private residence acquired by the college in 1937, Marshall Hall was now refashioned as the college's Pan-Hellenic Center.

Much of what had been achieved for the enhancement of the campus grounds was threatened on September 26, 1959, when a powerful storm of near-tornado strength swept through Monmouth, moving from the southwest to the northeast. Winds driving at more than 60 miles per hour shattered hundreds of large trees, uprooted smaller ones, and dumped torn limbs on cars and lawns. One man in town was killed by a falling tree, and four others were injured. Student volunteers quickly sprang into action, lifting limbs from crushed cars, directing traffic away from downed power lines, and clearing broken trees from the campus and neighboring yards. Nearly all the stately trees on the lawn fronting Wallace Hall were lost to the storm, as were many that had shaded the residence halls for years. The beauty of the campus had suffered a severe blow, but the enthusiastic efforts to clear the debris showed the resilience of the college community.

The triumph over adversity in the storm of 1959 might be seen as a theme for another area of Monmouth life during this period: collegiate sports. Although the 1950s and early 1960s were not the strongest era for Monmouth athletics, the Fighting Scots recorded some notable victories. In 1954, the Monmouth track team won the Midwest Conference championship under the leadership of coach Glenn "Jelly" Robinson. The team won the championship once more in 1961 under the direction of athletic director Chuck Larson. Basketball was another sport with memorable high points. In 1955, Pete Kovacs's

*Visiting high school seniors were entertained by a talent show in the Auditorium in the spring of 1959.*

**Monmouth in Transition 1952–1964**

## Class Warfare

THE COLOR RUSH, an annual collegiate battle between freshman and sophomore classes, was a time-honored tradition at many colleges beginning in the late nineteenth century. At Monmouth, it took the form of a "pole scrap" in which the sophomore class nailed its colors to the top of a telephone pole and fended off waves of freshmen trying to climb the pole and tear them down. At stake were bragging rights and, in later years, the freshmen earning the privilege to dispense with wearing the hated "freshman cap."

The first recorded Monmouth Pole Scrap occurred October 20, 1902, when the sophomores tacked their colors on top of an abandoned utility pole in front of campus. After the regular morning chapel, the sophomores goaded the freshmen, who rose to the challenge they could hardly escape. The first scrap ended when the pole was broken off and the sophomore colors were ingloriously dragged away.

The date of the annual event was a closely guarded secret. Early on the designated morning, a few weeks after the opening of the fall term, the old steam whistle on the heating plant would sound, signaling the suspension of classes and notifying contestants and spectators to assemble in front of Carnegie Library where the festivities would commence. A crowd of students and townspeople, often numbering more than 2,000, would gather as freshman and sophomore men, stripped to the waist, prepared to do battle. The biggest fear among the scrappers was losing one's pants, so contestants appeared with yards of adhesive tape wrapped securely around thighs and ankles.

As the Pole Scrap tradition became entrenched, formal rules were introduced and offensive and defensive strategies were developed. There were two periods of 20 minutes each. In the first, the freshmen were given an advantage of 10 men. In the first half of the second period, each class was allowed an equal number of men. In the second half, the freshmen could have an advantage of two to one. One of the best offensive plans involved assigning one or two freshmen to a sophomore according to size, with three men tackling the larger football players. With the principal combatants occupied, a concealed freshman would emerge from the bushes equipped with climbing irons and make short work of climbing the pole.

With the coming of World War II, the Pole Scrap had to be discontinued due to a lack of men on campus. Instead, freshman and sophomore women staged an annual tug of war. The Scrap was revived in 1946, but six years later it was outlawed by a vote of the student government, who deemed it old-fashioned and dangerous.

*The final Monmouth College pole scrap was staged in the fall of 1952. Students considered the annual contest old-fashioned if not barbaric, and they gladly exchanged the traditional school holiday for a four-day Thanksgiving weekend.*

*A favorite student hangout beginning in the 1960s was Pinney's Tap, located just two blocks from campus on Eleventh Street. Today the former tavern is part of the Monmouth College maintenance garage.*

number 36 was retired in honor of his many basketball scoring records, which culminated in a total of 1,499 points during his basketball career. Two years later, the Monmouth basketball team was invited to the NCAA regionals, but it lost to the eventual tournament champion, South Dakota. For most of the 1950s, the football team battled valiantly under coach Joe Pelisek, although winning seasons proved elusive. What did not wane was the spirited football rivalry with Knox College in the annual Bronze Turkey gridiron game and the passionate loyalty of Monmouth's fans.

It was a women's sport, however, that achieved the most distinctive success in these years. Women on the rifle team coached by Professor Garrett Thiessen won repeated national rankings, beginning with Hazel Hatch's first-place victory in 1948 and continuing to Joan Phifer's number-one ranking in 1954. The rifle team also won first place in the National Intercollegiate Women's Prone Rifle Match in April 1954, bringing home Monmouth's only national sports championship.

### The Passing of an Era

By 1963, the accumulating changes in Monmouth's institutional life were beginning to be fully felt. The student body and faculty were growing rapidly in size. New courses were reshaping the traditional liberal arts curriculum. Shifts in values and expectations among both faculty and students were signaling more dramatic changes to come. In this environment, President Gibson announced that he would retire in 1964. The president had led the college a great distance in 12 eventful years, and he felt satisfied with what had been achieved. He had exemplified the traditional values most desired in Monmouth's presidents—deep Christian faith, generous personal manner, and earnest commitment to a sound educational experience. Monmouth's next president would need to build on Gibson's record of thoughtful transition and face increasing challenges in the years to come.

*By the 1950s, instead of just having its own class colors, each freshman class got to wear a Scottish cap with a unique tartan design.*

**Monmouth in Transition 1952–1964**

# The Impact of
## 1964-1974

# Change

# Chapter 8

Monmouth in the mid-1960s was riding the crest of a surge in college population and a dramatic expansion in American higher education. The college had reformed its curriculum and planned for dramatic growth to meet the opportunities of the times. But the combined effects of war in Southeast Asia and economic fluctuations at home placed all of these expectations at risk. Throughout a decade of rapid and disruptive change, Monmouth was forced to reassess its most basic values and reshape its plans for the future.

PRECEDING PAGES
*Braving 60-below-zero wind chills, 800 students and 68 faculty members carry 130,000 volumes down the hill from the old Carnegie Library to the new Hewes Library on January 21, 1970. Classes were cancelled for the day-long marathon, which had been meticulously planned by the Blue Key organization and the faculty library committee. A color-coding system, devised by librarian Harris Hauge, directed the books to the proper location. Students celebrated that evening with a dance, after having dined on a giant Jell-O mold in the shape of a book.*

OPPOSITE PAGE
*A 1968 rally in Monmouth's West Park saw students demonstrating on both sides of the Vietnam issue.*

## Generational Succession

Robert Gibson's decision to retire after 12 years as president left many challenges for his successor. The new president would need strong leadership and managerial skills to develop the 3–3 curriculum, expand the faculty, increase the student body to its projected size, construct new buildings in accordance with the campus plan, and secure the necessary financial support for this unprecedented growth.

The person selected by the search committee in 1964 was fully prepared to meet these expectations. A 1946 graduate of the University of Oregon, Gordon Duncan Wimpress had taught journalism and public relations at Whittier College in California. In 1950, he earned a master's degree and served as assistant to the president of the Colorado School of Mines. After completing a doctorate in speech at the University of Colorado in 1958, he accepted the presidency of Monticello College (later Lewis and Clark College) in Godfrey, Illinois. In combination with his experiences in California and Colorado, his five years of leadership at Monticello had made him eager for enlarged administrative challenges.

The selection of Wimpress was a sharp departure for Monmouth. Not only was he the first layman appointed president of the college, but at 41 years of age he was a full generation younger than 68-year-old President Gibson. He flew airplanes, loved driving sports cars, played the drums, and belonged to the Young Presidents Organization, a select group of those who had become presidents of institutions before the age of 40.

The new president's natural sociability was enhanced soon after his arrival in 1964 by Ivory and Betty Quinby's gift to the college of Quinby House to serve as the president's residence. This beautiful Victorian mansion standing on the rise north of campus was an ideal place for displaying the furniture and chess sets that Wimpress collected. It also became a congenial setting for social occasions involving faculty, alumni, and friends of the college.

Wimpress' congenial personality and confident demeanor had an immediate effect on Monmouth. He reaffirmed the commitment to the liberal arts made during the Gibson administration and assured faculty members that their teaching and research were essential components of the college's continued success. He became active in the Monmouth Rotary and helped present a fresh image of the college to the community.

*Duncan Wimpress was just 41 years old when he assumed the Monmouth College presidency in 1964. He was the first president who was not an ordained minister, and his administration would usher in an era of increased secularization and expansion for the institution.*

*Departing from its long tradition as a strictly Presbyterian school, Monmouth College by the mid-'60s had taken on a more ecumenical flavor. Comprising the religion department in this 1967 photograph were, from left: Father Paul Showalter, a Catholic priest and lecturer; the Reverend Stafford Weeks, professor; Rama Manandhar, a former Nepalese ambassador; the Reverend Paul McClanahan, assistant professor and chaplain; the Reverend Charles Speel, professor; and Abraham Kotsuji, a visiting Japanese lecturer.*

# Quinby House

LAWYER, MERCHANT, BANKER, land speculator, judge—Ivory Quinby was all of these, but to Monmouth College he was much more. A member of the college's first board of trustees, Quinby gave generously of his money and sage business advice to help the fledgling college prior to his premature death in 1869. His legacy lives on at Monmouth College, however, in the home he had built just two years earlier.

Quinby House, an imposing Italianate mansion that stands on a rise overlooking the northwest corner of campus, remained in the Quinby family for nearly a century. Ivory Quinby's widow, Mary, lived there until her death in 1907. It then became the home of her son, Ivory II, a longtime member of the college's board of trustees, and her grandson, Ivory III, who succeeded his father on the board in 1929 and remained a trustee until 1964.

In 1965, Quinby and his wife, Elizabeth, proposed to deed the family home to Monmouth College to be used as a presidential manse. In exchange, the college agreed to let them live their remaining years in a handsome college-owned cottage near the campus. The first new residents of Quinby House were President and Mrs. Duncan Wimpress, who furnished it with choice antiques and made it the setting for frequent elegant receptions and dinner parties.

By the early 1990s, time had finally begun to take a toll on the mansion. Despite ongoing maintenance efforts by the college physical plant staff, trees and foliage surrounding the house had grown dense and led to rotting and mildew. The house's mechanical systems were outdated and potentially dangerous. At the suggestion of physical plant director Pete Loomis, the college applied for and received a historic preservation grant from the Illinois Department of Transportation. The grant, which recognized the first Ivory Quinby's role in helping establish the Peoria and Oquawka Railroad (later C.B. & Q.), funded the major portion of a two-year project, in which the house was gutted and rebuilt from the inside out.

Today, Quinby House is not only a college landmark, but a national one, thanks to the foresight of its third presidential resident, DeBow Freed, who in 1979 asked his administrative assistant Eileen Sandburg Loya '40 to prepare a nomination for listing the house on the National Register of Historic Places. Her yearlong research project uncovered a wealth of information, especially about the architect, John C. Cochrane, whose Chicago firm had designed dozens of important public buildings, including the Illinois and Iowa State Capitols. Fortunately, the Quinbys had retained an extensive archive of family documents, including Cochrane's original plans for the house.

A dedication of the renovated house at homecoming 1997 drew a large crowd of interested townspeople and dignitaries. Cutting the ribbon were the daughters of Ivory and Elizabeth Quinby, Jane Lowell '48 and Anne Dyni '56, who maintain a love for the house and have donated family heirlooms for display.

*Elizabeth and Ivory Quinby III in 1948.*

*Designed by the noted Chicago architect John C. Cochrane a century earlier, Quinby House fittingly reflected President Wimpress' inaugural theme, "A Touch of Elegance," when it was presented by the Quinby family as a presidential residence in 1965.*

*Chester Hewes (right), who with his wife, Mabel, provided the $1 million naming gift for Hewes Library, talks with director of development Glen Rankin (left) and chaplain Paul McClanahan at the library's dedication. (Hewes was enticed to marry Mabel after her brother created a mixture of Vaseline and coal dust in 1913 to darken her pale eyelashes. Two years later, the Maybelline company was founded by her brother, deriving its name from Mabel Hewes and Vaseline.)*

*An aerial photo of Monmouth College in 1966 shows the initial stages of President Wimpress' vision for the modern campus. Three new residence halls — Gibson, Cleland, and the Fraternity Complex — had been recently completed. Liedman Hall would follow in 1968, while construction of Hewes Library and Haldeman-Thiessen Science Center would commence shortly thereafter.*

The Wimpress administration also adopted a new stance of greater independence from the United Presbyterian Church. Shortly after his arrival, Monmouth secured the synod's approval for a change in the organization of the Senate. The controlling church judicatory would no longer have any role in nominating, confirming, or denying approval for membership in the Senate. Instead, Monmouth would have a self-perpetuating college board that would select 30 of its 33 members, the other three being selected by the alumni of the college. Henceforth, the church's synod would be an affiliated synod, not a controlling synod.

The increasing secularization this change reflected was accompanied by a further reduction in official religious observances on campus. By 1964–65, the Ichthus Club, gospel teams, and college "Y" groups had ceased to function. Now, by a vote of the faculty, weekday chapel services were discontinued, although vesper services would still be offered once a month on Sunday afternoons.

### College Expansion

President Wimpress' first priority was implementing the college expansion plan developed by the Gibson administration. National trends put Monmouth in a favorable position to accomplish this goal. As the national student population swelled in the 1960s, East Coast colleges and universities could not meet the growing demand for admission. Students denied access to crowded eastern institutions turned elsewhere for their college education, and Monmouth stood ready to accommodate them.

Monmouth's recruiting had already shifted away from western Illinois to include more students from Chicago and its suburbs. Now a diligent effort was made to attract a larger number of students from eastern states, especially New York, New Jersey, Massachusetts, and Connecticut. By 1965, Monmouth had 1,128 students, an increase of 249 from the year before, and enrollment peaked in the fall of 1968 at 1,350 students.

In undertaking this initiative, President Wimpress drew on the expertise of key members of his administration. David Fleming, director of development and assistant to the president, was in charge of fundraising efforts and was in close contact with alumni, corporations, and government. Glen Rankin, director of admissions and a former football, basketball, and track star for the Fighting Scots, led the successful recruitment of

*A decision by the Monmouth College administration to modernize and consolidate fraternity living resulted in the 1966 construction of an interconnected complex, financed by a government loan, that housed the Tau Kappa Epsilon, Sigma Alpha Epsilon, and Sigma Phi Epsilon fraternities. Each organization had its own lounge, chapter room, dining room, and kitchenette. The imaginative structure satisfied federal loan requirements as a single building while allowing each fraternity to retain its individuality.*

eastern students. Rankin's efforts produced not only a larger student body but also an increase from 12.3 to 29 percent in the number of students graduating in the top 20 percent of their high school class.

Dean of the college Frank McKenna was responsible for recruiting the best faculty members available, at annual salaries that quickly rose from an average of $8,260 to $12,630. Under Dean McKenna, the faculty grew 23 percent from 68 to 82 members. Most of the new faculty members had doctorates or were within a year of receiving the degree. Resources to support their teaching also needed to be improved. Annual purchases of equipment doubled, and the size of the Carnegie Library holdings soon rose from 80,000 to 120,000 volumes.

### Building on a New Scale

The rapid success of the expansion program accelerated plans for construction of new residence halls on campus. Cleland Hall, a women's residence named for John and Eva Cleland, the former dean and former professor of English, opened in 1966. Gibson Hall, a modern-style men's hall named for the college's recently retired president, had opened the previous fall. Distinguished by outside balconies around the perimeter of each floor and exterior entrances to rooms, it was quickly dubbed the Holiday Inn and, in a long-remembered stunt, students mounted an authentic Holiday Inn sign in the central court just before the building's official dedication. A third residence, Liedman Hall, opened in 1968. Named for former professor and dean of women Jean Liedman, the building had two towers and four-room suites.

The growth of campus residential facilities also affected Monmouth's fraternities. In 1966, the college completed construction of the Fraternity Complex at the northeast corner of the campus. Consisting of a three-wing building with living and meeting space, the Fraternity Complex became the new home of three of Monmouth's five fraternities: Sigma Alpha Epsilon, Sigma Phi Epsilon, and Tau Kappa Epsilon. The SigEps and TKEs were already well-established, but SAE had been formed only a few years earlier and received its charter from the national organization in 1963.

Plans were developed for an additional complex to house Monmouth's two other fraternities, Alpha Tau Omega and Theta Chi, plus a possible sixth fraternity, but these were not realized; another fraternity was organized, however, and became a chapter of the national Zeta

*Parents Weekend 1966 will be remembered in the annals of Monmouth College history not for the dedication of Gibson Hall but for the elaborate prank pulled by a group of students. The modern residence hall, which looked remarkably like a Holiday Inn, with brightly colored doors opening onto tiered balconies, received a surprise addition the day of the dedication: Students Bill Warneck '67, Bob Ballad '68, Bob Shippen '69, and Andy Marshall '70 transported an actual Holiday Inn billboard to the site from a factory in Indiana.*

*The Impact of Change 1964–1974* 123

ABOVE *Looking forward to their new "digs," members of the science faculty and the librarian pose on the patio of the newly completed Hewes Library in 1970 as crews complete construction of Haldeman-Thiessen Science Center. From left are Robert Buchholz, biology; Glen Merrill, geology; Jim Wills, geology; Harris Hauge, librarian; and Franklin Johnson, physics.*

PRECEDING PAGES *Wearing black skirts and sweaters, heels and pearls, these Alpha Xi Delta initiates were the height of fashion in the fall of 1961. Front row, from left: Mary Lou Burrello, Sue Gibson, Marcia Dawson, Sandra Grube, Ann Lake, and Lesley Jones. Back row: Sharon Zipse, Judith Maxwell, Sharon Wehrs, Nancy Krause, Betty Moore, Marilyn Marshall, Kathy Sanders, Sue Spaulding, Virginia Hookham, Karen Brunke, Nancy Snell, Anna Gambino, and Lorrie Goldstein.*

Beta Tau in 1971. The Fraternity Complex opened at a time of renewed activity for the Interfraternity Council, which imposed new controls on pledging and social activities and helped the fraternities expand their positive influence in the Monmouth community.

With residence halls and fraternity quarters going up, the Wimpress administration moved ahead to raise funds for the college's new library and science center. In 1969, Hewes Library was completed. Built with support from a $1 million gift of Mr. and Mrs. Chester Hewes in memory of their son, Thomas Randolph Hewes, the new building placed Monmouth at the forefront of library facilities in the region. When fundraising fell short of its goal, President Wimpress decided to build the second story but leave its interior unfinished, anticipating correctly that construction costs would only rise in the years to come.

When the new building was ready for occupancy, the entire college community came together in a remarkable collaborative effort to move books from Carnegie to Hewes. On a bright, 20-below-zero day in January 1970, hundreds of student, faculty, and administrative volunteers formed a human conveyor belt moving down the hill and up again, carrying 130,000 books in countless armloads from one building to the other. Volumes were color-coded and quickly sorted on the proper shelves in the new library. The cheerfully shared task made it, as history professor William Urban later wrote, "one of the great days of Monmouth history, perhaps the greatest day ever."

Once emptied of books, Carnegie Library was converted for other essential functions. Space was made available for the student deans, the *Oracle*, the history and government departments, and the college bookstore.

Construction had also begun on the new science center, its steel frame rising just to the west of Hewes Library. Completed in 1970, the Haldeman-Thiessen Science Center building was designed in close consultation with

# Monmouth Looks to the East

ESTABLISHED IN 1963, Monmouth College's respected East Asian Studies program grew out of a faculty committee report adopted by the College Senate that concluded, "The study of people and cultures outside the Western world is a necessary dimension of liberal education." With funding from the Ford Foundation and the strong support of Dean Harry Manley, a proposal was developed.

The idea to focus interest on East Asia was promoted by Takashi Komatsu, class of 1910, who later earned a degree from Harvard and became a leading steamship executive in Japan. Katharine Phelps Boone '30 and her husband, Gilbert, a Navy commander, helped push the proposal to fruition. Stationed for many years in Japan, the couple retired to Monmouth in 1960 with an important collection of Asian art and artifacts.

The Boone Oriental Library and Fine Arts Collection, which now resides in Chicago's Field Museum of Natural History, contained more than 3,500 pieces dating from the ninth century to modern times. Its pieces, which had been carefully selected for their educational value, were used extensively by the Boones in teaching Asian art courses. Their legacy lives on in Boone House, the museum-like home they constructed near the college.

The East Asian Studies program consisted of courses in Japanese language, philosophy, religion, government, history, and sociology. The program brought visiting lecturers from

*Commander and Mrs. Boone conduct a seminar in the library of their home in 1968.*

throughout Asia. Monmouth students were also given the opportunity to study for a year at universities in Asian countries.

Cecil Brett, an expert on Asian governments who had served two years with the British army in Southeast Asia and China, was hired to administer the program.

One of the program's memorable highlights was an exchange program with Tamagawa Gakuen, a well-known Tokyo institution, which first brought a group of 34 Japanese high school students to Monmouth in 1965 for 14 weeks of immersion studies.

But the East Asian Studies program would not survive the 1970s, when financial cutbacks and the end of the Vietnam War shifted the nation's attention to concerns at home such as Watergate.

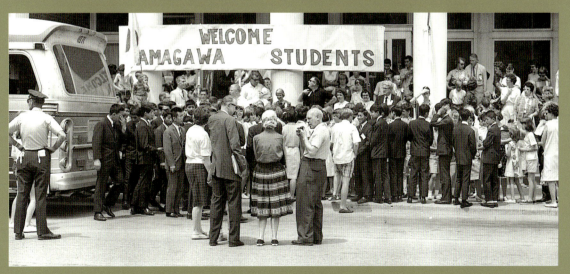

*A welcoming party on the steps of the Colonial Hotel greets arriving high school students from Tokyo's Tamagawa Gakuen in August 1965.*

*Professor Charles Skov demonstrates the complexities of the Lorentz Transformation to a physics class, circa 1967.*

*By 1966, one of the most prestigious off-campus study opportunities for Monmouth College students was the semester at Argonne National Laboratory in Chicago—one of the nation's three major centers of nuclear research. Initiated by the Associated Colleges of the Midwest in 1960, the program selected only 10 top math and science students from the 10 ACM colleges each semester.*

RIGHT *From left, biology faculty John Ketterer, David Allison, Ben Cooksey, and Robert Buchholz show a visitor from the Army Corps of Engineers the new Monmouth College Ecology Field Station near Keithsburg, Illinois. Located on the backwaters of the Mississippi River, the station was established in 1969.*

Monmouth's scientists and named for the college's most notable science professors. The new facility provided modern laboratories, classrooms, a fourth-floor greenhouse, and faculty offices for the science departments, all arranged around a central utilities core. The latest experimental equipment was also installed—a nuclear magnetic resonance spectrometer, chromographs, an X-ray diffusion unit, seismic and resistivity equipment, and X-ray diffraction and petrographic microscopes.

The new buildings gave physical form to a continuing expansion of academic offerings at the college. Asian studies received particular

attention. The Liberal Arts Festival of 1963 was devoted to East Asia, and its success led to the creation of a Japanese studies program. Additional new courses were added to the curriculum, faculty members went abroad to study, and new professors with expertise in Asian subjects were recruited. From 1965 to 1969, another popular program brought high school students from Tamagawa Gakuen, a famous Tokyo institution, to live in Monmouth and study at the college during the summer.

New approaches in education led to the creation of the Extra-Curricular School in 1968. Noncredit courses were offered in subjects such as medieval history, black history, and Freud. These in turn led to re-evaluations of existing courses and the creation of new offerings. In 1970, the Faculty Senate was created, allowing for the broader distribution of decision-making power and placing voting student representatives on each of the committees except Faculty Development.

Although the freshman reading program had lapsed by the late 1960s, faculty members William Urban and Paul Barks developed a plan to allow volunteer faculty to teach a freshman honors program. Adopted by the faculty in early 1970, the program proved to be popular with students, and it led to other developments, including courses at the 250-level that any faculty member could teach once with the approval of the Curriculum Committee.

# Calm in the Eye of the Storm

PEACE AND CIVIL RIGHTS—two of the key issues that defined the decade of the 1960s—created the potential for explosive tensions at Monmouth College, an institution that was born of Christian values such as pacificsm, academic freedom, and racial tolerance but was also grounded in the conservative values of family, God, and country. Yet as the death toll mounted in Vietnam and race-related rioting escalated at home, life on campus remained relatively serene.

The '60s had seen a major shift in the composition of the student body and faculty. A third of the students now came from the East Coast, and most of the faculty were no longer Presbyterians. Everyone at Monmouth was keenly aware of the emerging civil rights movement and the growing conflict in Southeast Asia, but values did not change as radically or quickly as might be expected.

Most of Monmouth's students still came from small towns and suburbs and were somewhat detached from the turmoil in the cities and at large universities. Additionally, some students sought out Monmouth's small-town atmosphere specifically to escape such problems.

Perhaps most significant to Monmouth's sense of calm in this encroaching storm was President Wimpress' decision to support demonstrations as long as they were legal and in good taste. This was not an easy step for him to take, because he was personally revulsed by what could be seen on television nightly, such as sit-ins that disrupted campus life and teaching, as well as riots and political hyperbole. But his policy resulted in Monmouth College remaining open even through the terrible spring weeks of 1970, when demonstrations following the Cambodian incursion and the Kent State shootings closed most of the other institutions in the Associated Colleges of the Midwest.

By that time Monmouth's percentage of black students had increased significantly, minority speakers were attracting large audiences, and more courses were giving attention to race issues. However, new and more militant concerns were emerging—Black Power, women's liberation, nuclear disarmament, and the preservation of the environment.

Meanwhile, many at the college were of two minds regarding Vietnam, which had the potential of escalating into an even larger conflict. Those who still supported the war were unable to articulate an alternative strategy for ending the stalemate. No one particularly liked the draft with its obvious inequities, and grade inflation followed faculty reluctance to expose young men to academic suspension. Many young men went to college (and some studied harder) to avoid becoming part of a war that was losing popularity.

Not surprisingly, the peace movement collapsed almost entirely in 1973 when the draft was ended. As pressure to stay in college eased, fewer students came to Monmouth or dropped out more quickly. What had been a contest over values soon evolved into an economic crisis with declining government support for education.

Campus interest in civil rights and peace further declined as identity politics became dominant nationally and the communists in Indochina proved themselves as evil as the "war mongers" had portrayed them. The moral clarity of those issues had at length become murky, making it easier for new concerns to replace them.

*One of the first organized Monmouth College protests of the Vietnam War was a November 1967 peace vigil behind Grier Hall, in which 30 students participated.*

*The Impact of Change 1964–1974*

RIGHT *A figure-drawing class meets in the former Art Center, circa 1966.*

BELOW *Converted from a former chicken hatchery, the Monmouth College Art Center housed classrooms, studios, and a public gallery during the 1960s and '70s.*

### *Protesting the War*

While Monmouth's ambitious expansion program moved ahead, America was entering a period of social and political upheaval. The civil rights campaign, which had reached its greatest success in the passage of the Civil Rights Act of 1964, split into a struggle between integrationists and advocates of black power and separatism. The rising toll of battlefield casualties in Vietnam, combined with an unclear strategy for victory, spurred growing demonstrations against the war and the draft. New attitudes reshaped every aspect of American culture, upending popular music and art and encouraging experimentation in drugs and sexuality.

Denominational traditions and geographical location kept Monmouth relatively isolated from many of these trends at the outset, but by the late 1960s social change in all of its forms was beginning to have a significant effect. Students resisted rules that defined living conditions and regulated interactions between men and women. Many demanded the right to participate in decisions affecting their education and challenged those in authority. A younger generation of faculty members found itself increasingly at odds with older professors, and some joined students in speaking out against the war and established institutions.

Monmouth's first public antiwar protest came in November 1967, when 30 students and one faculty member held a silent vigil. Local demonstrations continued in this restrained pattern, even in 1968–69 when antiwar protestors carrying the American flag began marching into downtown Monmouth, where they ringed the courthouse square and stood in silent vigils. The restraint of the protestors was partially in deference to the strong conservatism of the community, but it also reflected the religious convictions of those like Paul McClanahan, the new college chaplain, who quietly and thoughtfully questioned American involvement in Vietnam.

Conservative residents of Monmouth had called for the dismissal of faculty members who made statements about racial discrimination in the community, and these outcries were revived against faculty members who spoke out against the war. President Wimpress steadfastly resisted any threat to academic freedom and announced that while he was not in agreement with these faculty members' actions, he would support them as long as their actions were legal and respectful of those with other views.

On the Monmouth campus, as elsewhere, teach-ins were announced, and entire days were set aside from the regular class schedule for a coordinated program of lectures on topics such as Vietnam, the morality of war, and the concept of a just war. By early 1970, many faculty members had become convinced that the war was a mistake, and even some residents in the conservative community of Monmouth began to change their views.

The United States's invasion of Cambodia on April 30, 1970, and the shootings of four students by National Guardsmen at Kent State University on May 4 sharply increased tensions on all American campuses, including Monmouth. Student committees were formed to debate issues and plan demonstrations. A mass assembly attended by most of the college community was held in the gymnasium, where students expressed their concerns and called for action. In the following days, hundreds of students gathered to hear speeches in front of Wallace Hall, the Student Senate passed resolutions, and discussions ran late into the night. Although some classes continued to meet regularly, many were cancelled, and attendance was poor.

Students occupied the Student Center in protest, but they remained for only a few hours. When some students threatened to take over the Administration Building, President Wimpress announced emphatically that he would call in whatever force was necessary to evict them. In the end, the sit-in did not take place, and Monmouth was one of only two ACM colleges to continue to operate uninterrupted throughout the crisis. But the heightened tensions of the war and the confrontations they provoked had left their mark on relationships within the college community.

### Challenges and Reversals

Even as debates over the war accelerated in the late 1960s, President Wimpress pressed ahead to further Monmouth's planning process. In 1969, Wimpress accepted an invitation from the American Foundation for Management Research to be one of four colleges to receive the organization's consulting services. Wimpress saw the invitation as a chance to evaluate how Monmouth's growing enrollment could be sustained and to determine whether it might be allowed to rise still further to 2,000 students.

The first conference involving Wimpress, several professors, administrators, and student body president Sarah Wyant '70 was held in Hamilton, New York, in July 1969. This was followed by the collection of data for computer analysis in the fall of 1969 and a second conference session in Hamilton with President Wimpress and a different group of Monmouth representatives. The consultation produced a series of action assignments and planning for a renewed fund drive to complete the college's expansion program.

But just at this juncture in the spring of 1970, President Wimpress stunned the college by announcing his resignation. He had been offered the presidency of Trinity University in San Antonio, and despite the difficulty of leaving Monmouth, he felt he needed to accept the opportunity offered by the new position.

With the recent creation of a Faculty Senate and Student Senate, more points of view now needed to be incorporated within the search process for a successor. Three committees representing the College Senate, faculty, and students reviewed each of the candidates. Many faculty members in particular wanted the new president to be willing to listen to professors and students and incorporate their concerns into decision-making. Only in this way, some faculty felt, could Monmouth achieve its goal of becoming a distinguished small liberal arts college.

*Richard Stine came to the Monmouth presidency during a period when private colleges were reeling from student unrest, a nationwide recession, and increased competition from public universities.*

The man selected as Monmouth's eighth president was Richard Dengler Stine, a 44-year-old layman of Quaker background who had earned a doctorate in American civilization from the University of Pennsylvania. He had extensive experience in college management and training, and at the time of his selection he was a principal of a New York firm specializing in advising colleges on financial and educational policy.

While the college greeted President Stine's arrival with anticipation, he took office just as America's economic prosperity and the growth of student populations had begun to decline. By the fall of 1970, the first signs of a drop in enrollment were evident. By 1972, erosion in enrollment had reduced the size of the student body by one-fourth. The decline continued, and by 1976, only 674 students were enrolled, a drop of 50 percent from the 1968 high.

The principal cause of this sudden drop in enrollments was attrition. The recession that accompanied the American withdrawal from Vietnam raised difficulties for some families in meeting Monmouth's relatively high tuition and made lower-cost state schools, especially the rapidly growing number of junior colleges, more attractive. Students who had been attracted to Monmouth from the East Coast and from urban locations were not always willing to remain for full four years. In addition, the end of the military draft and Nixon's withdrawal of troops from Vietnam gave male students more options than simply college or the military.

The erosion in enrollment had immediate and serious consequences for the college. Because so much of Monmouth's operating income was derived from tuition, the enrollment decline had a direct impact on the budget. The expansion of physical facilities just a few years earlier was based on the most optimistic assumptions of continued growth, but each new building now loomed as a continuing obligation that had to be financed in the face of a budget deficit. In order to pay the college's creditors, President Stine realized he might need to release 20 percent of the faculty in 1970–71.

A Task Force on Budgetary Planning composed of faculty, administrators, and students was convened to review the situation. The group's recommendations included a number of cost-cutting measures, but the most significant was the reduction of the faculty by 15 full-time positions. These reductions, made before the end of December 1970, began a decline in faculty morale that was to become a significant factor in the Stine administration.

In response, Stine launched the Rendezvous for Renewal program, a series of eight nationally known speakers who were brought to campus to discuss trends in modern education. Concluding in January 1972, the Rendezvous for Renewal lectures were intended to serve as a springboard for further discussion, but the faculty was unable

ABOVE *In the "pre-laptop" days, enjoying the spring sunshine while writing a term paper took some creativity.*

*For more than 30 years, the Sound of Five was one of the most visible student vocal ensembles, performing popular songs and reflecting the fashion trends of the day.*

*Sponsored by the Women's Athletic Association, the Dolphins were a club of accomplished swimmers that presented a water show each spring along with their male counterparts, the Barracudas. Members in 1968–69 were front row, from left: Patricia Kite, Deborah Hook, Cynthia Wallace, Virginia Phillips, and Susan Rayniak. Middle row: Catherine Mayer, Barbara Sharp, Barbara Puck, Ellen Arkis, and Virginia DenPree. Back row: Coach Mary Fleming, Louise Laine, Cheryl Conglon, and Janet Quinn.*

to shape them into a new program because of the college's restricted financial resources.

Enrollment in the fall of 1971 continued below expectations. In February 1972, the College Senate rejected President Stine's proposed deficit budget and gave him five days to produce a balanced budget for the coming year. By the end of March 1972, a move had begun to unionize the faculty.

At the invitation of President Stine and the local chapter of the American Association of University Professors, two faculty members from Bradley University and Northwestern University visited Monmouth in September 1973 to evaluate the situation from an outside perspective. After meetings on campus, the team developed recommendations, which were approved by President Stine, for a range of reforms addressing faculty concerns: appointment of a program budget committee, acceptance of faculty recommendations on promotion and tenure, creation of a grievance procedure, and introduction of a policy of evaluating administrators as well as faculty.

Just a few weeks later, in October 1973, President Stine announced his intention to resign. Despite the heightened antagonisms

*Bill Reichow, who would become the most winning football coach in Fighting Scots history with a record of 78–31–2, meets with the captains of his first team at Monmouth in 1966, Jerry Armstrong (80) and Terry Dobbins (62).*

**The Impact of Change 1964–1974**  133

of the previous three years, his decision still came as a surprise, and many were disappointed by his decision to leave. The College Senate reflected this sentiment when it declared, "The incoming administration will be able to implement and reinforce the policies now set up because the Stine administration has successfully guided Monmouth beyond the critical turning point in this effort."

But another blow was yet to fall. In November 1973, the Midwest Athletic Conference announced sanctions against Monmouth consisting of two years' suspension in football and basketball to be followed by a year of probation. The charges were that athletics had been overemphasized and that the college had not followed conference guidelines in its admission policies. A lengthy investigation by a special faculty committee determined that the physical education department was not guilty of any direct and specific impropriety, but that the administration had not been given sufficient direction to the athletic program. The admission charges revolved around efforts by coaches to fight enrollment erosion by aggressive recruiting and the formation of a local booster club to buy uniforms for athletes.

The sanctions came after several years when Monmouth's athletic teams had emerged as conference powerhouses. The 1972 football team under coach Bill Reichow was undefeated. The 1973–74 basketball team under coach Terry Glasgow won the conference championship, and one of the stars of the team, Donovan Hunter, was chosen an athletic All-American in 1974. Large crowds filled the football stands and gymnasium for the games, and the Fighting Scots had seldom drawn such sustained enthusiasm from the fans.

Now all that seemed imperiled as the sanctions were imposed. Activities in actual or apparent violation of conference regulations were discontinued, and the conference suspension was removed in the fall of 1976. Still, the combination of severe budgetary constraints and athletic sanctions reinforced the sense that the next era of Monmouth's history would require fresh resolve and a new sense of purpose.

OPPOSITE PAGE *Playing before more than 7,000 fans—only a handful of them from Monmouth—the Fighting Scots's Bennie Coleman shoots over a North Dakota State University player in the 1974 small college basketball tournament. The future All-American scored 17 points, but the Scots fell 73–67.*

LEFT *Arguably the greatest team in Monmouth gridiron history, the 1972 Fighting Scots had a 9–0 record, scoring 40 or more points in five of their games. At upper left are two Monmouth coaching legends, Terry Glasgow and Bill Reichow, while Bobby Woll is obscured by shadows in the front row, far right.*

# A Decade of R
## 1974-1985

enewal

# Chapter 9

As Monmouth College approached its 125th anniversary in 1978, it confronted the interwoven effects of institutional expansion, social upheaval, declining enrollment, and a weakened economy. Strong leadership and reaffirmed ideals were now summoned to meet these challenges. In a crucial decade of its history, the college found new financial stability, enlarged its endowment, and launched an imaginatively reconceived liberal arts curriculum. Monmouth emerged from these years of renewal with fresh confidence, ready to assume a position of distinction among its peers.

PRECEDING PAGES *Professor Dick Griffiths with his pop vocal and instrumental ensemble, the Sound of Five, in 1982.*

OPPOSITE PAGE *A former West Pointer, DeBow Freed's military style of leadership gained him immediate respect when he assumed the presidency in 1974 and began to address Monmouth's difficult financial circumstances. His wife, Catherine, known affectionately as Kitty, was widely admired for her graciousness, bringing an air of southern hospitality to Quinby House.*

### Disciplined Stewardship

Following the resignation of President Stine, a search committee of trustees, faculty, and students began its work under the direction of trustee Peter H. Bunce. The needs of the college were many and pressing, the expectations for the new president were high, and there was general agreement that the selection needed to be made without undue delay. In securing DeBow Freed in 1974 as its ninth president, Monmouth College attracted an experienced administrator of strong character with solid academic credentials.

A 49-year-old native of Hendersonville, Tennessee, Freed graduated from West Point in 1946 and entered the U.S. Army. In 1961, he received a master's degree from the University of Kansas, and in 1966 he was granted a doctorate in physics from the University of New Mexico. After returning to teach physics at West Point from 1967 to 1969, Freed was appointed the academic dean at Mount Union College in Alliance, Ohio, where he served until he was recruited to Monmouth's presidency. His wife, Catherine Moore Freed, held a master's degree from the University of Kansas and was an accomplished teacher with a deep interest in education. Both Freeds were active in the United Presbyterian Church, and Mrs. Freed was elected moderator of the Presbytery of Great Rivers, the largest non-urban presbytery in the nation.

Soft-spoken and courtly, President Freed quickly impressed Monmouth colleagues and staff with his discipline, command of detail, and systematic personal habits. Freed kept notes about key questions and projects on three-by-five cards, assigned responsibilities with precision, and checked to ensure tasks were performed to his expectations. Despite working long hours in his office, Freed took great care to remain informed on all aspects of campus life, and he and his wife shared daily meals with students.

President Freed's immediate and most formidable task was to address the college's finances. In 1974, Monmouth was in the midst of a three-year run of operating budget deficits. For too long, the college had compensated for the cyclical pattern of annual expenses common in all academic institutions by short-term borrowing during months of reduced cash income. Freed addressed this problem by establishing strict control over the college's budget, reducing costs wherever possible—even in the smallest increments—and building a cash reserve from the resulting surplus. It was said that President Freed deposited money in the bank on Friday and withdrew it on Monday just to get the weekend interest, but his aggressive management of the college's cash flow soon produced dramatic results. During 1972–73, the college had borrowed $60,000 in short-term loans, but by 1978–79, it was realizing income of $100,000 or more each year from short-term investment of its cash surplus.

While the cost of instruction per student continued to be relatively high due to the college's historic emphasis on a teaching-intensive liberal arts curriculum, President Freed believed that careful planning could assure balanced budgets without consequential losses to the academic program. By holding expenses down and closely monitoring income, Freed moved the budget out of deficit in 1975–76, and balanced budgets were maintained in the following years.

During this time, Freed also improved Monmouth's long-term financial prospects. In 1978–79, he announced a capital campaign to increase the level of alumni giving. Alumni participation rose from 18 percent in 1977–78 to 23 percent in 1978–79, and by the winter

*The Monmouth College Jazz Band, directed in 1975 by Steve Terrones, headed an active jazz program, which included the Jazz Combo, Jazz Vocal Ensemble, and the Sound of Five. A decade later, under the direction of John Luebke, the ensembles toured Europe and started an annual spring "Cherries Jubilee" festival, which featured fiery jazz along with flaming desserts.*

of 1980, $2 million had been raised toward a $3 million campaign goal.

### Evaluating Education

While finances were being stabilized, Monmouth focused attention on the recruitment and retention of students. The college's enrollment had fallen throughout the first half of the 1970s to a low of 647 students by 1976–77, but it stabilized in the range of 640 to 660 students, allowing Monmouth to weather the decade, while several other private colleges were forced to close.

In the fall of 1974, Monmouth reorganized its financial aid program to attract a larger group of prospective students. One aim was to fund as much financial aid as possible from outside sources. The other was to expand scholarship offerings with a new initiative, the Honor Scholar program. The program identified all applicants who met established criteria in high school class rank and aptitude test scores, showed high potential for college work, or possessed unusual talent. These applicants were then awarded Honor Scholarships regardless of need.

Under the new Honor Scholar program, the number of high school valedictorians and other students ranking near the top of their class climbed from eight entering students in 1974–75 to 18 in 1977–78 and 28 in 1979–80. The number of Honor Scholars rose from 16 in 1975–76 to 81 in 1977–78 and 199 by 1979–80.

Efforts to hold good students at Monmouth were enhanced by the enrichment of educational offerings. In 1974–75, a Visiting Scholar Series was created to bring ten scholars to campus for two- or three-day visits. In a typical visit, the scholar conducted three to five classes, gave one or two public lectures, and participated in informal meetings with faculty and students. Visitors came from a variety of institutions, including the University of Illinois, Tufts University, and Harvard University, and they presented lectures on religion, political science, math, art, psychology, and biology, among other fields.

Monmouth's educational program was recognized in 1978 in the North Central Association's

evaluation. In recommending the college's reaccreditation for ten years without qualification, the North Central evaluation team commended Monmouth's strong administration, financial stability, and well-trained and dedicated faculty. The team reported an unusual degree of harmony and unity on campus, with cooperative relationships between departments and genuine participation in governance by faculty and students. Recognizing that Monmouth's curriculum had not been formally reviewed since the adoption of the 3–3 course structure in 1963, the evaluators also recommended defining institutional goals more clearly and creating greater rigor and intellectual excitement in the teaching program.

The positive North Central evaluation reflected the upbeat mood on campus throughout the celebration of Monmouth's 125th anniversary in 1977–78. The commemoration began in May 1977 with an alumni banquet in the Student Center and continued into the fall of 1977 and spring of 1978 with two alumni lecture series on the topic "Scots in 20th Century Society." Leading alumni offered perspectives from their own fields and participated in discussions on the college's past and future. As part of the celebration, the college published *A History*

ABOVE LEFT *Organized by Blue Key, "Scot Sing" was an annual spring music and talent competition inspired by the popular Interfraternity Sings of an earlier era. Seen here in 1975, the tradition continues today under the name "Scotlight."*

ABOVE *The snack bar in the lower level of Stockdale Center has undergone several transformations since the building opened in 1963. Originally a standard hangout where students could study, listen to the jukebox, and smoke, by the end of the '60s it had developed a unique character. Its walls were lined with caricature portraits of students, and it was christened The Styx, in honor of the springtime floods that often soaked its carpeting. In the 1980s, it acquired a quieter décor and a new name—Scotland Yard.*

*An inveterate world traveler and photographer, Professor Mary Crow drew from tens of thousands of slides she had taken to illustrate many of her history lectures.*

*As late as the 1970s, freshmen and students on financial aid were not allowed to have automobiles on campus, so bicycles were a common sight. By the '80s, the regulations were relaxed, and cars had virtually replaced bikes. One of the last holdouts was Professor Bill Urban, who still can be seen pedaling to and from Wallace Hall most months of the year.*

*Professor John Ketterer, who retired in 1986 after 33 years on the faculty, regularly brought a wry sense of humor to his biology classroom and occasionally to his brief stint as dean of men.*

of Monmouth College: Through Its Fifth Quarter Century (1980), a lively account written by Professor William Urban with contributions by senior faculty members Mary Crow, Charles Speel, and Samuel Thompson.

The emerging sense of reassurance on campus was interrupted in September 1979, when President Freed announced his decision to leave Monmouth to become president of Ohio Northern University. Freed's contributions to the Monmouth renewal over five years were significant, and his judicious and focused approach was beginning to bring consistent results. His successor would now need to carry these initiatives forward to a broader fulfillment.

### The New Curriculum

On April 2, 1980, Senate chairman Peter Bunce announced the election of Bruce Haywood as the tenth president of Monmouth College. Born in Allerton Bywater, West Yorkshire, in 1925, Haywood had attended school in England before joining the British army in 1943 and serving in U.S. counterintelligence in Germany from 1945 to 1947. After receiving his bachelor's and master's degrees from McGill University, Haywood completed a doctorate in German at Harvard University in 1956.

Following several years of teaching at Harvard, Haywood joined the faculty of Kenyon College as professor of modern foreign languages and literatures in 1954 and was successively appointed dean of the college and provost at Kenyon. He also became involved in working with the College Entrance Examination Board, the Woodrow Wilson Fellowship Program, the Board of Consultants of the National Endowment for the Humanities, and the Lilly Endowment.

An emphatic proponent of the liberal arts, Haywood saw Monmouth as a college with rich potential for educational growth. He found common cause with many members of the faculty and also had a strong ally in Dean William O. Amy, who had served as acting president of Monmouth from December 1979 until Haywood's arrival in the summer of 1980. Under Dean Amy's leadership, the faculty had already begun an extended evaluation of the college curriculum. Haywood now joined the dialogue, adding his own perspective as the recent head of academic affairs at Kenyon and as a participant in national debates on educational policy.

Haywood and Amy saw Monmouth's curriculum awkwardly divided between liberal education courses in the first two years and subject-major concentration in the last two years. Liberal arts had become a set of requirements to get "out of the way" before students narrowed

*Although a native of West Yorkshire in England, President Bruce Haywood was thoroughly American in his philosophy and lifestyle. His British accent commanded respect, but it was his genuine commitment to the liberal arts that attracted the attention of major donors and helped solidify Monmouth's academic reputation.*

their interests to a major for graduation. Haywood, Amy, and key faculty members proposed to reverse this trend by refashioning the curriculum into a completely integrated four-year liberal arts experience.

On April 29, 1981, after more than a year of intensive discussion, Monmouth's faculty adopted the new curriculum by a 30–14 vote. While retaining the 3–3 trimester calendar, the curriculum defined four key elements in a liberal arts education: the freshman seminar, the required components in general education, the student's major program, and elective courses.

The freshman seminar, mandatory for all incoming students during their first term, focused on a common topic and set of readings. The general education requirements were distributed across the four years of college and divided into five thematic areas, each representing two courses: Language; Beauty and Meaning in Works of Art; the Physical Universe and Its Life Forms; Human Societies; and Systems of Thought and Belief.

Students would complete their subject majors as a single discipline or as a synoptic major study. For single-discipline majors, excessive concentration was limited by mandating that a department could require no more than 12 of its courses for graduation, and no more than 15 courses could be counted toward the 36 needed for graduation. For synoptic majors, 12 term courses were to be selected from two or more departments, providing extended study of a special interest. Electives outside the major

concentrations provided opportunities for broadened studies or a second major.

While the new curriculum was not achieved without intense debate, it represented an unusually broad faculty consensus. "We got better than a two-to-one margin," President Haywood told the student *Oracle*. "One faculty member noted that it was the strongest majority he's seen for anything since he's been here." The strength of the new structure was also noted beyond the campus. At a time when college reform was attracting fresh critical attention, Monmouth's curriculum put it at the forefront of new approaches to the liberal arts and brought increased national attention to the institution.

### Facilities and Resources

The vigor that President Haywood brought to curricular reform was also turned to the pressing physical needs of the college. In 1980–81, as part of Monmouth's three-year capital campaign, the Auditorium was substantially renovated. Funded in large part by a matching grant from the Kresge Foundation, the Auditorium project included extending and rebuilding the stage, relocating the organ pipes for improved sound, and redecorating the front lobby.

Also in 1981, a new athletic field was completed and named Bobby Woll Athletic Field in honor of Monmouth's most notable athlete and coach and the college's only football player to have his jersey number (29) retired. Woll Field

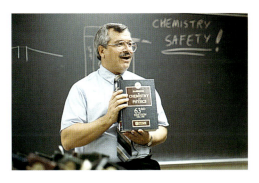

*After more than a quarter of a century in the chemistry department, Richard "Doc" Kieft remains a favorite of students and alumni alike, both for his style of teaching and for his camaraderie outside the classroom.*

*Four Monmouth College students take advantage of a tree uprooted by a windstorm in front of Liedman Hall, circa 1981. Toasting marshmallows in the resulting crater are, from left: Beth Miller, Kim Carlstrom, Linda Smith, and Martie Eckhard.*

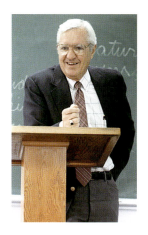

*A native of Ontario, Canada, William Amy was a minister for seven years before becoming a professor of philosophy and religious studies at Otterbein College. Seeking an academic administrator with a commitment to church relations, President DeBow Freed appointed him dean of Monmouth College in 1978. Amy held that post until 1988, when he returned to full-time teaching (and also became a U.S. citizen). He retired in 1993.*

*A Decade of Renewal 1974–1985*

*For decades, freshmen have been treated to a picnic at the president's house during orientation. Former physics professor Franklin Johnson chats with new students at the 1974 picnic.*

provided a 400-meter all-weather track, a football/soccer field, diamonds for baseball and softball, and an area for field events. The project included moving the football field to the north and relocating the bleachers to the bank on the east side of the field.

Two years later in April 1983, the Arthur Glennie Gymnasium opened, expanding the original 1925 gymnasium and providing much-needed modern indoor athletic facilities. The facility was funded by a principal gift of $500,000 from Larry and Nancy Glennie Beck '53 and named for Nancy's late father. Glennie Gymnasium increased the college's seating capacity for basketball games and events to 1,560, renovated the swimming pool, and added space for locker rooms, workout rooms, handball/racquetball courts, and offices for the athletic department.

The physical needs of academic programs were not neglected. In 1985, the college completed a $250,000 renovation of McMichael Science Hall, which was renamed McMichael Academic Hall. The 75-year-old building was rehabilitated to house the art and political economy departments and the college career development center.

These welcome improvements came as Monmouth experienced one of the most significant advances in its history, the $5 million gift

ABOVE *The completion of Hewes Library in early 1970 provided an opportunity for the college bookstore to move from its cramped quarters in the basement of the Student Center to the former Carnegie Library. It would remain there until the 1980s, when it was moved again to the remodeled lower level of McMichael Residence Hall, in the area once occupied by the college dining hall.*

LEFT *The Sound of Five produced its second album in 1982. Arranged by Scott Stanton '73,* Takin' It to the Limit *was strong on horns and percussion and featured an original instrumental by Stanton.*

*A Thousand Hearts' Devotion*

# Mr. Fighting Scot

AS A STUDENT DURING THE 1930S, Bobby Woll's inspired performance on the football field and basketball court made him a Monmouth legend. Later, as a faculty member and coach, he would be an inspiration to generations of Monmouth College students.

"I doubt seriously that anyone else will do what Bobby has done—spend 60-plus years at one institution," said longtime athletic director Terry Glasgow following Woll's death in 1999. "That says something about you. I don't know that Bobby ever retired. He just didn't draw a paycheck."

A presence on campus long after his official retirement in 1976, Woll posted a record of 182–105 and won two conference titles in 17 years as head basketball coach. He was further distinguished by his 5-foot-4 frame, which seemed more suited to a waterboy than to a star athlete. Yet he was named to the UPI All-State football team in 1932 and 1933 and even led the nation in scoring.

How brightly did the Murphysboro, Illinois, native shine on the gridiron? A newspaper account, referring to Knox College's defeat by Monmouth on Thanksgiving Day 1932, said:

> The reason for defeat, which was by the greatest margin since way back in 1909, can almost be solely blamed upon a tiny 129-pound dynamo named Bobby Woll, who was scooting around the field during the entire day like a playful little puppy scampering among some children.

Woll gained 89 yards rushing in the contest and added punt returns of 55 and 30 yards, setting up all three Fighting Scot touchdowns.

Woll's exploits impressed not only Monmouth fans but his teammates as well.

*A Fighting Scots legend as both a player and a coach, Bobby Woll '34 was still a fixture on the sidelines long after his retirement.*

Following his senior season, his playing number, 29, was retired at their request—the only Monmouth football jersey ever accorded that honor.

It would have been futile to ask Woll, who also starred in basketball and baseball, what had prompted his teammates' action. By no means a self-promoter, Woll preferred to let his actions do the talking. That was still the case as he neared retirement, when he had a famous encounter with President DeBow Freed.

Impressed by the repainted bleachers at the football field (which now bears Woll's name) and eager to see some additional renovations, Freed approached Woll and said, "Why don't you get your crew and…" Whereupon Woll broke in, surprised, and asked, "What crew?" He had been doing the work all by himself.

At a 1975 recognition dinner for Woll, Professor David Allison concluded his remarks with reverence to Woll's loyalty and tireless, behind-the-scenes service: "To many, Bobby Woll *is* Monmouth College and what she stands for."

## Keeping the Classics Alive

THE STUDY OF CLASSICS has had a significant presence at Monmouth College since its earliest days, when the training of Presbyterian ministers and teachers was a primary objective. For many decades, the faculty boasted two classicists—a professor of Latin and a professor of Greek—and until 1937 courses in Latin or Greek were required for graduation. For many years, *koine* Greek was taught on a regular basis to students planning to enter the seminary.

The classics department maintained a faculty of two until the death in 1971 of Harold J. Ralston, professor of Greek. Until her retirement in 1981, Professor Bernice L. Fox struggled to offer a full classics program by herself. She taught all levels of Latin language and literature, plus classical mythology and word elements and occasionally added elementary Greek as an overload. She still managed to produce a number of outstanding graduates, several of whom made the teaching of Latin their careers, and at least two earned PhD degrees in classics or related fields.

The Monmouth College Gamma Omicron Chapter of Eta Sigma Phi, the national classics honorary society, was founded in 1956 by Professors Fox and Ralston. The chapter has been very active both on campus and nationally, hosting more national conventions than any other chapter.

In the early 1980s, the college received a challenge grant from the National Endowment for the Humanities to establish an endowed chair in classics. Thanks to a generous gift by

*During more than 30 years of teaching, Bernice Fox instilled her love of the classics in thousands of students.*

Keith Capron (personal secretary to legendary *Chicago Tribune* publisher Colonel Robert R. McCormick) in honor of his mother, Minnie Billings Capron, the chair in classics became a reality a few years later.

In 1984 the college hired Thomas J. Sienkewicz as professor of classics and offered him the endowed chair the following year. When he was interviewed, Sienkewicz was encouraged by both President Haywood and Dean William Amy to develop ways to make the classics more central to the Monmouth College curriculum and more attractive to more students.

In 1985 Sienkewicz radically changed the emphasis of the classics curriculum from a traditional language-based program to a more flexible one incorporating the study of the Latin and Greek languages into classics courses taught in translation. One advantage of the triad course, which has since been adopted at several other small liberal arts colleges, is that a small faculty can maintain core courses in language and literature for majors and minors while still offering courses in translation for the general student body.

In 1987 Keith Capron provided additional funds to create a dedicated classroom for the teaching of classics with state-of-the-art equipment.

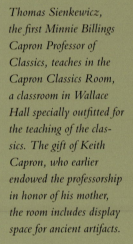

*Thomas Sienkewicz, the first Minnie Billings Capron Professor of Classics, teaches in the Capron Classics Room, a classroom in Wallace Hall specially outfitted for the teaching of the classics. The gift of Keith Capron, who earlier endowed the professorship in honor of his mother, the room includes display space for ancient artifacts.*

*A Thousand Hearts' Devotion*

of alumnus Walter S. Huff Jr. The gift could not have been better timed. When President Haywood took office in 1980, the accumulated debt from Monmouth's expansion in the 1960s had left the college owing the federal government a sum greater than its $4.4 million endowment. If Monmouth hoped to attract new students, hire skilled faculty, and enhance its physical plant, it was urgent that the debt be retired and the endowment be expanded.

With these needs in mind, President Haywood approached Walter Huff of Atlanta, Georgia, the founder and chairman of HBO & Company, an information systems firm for the health care industry. Monmouth's alumni had not been giving in sufficient amounts, and the college trustees were also reluctant to make large gifts. What was needed, President Haywood told Huff, was a dramatic gesture that would encourage alumni, trustees, and friends of the college to invest in the college's future. Huff's dramatic response was a commitment of $5 million, the keystone gift in a new Monmouth capital campaign to raise $15 million.

Huff's pledge was initially kept a close secret, with only the executive committee of the trustees alerted. The formal public announcement came in the spring of 1983 at a campus-wide celebration of the 130th anniversary of the college. Speaking to a gathering in the new gymnasium (which Huff had also helped to finance), Professor Mary Crow summarized the history of the college, and chairman of the board Peter Bunce then stepped forward to announce the Huff gift, the largest in the college's history.

Huff's generosity had a galvanizing effect on other supporters of the college. Trustees responded with greater involvement in Monmouth's capital campaign, and alumni giving also began to mark an upward course. A crucial turning point had been passed.

The academic program was further strengthened by a multiyear $150,000 challenge grant from the National Endowment for the Humanities. With $450,000 raised from Monmouth donors, the combined $600,000 was directed toward endowing a faculty chair in classical languages, the first fully endowed faculty position in Monmouth's history. Monmouth received an additional grant of $300,000 in 1984, which supported development of new courses, two-week spring institutes in each of three years of the grant period, and the addition of three new faculty positions in the humanities.

The high quality of teaching by Monmouth's faculty also attracted substantial recognition. In May 1985, the first Burlington Northern Foundation Faculty Award for Teaching Excellence was presented to Professor William Urban of the history department. Continued annually in the years that followed, the Burlington Northern program provided a cash award to underwrite independent faculty research and travel.

With increased financial resources came further continuity in Monmouth's student enrollment. By the late 1970s, enrollment had been stabilized at between 600 and 700 students, and this level remained constant for 13 consecutive years, through the end of the 1980s. The relatively small base of tuition income, however, emphasized the need for the college to continue to increase its gift and grant support and to build the size of the endowment.

### Monmouth Takes the Field

In addition to strengthening academic offerings, the decade of Monmouth's renewal also brought increased participation in all types of athletic activities. By 1978–79, Monmouth was competing in ten intercollegiate sports for men and four for women. Nearly half the student body was actively involved in intercollegiate programs, and most of the remaining students were involved in intramural sports.

With the lifting of athletic sanctions in the fall of 1976, Monmouth once more entered into spirited competition with its traditional Midwest Conference football rivals. Coached by Bill Reichow, the football team responded immediately by racking up a 6–3 record and claiming a tie for the conference championship. Seven members of the 1976 team—Robb Curtis, Bob Reedy, Steve Graves, Mark Bradley, Rich

*Walter S. Huff Jr. '56 provided Monmouth College with the largest gift in its history—$5 million—in 1983. Nearly 20 years later, he would double that gift by giving an additional $10 million toward a new athletic center.*

Kucharz, Joe Levita, and Tim Lucas—were named to the all-conference team.

Women's sports were also strengthened significantly. Basketball had been played on an intramural basis, but in 1974 a varsity squad was organized. Women's softball was introduced as a spring sport, and in 1981 and 1982 the volleyball teams, led by Mary Day, Karen Friedrich, and Karen Spencer, won the Midwest Conference championship.

Men's sports also garnered their share of glory. The basketball team flourished with the skills of Roger "Sandman" Sander, who set Monmouth records for rebounds per game and season and ended his 1974–78 career with a record 939 rebounds. Sander was named an All-American in 1977 and 1978, following two of his teammates, Tom Gillhouse and Bennie Coleman, named All-Americans in 1975. The Monmouth basketball team reached the conference title game four straight times from 1980 to 1983, but it was not until 1985 that the team won the championship under coach Terry Glasgow. Team star Bill Seiler closed his career with the second highest point total in Monmouth's history.

Also under Glasgow, baseball teams were winning championships. In 1974, Monmouth tied for the conference baseball championship, and the next year it won the championship outright. The baseball team went on to win in 1980 (sharing the title with Lawrence), 1981, 1982, 1983, and 1985 (sharing with Coe).

The softball team won the conference championship in 1979, and the men's track team won the title in 1985. The men's golf team claimed trophies of its own, winning the Midwest Conference championship in 1975 and from 1977 to 1981. Monmouth's wrestling, swimming, and tennis teams also set high marks with strong performances during these years.

In sports, as in its educational program and its expanding level of donor support, Monmouth was demonstrating a newly found sense of spirit and purpose. The college had redefined its academic standards and redoubled its collective energies, and the years ahead promised further achievement.

ABOVE *Perhaps better remembered for his long and successful career as a basketball coach, Terry Glasgow had multiple conference championships and national tournament appearances as a baseball coach during the 1970s, '80s, and '90s.*

*Monmouth College's all-time leading rusher and scorer, Ron Baker '76 (shown with President Freed), was named to the Kodak All-American team and drafted by the Denver Broncos.*

148     *A Thousand Hearts' Devotion*

# The Rise of Women's Athletics

THROUGH THE FIRST three-quarters of the twentieth century, women in uniform at a Monmouth College athletic event were more likely to be cheerleaders than actual players. There were, however, a few notable exceptions. For many years, the college fielded a women's basketball team. Its first game on April 7, 1900, was lost to a Monmouth town team by a score of 9–6 (perhaps the team's long wool skirts made scoring difficult), but it later had success against colleges such as Lombard and Augustana. Monmouth women also participated in a wide range of non-intercollegiate activities, including swimming, track, baseball, field hockey, and synchronized swimming.

A girls' rifle squad, formed in 1938–39 by Professor Garrett Thiessen, produced the first national sporting champion in Monmouth history, Hazel Hatch Wharff '49. Five years later, Joan Phifer Hunt '55 duplicated Wharff's feat, while her team also won a national championship.

Monmouth's first official intercollegiate women's teams appeared in 1974, two years after President Nixon signed into law Title IX of the Educational Amendments of 1972, which states, in part, "No person in the U.S. shall, on the basis of sex be excluded from participation in, or denied the benefits of, or be subjected to discrimination under any educational program or activity receiving federal aid."

Volleyball was the first sport added at Monmouth, beginning competition in the fall of 1974. Basketball, tennis, and softball began official varsity schedules later that academic year.

The expansion and addition of women's sports required additional regulation, an idea the Midwest Conference recognized in the late 1970s. As one of the conference schools at the front of the women's athletic movement, Monmouth joined with several Midwest Collegiate Athletic Conference schools to create a new women's league to meet the demand and provide female athletes with a separate voice in controlling their athletic business. Subsequently, the Midwest Athletic Conference for Women was created in 1977 to conduct women's championship competition and regulate sports among the existing conference's member schools. (The separate men's and women's conferences were merged into a single Midwest Conference in 1994.)

In the past quarter-century, Monmouth women have often excelled on the playing fields. The volleyball and softball teams have each won conference championships, but no sport has matched the success of the track program, which has won a combined 12 indoor and outdoor league titles and seen 17 different athletes earn All-American honors, including Constance Jackson, who was second in the nation in the 200-meter dash in 2001.

Of the 96 Monmouth athletes in the M Club Hall of Fame, nine are women: Wharff and Hunt, as well as post–Title IX competitors Kim Mead '82, Karen Friedrich Pyatt '84, Mary Day '85, Ann Jamieson '85, Angie Hickerson '87, Kim Buckert Fox '88, and Heather Robertson '90.

*By the early 1980s, volleyball was rapidly becoming a popular women's sport at Monmouth.*

# Securing Foun

dations 1985–1994

# Chapter 10

By the mid-1980s, Monmouth College had reestablished its presence as a leading regional liberal arts college. Under the leadership of President Haywood, faculty were developing new courses, alumni and trustees were increasing their commitment to the college, and educational peers were recognizing the substantive advances being made. With growing assurance, the college was building the foundations for a broader and stronger institution.

Among President Haywood's strongest impressions upon arriving at Monmouth was the college's potential for further development.

PRECEDING PAGES *Alpha Tau Omegas and Theta Chis battle for position in a 1989 Greek Week "chariot" race.*

OPPOSITE PAGE *From left, Deletra Cross '92, Damon Hendricks '93 and Gloria Shaw '92 model the latest fashions at Reflections 1991, an annual dinner and style show sponsored by the Black Action Affairs Council.*

The bucolic appeal of the old "Valley Beautiful" between McMichael Academic and McMichael Residence was long faded, and many structures had outlived their usefulness, including the ancient campus heating plant and the old Nichol's chicken hatchery building that sheltered the art department. Faculty and student automobiles were an increasingly dominant presence at the college, and numerous roadways running through the campus added little to its visual appeal.

With the construction of Hewes Library and the Haldeman-Thiessen Science Center, the athletic fields had been moved farther north, creating a new enclosed campus green stretching from the expanded gymnasium on Seventh Street to the row of residence halls along Ninth Street. Although the second floor of Hewes Library had been left unfinished at the time of its construction, the art gallery was relocated there in 1980. In 1987, the gallery was extensively remodeled and renamed the Len G. Everett Gallery.

Also in 1987, a gift from the Beveridge family in memory of former math professor and dean Hugh R. Beveridge '23 and his wife, Dorothy, supported the construction of the Beveridge Rooms. This suite on the second floor of Hewes comprised the Monmouthiana Room, to house the collection started by librarian Mary McCoy in 1937, and the Rare Book Room, for the most valuable and important volumes in the library's collection.

*President Haywood (left) examines plans for the renovation of Carnegie Library with trustees and the architect in 1992.*

The Haywood administration's attention now turned to the buildings in the southeast quadrant of the campus and the open tracts of land along Ninth and Broadway. The first step was the refurbishing of Wallace Hall, made possible by a bequest from Rebecca Porter Wells in 1986. With these funds, Wallace was reconfigured with new offices for faculty members, remodeled classrooms, audio-visual studios for the speech department, student lounges, small seminar rooms, and an office suite for the president and vice president for academic affairs.

The Student Center was also renovated. The dining hall was upgraded with improved seating, more elegant windows, and a new stairway to provide easier access to the popular Highlander Room upstairs, which was also redecorated. At commencement in May 1989, the renovated facility was named in honor of retired Navy Vice Admiral James B. Stockdale, Class of 1946, a much-decorated recipient of the Congressional Medal of Honor who had been the senior naval prisoner of war in Hanoi during the conflict in Southeast Asia.

The Stockdale Center was further enhanced by a new landscaped terrace uniting it with McMichael Residence to the east, where the bookstore was now located. Dedicated on October 12, 1990, the terrace was named in honor of Robert "Bobby" Dunlap, Class of 1942, a cousin of Admiral Stockdale and himself a Congressional Medal of Honor recipient for heroism on Iwo Jima during World War II. The Dunlap Terrace featured handsome red brick paving interspersed with trees, planters, and casual seating. At its south end, a series of steps led to a revamped campus parking lot on the site of the former "Valley Beautiful."

The Wallace and Stockdale renovations and the creation of Dunlap Terrace were paralleled by steps taken toward an equally great need at Monmouth, a new campus theater. In 1987, President Haywood announced the receipt of a naming gift for the theater from the Ruth L. Wells Foundation of Camp Hill, Pennsylvania; Ruth Wells had been a graduate of the Class of 1923. A campaign was immediately launched

## Commander and Commando

GROWING UP NEAR tiny Abingdon, Illinois, the late Robert "Bobby" Dunlap '42 and James B. Stockdale '46 probably never heard of Iwo Jima or Hanoi.

However, it was in those distant places that the first cousins distinguished themselves as American heroes. Together, they comprise half the list of Monmouth alumni who have received Congressional Medals of Honor.

Dunlap, who attained the rank of captain in the Marine Corps, saw his first World War II combat in December of 1943. In 1945, he was sent to Iwo Jima. Intense fighting there left all but three or four members of his 285-man company dead, and Dunlap himself was also wounded. His bravery earned him the Purple Heart. He received his Medal of Honor for heroism from President Harry S Truman in a 1945 White House ceremony.

Stockdale was conferred the Medal of Honor for his valor as the senior Naval prisoner of war during more than seven years of imprisonment in North Vietnam.

After graduating from Annapolis in 1946, he became a naval fighter pilot. Shot down on his second tour of duty over Vietnam on Sept. 9, 1965, Captain Stockdale was captured and taken to the "Hanoi Hilton" POW camp. There, he endured severe physical and mental torture, spending four years in solitary confinement, two of which he was kept in leg irons. Yet he did not break, resolving to make himself a symbol of resistance.

In 1976, Stockdale was awarded his Medal of Honor by President Gerald Ford. He left the naval service as a vice admiral and its most decorated member, garnering 26 personal combat decorations, including two Purple Hearts.

Sixteen years later, Stockdale was again associated with the nation's highest office when he agreed to serve as a stand-in vice presidential candidate on his friend Ross Perot's independent ticket. When Perot suddenly decided to rejoin the race after earlier withdrawing, circumstances did not permit the naming of another running mate, and Stockdale became the official candidate. The team garnered an impressive 19 percent of the popular vote in the Presidential election.

*Cousins James B. Stockdale (left) and Robert "Bobby" Dunlap converse at the 1989 dedication of Stockdale Center.*

Dunlap and Stockdale are also linked by having adjoining campus landmarks named in their honor.

Though a student at Monmouth for less than a year, Stockdale was permanently associated with the college when the student center was named for him in 1989. A plaque at Stockdale Center reads, in part, "His life is a model and inspiration for the students of Monmouth College." Eleven years later, Stockdale was inducted into the Hall of Achievement, the college's highest honor.

In 1990, the terrace just outside Stockdale Center was named for Dunlap, but that was not a first for the M Club Hall of Famer. The Abingdon High School gymnasium is named in his honor, and the school adopted the nickname "Commandos." Also, the War Memorial on the Warren County Courthouse lawn was created in Dunlap's likeness.

"He was an American veteran," said his wife, Mary Louise Frantz Dunlap '45. "He thought the American people were worth fighting for."

For that, Monmouth College owes its veterans like Dunlap and Stockdale more than a medal or a name on a building could ever repay.

## Punchcard Pioneers

THE MODERN ERA of computing at Monmouth College began in 1975 when President DeBow Freed appointed math professor John Arrison as director of the computer center; and a suite of former classrooms in Wallace Hall was transformed into a center for academic computing and business data processing. Punchcards were the medium of data entry until physics professor Peter Kloeppel (who assisted Arrison) convinced the administration to purchase CRT terminals—to the dismay of some faculty who were convinced that the data needed to be stored on paper.

Kloeppel, who wrote most of the programming for the center using BASIC language, remembers booting up the system in a long and complicated sequence each morning. The maintenance agreement also required that the system be shut down if room temperature exceeded 75 degrees, which was often the case despite two large window air conditioners. The only disk drive in those days was a removable pack drive the size of a washing machine with a storage capacity of 40 megabytes.

History professor Bill Urban, who was one of the first non-science faculty members to embrace computer technology, credits Arrison for helping to put Monmouth at the forefront of academic computing: "He persuaded, cajoled, and forced his faculty members to use the computer in their classes," Urban said. "As a result, there are alumni today who learned useful computer skills long before a major was offered or word processing became fashionable."

Dick Reno, who succeeded Arrison in the early 1980s, recalls that his first official action was to purchase two additional disk drives so that faculty and administrative users could each have their own drive, and there would be an extra drive for the storage of software and backup. The used drives, with a total capacity of 80 megabytes, were purchased from another college for $17,000.

Just as Kloeppel had earlier faced resistance for purchasing CRTs, Reno felt the ire of some faculty when he suggested the idea of a campuswide computer network. "Putting software on each machine was a nightmare from a staff standpoint, plus a licensing standpoint," Reno said. "A network was the only way to manage a growing system, but faculty were worried that students could hack into their machines."

The client-server network idea finally became a reality under Reno's successor, current information systems director Daryl Carr '88. "We installed the network ourselves, stringing and burying coaxial cable all across campus," he said. "That system constantly got overloaded, though, and it was replaced with twin fiber-optic cables." Carr said a milestone in college computing history occurred in 1996 when there was finally a personal computer on every desk.

*Before the advent of personal computers, students in the computer lab used terminals connected to a mainframe computer.*

*LEFT: Douglas Rankin '79 and Helen Wagner Willey '38 helped inaugurate the Wells Theater in 1990 with their stirring portrayals of Henry II and Eleanor of Aquitaine.*

to secure the additional funds needed to erect the building. With a challenge grant from the Kresge Foundation in 1988, the campaign moved successfully toward its goal.

Plans for the new theater included a flexible stage for mounting either traditional proscenium or modern thrust-stage productions, an auditorium seating 150, a green room and backstage storage area, projection facilities and scene shop, and a public lobby and box office. As the walls of the new theater rose steadily on its site to the south and east of McMichael Academic, a surviving relic of Monmouth's earlier storied theatrical tradition finally met its end. In August 1990, the Little Theater was demolished, but not before pieces of its distinctive red exterior siding were salvaged to distribute as souvenirs to Monmouth's many theater alumni.

On October 13, 1990, the new Wells Theater was formally dedicated in honor of Ruth Wells. The following day, Sunday, October 14, the portico and plaza at the entrance of the theater were dedicated and named for Grace Gawthrop Peterson, Monmouth's reigning presence on the music faculty for more than 50 years. The premiere production at the Wells Theater on November 1 was James Goldman's *The Lion in Winter*, starring Douglas Rankin '79 and the well-known television dramatic actress Helen Wagner Willey '38. At the conclusion of the gala opening night performance, President Haywood announced to the audience that the Wells Theater stage would be named in Willey's honor.

### An Emerging Reputation

Monmouth's reinvigorated curriculum brought fresh energy to faculty instruction and the development of new courses. It also highlighted the importance of integrated approaches to learning and emphasized anew the significance of good teaching in a liberal arts college.

In 1982, Dean William Amy was successful in obtaining a National Endowment for the Humanities grant to help six faculty members develop six new courses in support of the senior capstone requirement of the new curriculum. The "Systems of Thought and Belief" component, Amy wrote, would require students "to face up to fundamental questions about mankind, society and God." The following year, the college received another NEH grant that supported summer work by faculty to develop new courses in language and literature, history, philosophy, and religion.

Interrelations among the arts and sciences were the focus of a special series of summer faculty institutes supported by a 1989 grant from the Lilly Endowment. The result of a successful proposal from the college faculty and the Institutional Development Committee, the Lilly

*A Monmouth boy who attended Monmouth College, David Allison '53 returned to his alma mater in 1962, where he began a long and distinguished career as a professor of biology.*

**Securing Foundations 1985–1994**

grant enlarged understanding of modern science among nonscience faculty through visits by distinguished speakers.

Monmouth continued to honor distinguished contributions in faculty teaching. Recipients of the Burlington Northern Foundation Faculty Achievement Award during this period included professors William Urban, Douglas R. Spitz, Esther White, Craig Watson, Richard Cogswell, Thomas Sienkewicz, and Rajkumar Ambrose.

In 1988, Monmouth received funding to establish a second annual faculty award program, the Sears Roebuck Foundation Award for Teaching Excellence and Campus Leadership. The first Sears Roebuck award was given to Richard L. Kieft, associate professor of chemistry. Other recipients in the initial years were George Arnold, Harlow Blum, James De Young, and Jeremy McNamara. Besides marking individual accomplishment, Monmouth's two faculty awards encouraged further enrichment of the college's teaching and learning environment.

In reshaping the liberal arts curriculum, the Monmouth faculty affirmed its historic commitment to a broad and well-grounded college experience. President Haywood continued to build on the strength of this collective achievement by championing the significance of Monmouth's new program to its public constituency. Whether addressing alumni, trustees, donors, community residents, or fellow college presidents, Haywood eloquently reaffirmed the college's commitment to the individual and social value of the liberal arts. The president's high profile in academic circles and in public meetings and press interviews was a substantial factor in reshaping general perceptions of the college's achievement and potential.

Monmouth's rising educational reputation was evident in many ways, especially in the increasing financial support of alumni and trustees. But nothing captured the public imagination more than Monmouth's appearance among the "top 25 regional liberal arts colleges" in *U.S. News & World Report*'s annual college rankings. First listed in 1987, Monmouth went on to successive annual appearances in *U.S. News*, ranking fifth among the top ten Midwestern liberal arts colleges in 1989 and fourth in 1990.

In 1990, Monmouth was included in Barron's *300 Best Buys in College Education,* and in 1992 and 1993 it was featured in the *Guide to 101 of the Best Values in America's Colleges and Universities.* Beginning in 1991, it was also selected as one of

*President Haywood takes a moment from his busy schedule to chat informally with students.*

*A coed residence hall with its doors opening onto balconies, Gibson Hall was the dormitory of choice for students in the 1980s and '90s.*

158　　A Thousand Hearts' Devotion

300 colleges and universities in *Peterson's Competitive Colleges*, a nationwide evaluation based on the quality of a college's student body. Rankings like these reflected perceptions that change was afoot at Monmouth and that the college was successfully redefining its place in the educational community.

### Campus Diversity

Despite Monmouth's geographical location in western Illinois, far from the Midwest's urban centers, it had never been an intellectually or culturally isolated institution. Its early presidents and faculty members were drawn from a national Protestant community that played a significant role in defining America's political and social values. Monmouth's Presbyterian heritage reinforced this cosmopolitanism with its rich historic emphases on Scotch-Irish roots, western frontier pioneering, overseas missions, and educational ventures at Assiut College in Egypt and other international locations.

Though Monmouth's student body had been drawn largely from its regional base in the Midwest, its graduates were dispersed across the country and beyond. Some served the church as ministers and teachers, while others found careers in public and private education, business, industry, commerce, government service, and many other fields. The influx of students from the eastern United States during the college growth of the 1960s had brought in large numbers of students from a broader geographical area.

By the 1970s and 1980s, increasing racial, ethnic, and religious pluralism in American society, along with improved access to college education for students from all economic and social backgrounds, gave Monmouth a noticeably more diverse faculty and student body. As Monmouth entered the 1980s, minorities composed less than two percent of the student body. By 1991, the minority population had increased more than sevenfold, and Monmouth had become one of the most diverse colleges in the Associated Colleges of the Midwest.

This growing diversity was reflected in a range of programs, organizations, and events that encouraged openness to different beliefs and cultural traditions. The Liberal Arts Festivals of the 1960s, foreign language instruction, East Asian Studies program, and off-campus studies programs were all important steps in this direction.

Equally significant was the opening in 1988 of Hubbard House, the Monmouth College Center for Cultural Diversity. The gift of Willis Hubbard '62 and Marilyn Kessinger Hubbard '64, the Victorian house on the corner of Broadway and South Seventh Street had been home to three generations of Monmouth alumni and more than 75 Monmouth College students who roomed there over the years.

Under the leadership of Dean William Julian, a Hubbard House Board was formed consisting of faculty, student, and community representatives. Student members included Cheryl Conaway '90, president of the Student Association; Carlos Smith '90, president of the Black Action Affairs Council; and Soon Chye Yap '90, president of the International Relations Club. Subcommitttees of the board set out to address programming for the larger Monmouth community, especially its African-American and Hispanic American members, ethnic minority students, and international students.

In 1990, a special celebration marked the twentieth anniversary of the founding of the Black Action Affairs Council. Returning to campus for the event, 24 African-American alumni who had founded BAAC established the African American Alumni Network to work with the college to enhance the African-American experience on campus. In conjunction with the celebration, Monmouth announced the appointment of minority affairs director Robert L. Mason '74, who also became president of the newly formed AAAN.

The early 1990s saw a wealth of international scholars on campus. Gabriel Adeleye, a Nigerian with a doctorate from Princeton University, taught courses in African history as a Fulbright scholar-in-residence in 1991–92. Another Nigerian, Julius Umennachi, taught in the philosophy and religious studies department,

# The Battle for the Bronze Turkey

*The 100th meeting of the Fighting Scots and the Siwash played to a packed house at the Knox Bowl on November 4, 1989. Monmouth won the much-publicized contest, 14–0.*

RIGHT *Battered, bent and missing its original base, the Bronze Turkey remains a revered symbol of the Knox-Monmouth rivalry, and stays locked in the vault of the victorious school.*

THE EXACT DATE OF THE FIRST GAME may have been forgotten, but the rivalry between Monmouth and Knox Colleges that began on a football field in 1891 is etched in the collective memory of the two schools. The 112-game series is the second-oldest west of the Allegheny Mountains, the fourth-oldest among NCAA Division III schools, and the seventh-oldest in college football.

Perhaps even more storied than the rivalry itself is the traveling trophy introduced in 1928. Presented by the two local newspapers, the *Monmouth Review Atlas* and the *Galesburg Register-Mail*, the trophy was topped by a large bronze turkey, symbolizing the fact that the annual game was then held on Thanksgiving Day. Each year, the Bronze Turkey was formally presented at the home basketball game of the victor—that is, when the bird could be found.

The first in a long line of bird abductions occurred in the early 1940s, when the trophy went missing for five years. Finally, Monmouth officials were tipped off that it had been buried under the old dirt running track in the basement of the gymnasium. In 1965, the turkey was stolen from the Monmouth trophy case during a daring daylight raid. Two Knox students pretending to be reporters for the Monmouth student newspaper convinced the student center director to take the trophy outdoors for a photograph. Just then, the director was called to the phone, and the thieves made their getaway. Monmouth students retaliated by publishing a spurious issue of the Knox newspaper and dropping copies over the Knox campus from an airplane.

In the spring of 1984, the trophy was not so cleverly liberated from the Monmouth trophy case by breaking the glass. The *Register-Mail* purchased a smaller replacement trophy for the 1985 game, which was won by Knox. That possession was brief, however, as Monmouth won the next seven games. Just as mysteriously as it had disappeared, the original trophy then resurfaced in 1993 when it was returned to a Monmouth class reunion at homecoming. Today, the replacement trophy is put on public display, while the original—severely bent, battered, and missing its original base—remains safely locked in the vault of the victorious school.

The Battle for the Bronze Turkey drew national attention in 1989 when the 100th contest between Monmouth and Knox was played at the Knox Bowl. Monmouth won the much-hyped game 14–0 on two late fourth-quarter touchdown drives, leveling the all-time series record at 45–45–10. The Fighting Scots then won three straight to open up their first lead in the series, but Knox struck back later with four consecutive wins to go ahead by one.

A thrilling 27–26 victory in coach Kelly Kane's final game on the Monmouth sidelines tied the series in 1999, and coach Steve Bell won his first two Bronze Turkey games in 2000 and 2001 to put the Scots ahead 52–50–10.

*Jeff Houston (33), celebrates a basketball conference championship in 1988.*

as did Ed Scott, an African-American with teaching experience in Africa, and Chenyang Li of China.

The international scope of diversity became the focus of a multicultural festival, "Celebrating the World," held during 1991–92. The year-long event began in late September with "Magic, Minstrels, and Merrymaking," an event featuring European folk music, folk storytelling, Korean woodcarving, Chinese calligraphy, and other crafts, as well as a multicultural dinner.

Professor William Urban, an authority on the history of the Baltic States, spearheaded an effort to increase Monmouth's connections with that often-overlooked but increasingly important region of the world. *The Journal of Baltic Studies,* a prestigious scholarly journal, became based at Monmouth College, with Urban and modern foreign languages professor Roger Noël serving as co-editors. Urban directed off-campus studies programs in Yugoslavia and Czechoslovakia, and often brought guest lecturers to campus to speak about the region.

### A Golden Era

As the college rallied in the 1980s and early 1990s, the Fighting Scots athletics teams certainly kept pace, producing quite possibly the best ten-year span in school history.

The Scots crowned their first male national champions—high jumper Eric Ealy and hurdler Charles Burton—during the era, and Burton was part of a 1992 squad that placed seventh in the nation. Entering the 1985 season, Monmouth had won just three Midwest Conference titles in track, but under coach Roger Haynes '82 the team added five more through the '92 season, and the women got into the act in 1993, winning the program's first title.

The marquee sports of football and basketball also fared well. Under the leadership of coach Kelly Kane, the Scots won 26 straight regular-season football games from 1986 to 1989, and they appeared in three straight conference championship games during that span. Quarterback Mark Reed, who had played for Kane in high school, led Monmouth's gridiron resurgence.

*An all-conference player in three sports, Heather Robertson '90 holds the all-time scoring record for both a season and a career in women's basketball.*

*Hall-of-fame pitcher Kim Buckert led the Fighting Scots to a softball conference championship in 1987.*

**Securing Foundations 1985–1994**

*Quarterback Mark Reed '88, known as much for his running as his passing, led a Fighting Scots resurgence in the mid-1980s.*

Coach Terry Glasgow's basketball teams, led by 1,000-point scorers Juan Mitchell, Bill Lavery, John Herman, and Brant Carius, also excelled, winning league titles in 1988 and 1990 and qualifying for three straight national tournaments.

The national selection committee wasn't as kind to Glasgow's baseball teams, but the Scots certainly racked up wins, compiling a 142–39 record and winning six Midwest Conference crowns from 1987 to 1993. Hitters like Chris Wheat and Travis Wyatt and pitchers Arnold Gonzalez and Jake Libby were the stars of the era.

On the individual scene, Angie Hickerson and Dan Schisler became the first Scots to win the Midwest Conference women's and men's cross country meets, and wrestler John Chapman took second in the nation. High scorers Heather Robertson and Penny Rowan dominated the women's hardwood, and Kim Buckert pitched the Scots to a 1987 Midwest Conference softball title.

### Academic Adjustments

Retaining good students in a challenging academic setting was an important part of Monmouth's efforts during this era as well. In the fall of 1986, the college instituted the Distinction Program to provide independent study to its most academically talented students. Incoming students designated as Senate Scholars were invited to participate in the Distinction Program through a formal selection process that began in the second term of the freshman year.

A special Distinction study group topic was offered each term, with students reading a common set of materials, engaging in discussion, and writing papers. Distinction Program students were also given the opportunity to serve as Freshman Seminar associates, leading freshman discussion sessions and evaluating freshman

*Monmouth College's first intercollegiate women's soccer team took the field in 1994.*

papers with the faculty seminar leader. The Distinction program culminated in a two-term seminar for seniors, "Continuity and Change in the 20th Century," and those who completed the program received special recognition at the honors convocation and commencement each year.

As the Haywood administration entered the 1990s, the character and scale of Monmouth's academic program continued to be the focus of discussion and debate. By the fall of 1991, Monmouth was able to announce its largest student body on campus in 20 years, 724 students, of which 252 were entering freshmen. Still, the gains in class size from the lowest point in the mid-1970s remained modest, and development of a program for stable recruitment was a continuing challenge.

The revision of the curriculum was a major educational achievement, but it also made Monmouth's courses more intellectually demanding and placed a greater premium on individual student initiative. Some types of students that Monmouth had traditionally attracted in the past found the transition to the new curriculum too difficult, and the college's retention rate suffered.

In evaluating these changes, many faculty members believed Monmouth's 3–3 trimester was a key issue. While the 3–3 system offered focused study in a greater number of course offerings, it also limited the range of topics that could be covered in any one course. Faculty in the humanities found that 3–3 courses left too little time for themes and concepts to be developed, and science faculty were frustrated by the fact that a ten-week trimester made lengthy laboratory experiments difficult.

In May 1989, after 26 years with a 3–3 schedule, the faculty voted to return to semesters. Under the new "early semester" calendar, the first term began in late August, followed by a month-long break from mid-December to mid-January and then a second term that ended in mid-May. Dean Julian pointed out that in addition to creating 15-week fall and spring terms, the semester plan would also make it far easier to

participate in off-campus programs of the Associated Colleges of the Midwest, which were run entirely on the semester system. Monmouth implemented the semester system in 1990–91.

Other changes were also proposed to strengthen Monmouth's academic program. President Haywood hoped to move toward a coalescence of academic departments into divisions uniting all the humanities or sciences. The concept appealed to those who believed that education would benefit from more interdisciplinary efforts. However, many faculty members were equally concerned that blurring distinctions between academic departments would cause faculty to lose their professional identity and frustrate students who wanted to work toward a clearly defined subject major.

Further disagreements over directions in academic policy and allocation of resources emerged in 1992, when several years of below-700 enrollments forced the college to face difficult choices. After conferring with the trustees, President Haywood reduced the instructional staff by several positions to balance the budget, causing some faculty members to question both his decision and the administrative priorities that had led to the cuts. The challenge of creating a new academic environment was producing stresses as well as satisfactions, and the pattern of enrollment that had seemed stable a few years before now appeared inadequate to sustain the expansive hopes of the Haywood administration.

The only effective way to address the problem of flagging enrollments, President Haywood

*A former professor of political science, Dean William B. Julian presided over the faculty during the difficult period of retrenchment in the early 1990s.*

*Lee L. Morgan, retired CEO of Caterpillar Inc., was chairman of the Monmouth College Senate from 1969 to 1975. A member of the Senate Executive Committee during five presidential administrations, he established a faculty chair in history and international studies in 1994.*

*A perennial Midwest Conference powerhouse, the Fighting Scots track team in the spring of 1994 included, from left, Bob Strabley '97, Dan Schisler '94, Aaron Venters '97, Ryan Moore '98, and Matt Jenkins '97.*

concluded, was to help address the financial concerns of families with potential Monmouth students. Many middle-income families were no longer eligible for many college aid programs; they earned too little to afford private college tuition yet earned too much to qualify for financial aid.

To meet this need, in 1993 President Haywood announced the creation of the Monmouth Plan. This new program would underwrite more than 47 percent of the cost of a Monmouth education and bring the total expenses to a level comparable to that of a state university. Funded by generous gifts from Monmouth alumni, the Monmouth Plan was based solely on the student's academic admissibility, could be renewed each year, and was not affected by any change in a family's income or assets. The plan also offered the student additional financial assistance opportunities as well as a payment schedule that could be tailored to a family's specific needs.

The Monmouth Plan, which would later be copied by dozens of private colleges, was perceived to be both simple and fair, and it overcame one of the principal obstacles many potential students faced in considering Monmouth.

To help implement the plan, Monmouth sought out a veteran admissions dean who had recently helped institute a dramatic enrollment increase at Arkansas College. Richard Valentine of Batesville, Arkansas, immediately began an aggressive recruiting program that in 1994 attracted the largest freshman class in 20 years.

### Campaigning for Monmouth

As improvements were made in recruiting efforts, success was also being achieved in two major capital campaigns during the Haywood administration. In 1983, Walter Huff's gift of $5 million had launched the "Campaign for Monmouth College" with a goal of $15 million. The campaign concluded in June 1986 having raised $15.1 million, $12.9 million of which was dedicated to the college endowment. Funds from the campaign also retired the last of the college's expansion debt from the 1970s, underwrote the improvements in campus facilities, and supported the creation of new scholarships.

In 1991, Monmouth began planning the formation of an even larger capital campaign. Publicly announced in the spring of 1992, "Forward to the 21st Century" had a goal of raising $25 million by June of 1994, $11.5 million of which was earmarked for support of the capital improvement program and $13.5 million for enlarging the college endowment. President Haywood determined to commit 70 percent of his time to the campaign and began a series of cross-country trips to 35 cities to meet with alumni and friends.

The stronger support being garnered by the college made possible the establishment of four new appointments to four endowed faculty chairs. Based on groundwork laid by the Freed administration, President Haywood was able to secure the Minnie Billings Capron Chair in Classics. Thomas Sienkewicz was appointed the first incumbent of the Capron Chair in 1985. An appointment to a second endowed chair was made in 1986, when Andrew Weiss was named the Edwin A. Trapp Jr. Professor of Business Administration. Seven years later, in the fall of 1993, Susan F. Holm became the first incumbent

*Students enjoy a spring day in 1994.*

of the Dorothy Donald Chair for Romance Languages and Literature, a position honoring the former chair of Monmouth's modern languages department. In the spring of 1994, a fourth endowed chair was announced when William Urban was appointed the Lee L. Morgan Professor of History and International Studies, named in honor of a former chairman of the board. In helping raise the profile of Monmouth's distinguished teaching faculty, these four chairs also marked the significant advances made during the Haywood years in reinforcing the future prospects of the college.

In 1993, President Haywood decided to retire the following year. His substantial effect on the financial well-being of the college during his 14-year tenure was clear. The size of the college endowment grew from $4 million to $24 million, and the proportion of alumni contributing to Monmouth increased from 16 percent to 40 percent. The physical environment of the campus was enhanced with modern heating and utilities, improved roadways and parking, renovated academic and residence halls, new athletic facilities, a reshaped student center, and the amenities of Dunlap Terrace and the Wells Theater.

More than this, in reconceiving its curriculum and attracting a broader and more diverse student body, Monmouth redefined and strengthened its identity as a national liberal arts college.

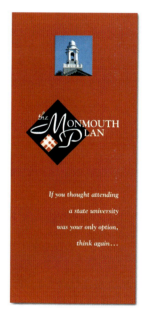

*A 1993 brochure described the benefits of the Monmouth Plan, a novel financial assistance program that helped spark a dramatic enrollment increase.*

**Securing Foundations 1985–1994**

# Into the Twent
## 1994–2002

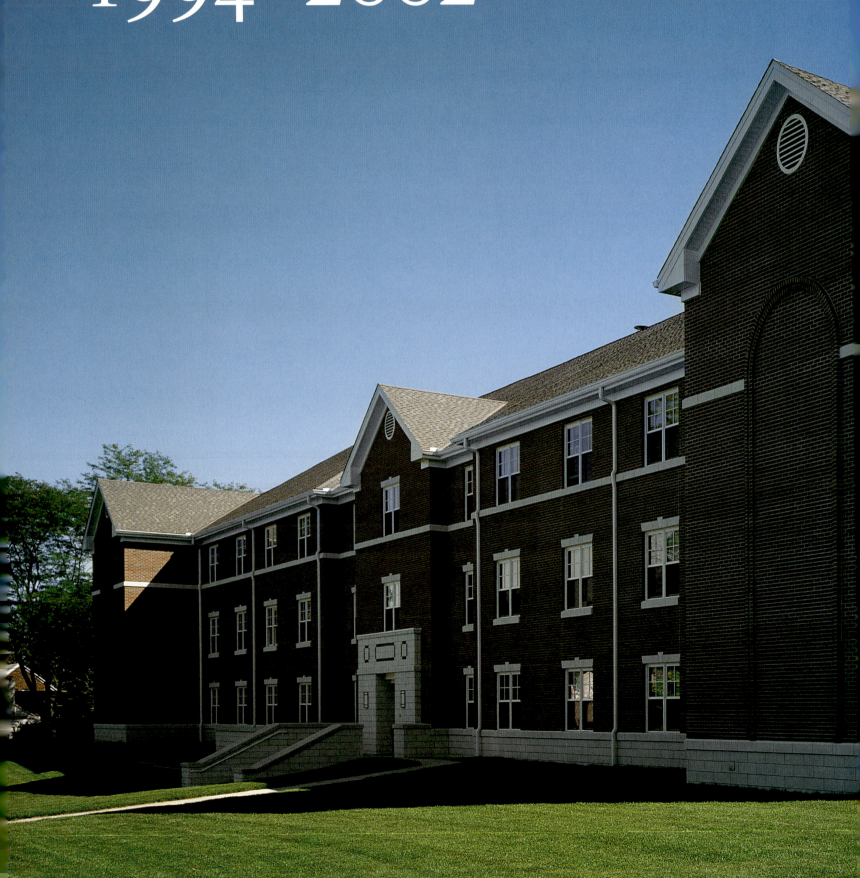

y-first Century

## Chapter 11

The last years of the 1990s brought a quicker tempo of events to the Monmouth campus. A major fundraising campaign was concluded with unprecedented contributions from alumni and friends as well as a record number of grants. Enrollment was increasing, and a master plan began shaping an enlarged and technologically advanced campus. The college took stock of its traditions and achievements and defined its goals for teaching, learning, and community life as the campus looked ahead to the promises of the twenty-first century.

PRECEDING PAGES *Board chairman David A. Bowers '60 provided the naming gift for Bowers Hall, a coeducational residence completed in 2001. Its innovative design incorporates a series of two-bedroom suites, each with its own bathroom and a living room.*

OPPOSITE PAGE *The renovated dining hall in Stockdale Center offers students a vast array of meal choices, from vegetable wraps to rotisserie chicken. Students can also use their meal cards to purchase specialty foods such as Mexican, deli sandwiches, and pizza in the Scotland Yard snack bar.*

### Dialogue and Diversity

Bruce Haywood's decision to retire launched a lengthy search for his successor. Over 10 months in 1993–94, a committee composed of Senate members, faculty, and students sought, as its chairman David Bowers '60 later wrote, "a fervent proponent of the liberal arts and a consensus builder who could establish an atmosphere of communication and cooperation on campus."

Sue Ann Huseman, Monmouth's eleventh president, met these criteria. Born in St. Louis in 1946, Huseman graduated from the University of Missouri–Columbia and earned a master's degree at Indiana University as well as a doctorate at the University of Illinois at Urbana-Champaign. She began her academic career at Illinois Wesleyan University teaching French, and by 1975 she became the chair of the foreign languages department at the age of 29. She was subsequently appointed director of the humanities division, co-director of the international studies program, and associate dean for academic affairs. In 1989, Huseman moved to the University of Maine at Farmington, where she became vice president for academic affairs and interim president in 1992. Two years later, she became the first woman to assume the Monmouth presidency.

President Huseman believed that the best college curriculum gave students a holistic educational experience and the ability to think and learn across academic disciplines. With the cooperation of trustees and faculty, she developed an atmosphere of mutual understanding and broader collaboration. She called on the college to strengthen its commitment to traditional values while increasing diversity and inclusiveness.

### Putting Students at the Center

Through the end of the Haywood administration, more than $17 million had been raised for the "Forward to the 21st Century" campaign launched in 1991. Included was a gift from college trustee Harold A. "Red" Poling '49 for the conversion of Carnegie Library into a student services center to be known as Poling Hall. A campaign gift from former basketball coach George Trotter '47 and trustee Maxine Murdy Trotter '47 was recognized with the naming of a new computer center in Wallace Hall in their honor.

President Huseman focused the final effort of the fundraising campaign on projects directly benefiting students. Under the slogan "Putting Students at the Center," the college completed a $5.5 million mini-campaign for funds to remodel and rehabilitate McMichael Residence Hall, Hewes Library, the former Carnegie Library, and Stockdale Center, in addition to upgrading the college's information technology infrastructure.

In October 1996, Poling Hall was formally dedicated during homecoming weekend. Included in the building was an elegant meeting room funded by a contribution from former Senate chair Lee L. Morgan. Adjoining the Morgan Room was a student career and leadership center, the gift of trustee Frederick W. Wackerle '61. When Harold Poling unveiled the new Poling Hall sign at the dedication, it was covered by a piece of tartan fabric—the college's first commissioned tartan, manufactured in Scotland and registered with the clan chieftains. The striking new plaid—a combination of red, black, and white—supplemented the college's traditional red and white Menzies plaid, which remained the ancient tartan.

### Reinvigorating Tradition

President Huseman's theme during her first year in office was "Creating Community: Celebrating Our History, Building Our Future." The academic year opened with a back-to-school celebration at which employees were the focus. For the first time in many years, employees were recognized for their years of service in a morning ceremony, and in the evening they were treated to a family barbecue. During the afternoon, the newly reopened and refurbished Graham Hall was formally dedicated.

At the first convocation of 1994, President Huseman opened a time capsule discovered in Grier Hall and invited former students and faculty to offer reminiscences about its contents.

*Upon assuming the presidency in 1994, Sue Ann Huseman used her talent for consensus building to engage the faculty in thoughtful discussions about the future size, appearance, and curriculum of the college.*

# The Freshman Walkout

IN 1995, UNDER THE DIRECTION of President Sue Huseman, the Freshman Walkout was one of several old Monmouth College traditions to be revived.

The walkout originated as an informal torchlight parade early in the twentieth century. By the 1920s, it had evolved into more organized event. Held on the first night of the fall semester, the walkout paired freshman men and women for an introductory tour of the town. Led by upperclassmen, the procession left from Wallace Hall and headed uptown along Broadway, winding its way through the president's mansion and fraternity houses along the way.

A favorite destination was the Rivoli Theater, where the movie would be stopped and the lights would come up as the audience applauded the new students. Before heading back to campus for a bonfire and dance, the entourage would often take an instructive tour through the local jail.

The 1955 *Ravelings* commented on the popular tradition as it existed in those times:

> *Every fall, Monmouth College devotes the first week to introducing the freshmen to the campus and to the town. One of the outstanding features of Freshman Week is the "Walkout." Led by the pep club members and fraternity torch-bearers, the freshmen toured the downtown section of Monmouth. Then, near the Public Square, they were addressed by the civic leaders of the town and by the college "YM" and "YW" president… To begin the annual Walkout, freshmen formed a double line in front of Wallace Hall. The evening culminated with a tennis court dance.*

But early in the 1970s, the walkout was discontinued due to lack of interest. By that point, it had become an afternoon affair and largely a promotional event for Monmouth merchants.

Since its recent revival, the walkout has remained in the afternoon, and although one of its purposes continues to be freshman bonding, it also helps the college foster its relationship with the town of Monmouth by introducing scores of new consumers to local businesses. Once again a popular part of freshman orientation, a recent walkout included participation by 54 local merchants, organizations, and industries. Approximately 300 freshmen and transfer students completed the route, filling shopping bags with coupons and handouts while sampling pizza, popcorn, and chocolate-covered strawberries.

*Above and below: The climax of orientation weekend is the Freshman Walkout, which starts at Dunlap Terrace and proceeds up Broadway to the business district.*

*Students conduct their own Scots Day celebration away from the raucousness of some of the planned activities.*

Huseman also began three projects to support Monmouth's history: the reorganization of the Monmouthiana Room in Hewes Library to make it a more useful historical resource; an oral history project to capture reminiscences of older alumni; and a revival of the college's pipe and drum band.

The Huseman administration also successfully secured support for a reinvigoration of Monmouth's religious heritage. Barbara Watt Johnson '52 provided principal funding toward a permanently endowed college chaplaincy, and the fund's growth was further enhanced in 1997 by a challenge gift made by Ruth Huseman, the president's mother.

### Education and Community Service

Monmouth's academic reputation continued to grow. In successive years, Monmouth was ranked by *U.S. News & World Report* as an outstanding national liberal arts college and was selected as one of the best colleges for the study of science and math in Peterson's *Guide to Top Colleges for Science* in 1996. *Money* magazine listed Monmouth in October 1995 as one of the top 10 schools in the country awarding the largest percentage of its funds in scholarships and grants. Barron's *Profiles of American Colleges* followed with a "competitive plus" rating and a recommendation of Monmouth among its 300 selected "Best Buys in American Colleges."

Equally significant was the steady rise in student enrollment. Much of the improvement could be credited to the innovative Monmouth Plan. Introduced in 1992, it assured that, for most students, a private college education at Monmouth would cost no more than a degree from their state university. Enrollment had hit a low of 670 students before the Monmouth Plan was introduced. By 1995–96, enrollment reached 925, and a student body of 1,000 no longer seemed unlikely.

In 1995, Huseman established the Alternative Spring Break, reviving a tradition of student service that was first implemented during the 1960s. That year, 13 Monmouth students traveled to the impoverished Appalachian community of Max Meadows, Virginia, where they cleared brush and helped build a community recreation center. In the spring of 1996, 19 students went to work on the Wahpeton-Sisseton National American Indian Reservation in South Dakota, while a second group of student volunteers returned to Max Meadows.

On campus, the college's renewed focus on community service led to the formation of Students Organized for Service (SOS) in 1996. Led by co-chairs Ginny Martin '96 and Bob Grimm '96, SOS participants performed more than 1,200 hours of community service in the group's inaugural year.

### Transition to New Leadership

In the fall of 1996, President Huseman announced her decision to leave Monmouth to become the vice chancellor for academic affairs of the University of Maine System. During her brief, three-year tenure, Huseman had successfully

*A sure sign of spring on the Monmouth campus is the sudden appearance of improvised lawn furniture.*

# From ScotOlympics to Ceilidh

FOR MORE THAN A CENTURY, Monmouth College students have welcomed spring with a special day devoted to outdoor activities. Now known by the Celtic word "Ceilidh," which means "a gathering," the celebration has taken many forms over the years—from the innocence of dancing around a Maypole to the relative decadence of a "Streakers Weekend" in the 1970s.

After the traditional May Fete went out of style in the 1950s, students tried to initiate "Skip Day," in which they took a holiday from classes, but faculty resistance shot it down. In 1962, Blue Key held its first Scots Sing, a springtime musical competition that remains popular to this day under the name "Scotlight." The following year, the first-ever ScotOlympics debuted on the athletic field following the Monmouth-Knox track meet. The inaugural Olympics included bicycle races and a swim meet, and the day concluded with an all-school dance in the gymnasium.

As the "flower power" movement blossomed, so did a popular springtime phenomenon on college campuses known as the Festival of Life. Monmouth's first such festival took place on May 1, 1971. The all-night affair, featuring folk and rock performances, was to run from 7 p.m. until 7 a.m. on the Wallace Hall Plaza, but fear of police intervention eventually drove the affair into the gym. The ScotOlympics of that year were an equally ambitious undertaking, featuring evening concerts by REO Speedwagon and the Ides of March.

Combining the back-to-nature appeal of the Festival of Life with the zaniness of ScotOlympics, students in 1974 celebrated a "Festival Olympics" with outdoor movies and concerts on the library terrace. Participants brought sleeping bags and spent the night in People's Park. The same year was also notorious for its Streakers Weekend, when Ray Stevens serenaded the nation with his novelty song and Monmouth students shed their clothes, running a gauntlet between Gibson Hall and Winbigler Hall.

The 1980s saw the emergence of Scots Day as an integral part of the school year. The date of the event was kept a closely guarded secret, only revealed to the college community when a bagpiper would stroll through residence halls at 7 a.m., blasting students out of bed. Teams would then gather for breakfast on Wallace Hall Plaza in their pajamas, and a day of games, from tug-of-war to Jell-O wrestling, would ensue.

By 1993, the value of Scots Day was being questioned. Faculty did not like the idea of students dictating when classes would be cancelled, and the administration worried that the "secret" date for the celebration was leaking out, leading to student drinking binges the night before. The following year, the event was replaced with "Scots Weekend" so that class attendance would not be compromised.

President Huseman took office in 1995 under the theme "Creating Community." She believed that instilling a campus-wide sense of pride in the college's heritage would help bring students and faculty together. Scots Weekend was scrapped and Scots Day was reinstated as a planned event featuring Honors Convocation, Scottish food in the dining hall, a trip to South Henderson Church (where the college had its roots), music, and games. By 2000, the celebration had become well established, changing its name to Ceilidh and placing a new emphasis on competition in traditional Highland games.

*The Kappa Deltas show fierce determination in the tug of war during the 1981 ScotOlympics.*

*Three former Monmouth College presidents helped celebrate Richard Giese's inauguration in 1987. From left are President Emeritus Bruce Haywood, Giese, Sue Huseman and DeBow Freed.*

completed the largest capital campaign in Monmouth history, built the endowment to $30 million, rearticulated the college's educational mission, and met the enrollment goal of 1,000 students.

The presidential search committee reviewed the qualifications of 150 candidates, looking for individuals with expertise in administration and management, experience in fundraising and admissions, and the ability to direct strategic institutional planning.

Following a seven-month search, the committee selected Richard F. Giese as Monmouth's twelfth president. Giese came to Monmouth with 21 years of experience in teaching, coaching, and college administration in private, church-related liberal arts colleges. After receiving his bachelor's degree from Concordia College and a master's from Concordia Seminary in Exile, Giese went on to earn a master's degree in kinesiology and exercise physiology from Washington University in St. Louis, and in 1986 he received a doctorate in college and university administration from Kent State University.

Giese held a brief coaching position at Averett College in Virginia before moving to Alliance, Ohio, in 1978 to become a physical education instructor and the head men's basketball and tennis coach for Mount Union College. Within a few years, his responsibilities increased in successive appointments as director of student financial services, dean of enrollment services, vice president for enrollment services, and vice president for institutional advancement. Thus, Giese brought to Monmouth an unusually broad range of experience in teaching and academic administration.

President Giese was formally installed in office during the 1997 homecoming festivities. Delegates from 40 colleges and universities, representatives of every Monmouth class from 1920 to 2001, and his three predecessors in office—DeBow Freed, Bruce Haywood, and Sue Huseman—participated in the inauguration ceremony.

A highlight of the weekend was the dedication of Quinby House, which was closed in 1992 for major renovations and repairs. The Victorian presidential home, donated by a descendant of Ivory Quinby, was now occupied by President Giese and his family.

### Strategic Initiatives for the Future

As Monmouth entered the final years of the twentieth century, planning turned to the demands the college would face in the future. In consultation with senior administrators and members of the faculty, President Giese began a systematic review of Monmouth's educational program, physical plant, and financial resources.

Based on this review, President Giese proposed a set of five strategic initiatives: develop a curriculum for the future; expand and enhance the residential experience for students; improve the college's fiscal strength; increase enrollment; and strengthen the institution's national reputation and visibility.

In focusing on these objectives, President Giese was backed by an experienced cabinet that included George Arnold, vice president for academic affairs; Richard Valentine, vice president for external relations; Jacquelyn Condon, vice president for student life; Donald Gladfelter '77, vice president for finance and business; and Marybeth Kemp '93, vice president for admission.

### A Master Plan for the Campus

The first step in pursuing these initiatives was the development of a campus master plan. Four possible plans were developed and unveiled in a campuswide meeting in March 1998. Each called for the addition of a fine arts center, new residence hall space, a new recreation center, a new main campus entrance at Broadway and North Seventh Street, and additional parking lots.

After consultation with faculty, students, trustees, and alumni, the Giese administration identified three clear campus priorities: modernization and renovation of Hewes Library, expansion of Stockdale Student Center, construction of a recreation center, and expansion of the campus west to North Sixth Street.

Substantial progress was made in refitting existing buildings to meet new college needs. In 1998, McMichael Residence Hall was reopened after a yearlong renovation project. The following year, the 70-year-old building that once housed Alpha Tau Omega fraternity was converted into the Edward A. Mellinger Teaching and Learning Center with a grant from the Mellinger Foundation of Monmouth. The building became headquarters for the English department, a tutoring center, and the home of a 24-hour computer lab. Also that year, the first phase of a renovation of Stockdale Student Center was completed. The crowning touch was a newly refurbished Highlander Room, a meeting and banquet facility on the top floor, the gift of the Whiteman and McMillan families. One of the Whitemans, Ralph '52, was the student center's first director, serving from 1963 until 1966.

In 2000, the college was presented with Boone House, the former home of faculty members Commander Gilbert Ebbett Boone and Katharine Phelps Boone '30. Given by Mrs. Boone's nephew Dr. Hugh N. Phelps '63, and his wife, Norma, the house was memorable for many Monmouth alumni as the setting for East Asian studies seminars taught by the Boones between 1965 and 1977. Situated in a secluded wooded setting just a block from the campus, the house, which had been hand-built by the Boones as their retirement home, offered an ideal location for a college retreat center. A gift from Tina Hartwig '68 financed renovation of a display gallery honoring former art professor Harlow B. Blum, and the former dining room was named the Ruth Huseman Meditation Room.

### Athletic Fields and Nature Trails

By 2000, the college's central campus had been expanded to 15 square city blocks, including all the property from Broadway north to Euclid Avenue and nearly the entire expanse from North Sixth to North Ninth Streets.

Sports facilities greatly improved in 2000, when a gift from former Senate chair Safford Peacock and his wife, Betty, underwrote the costs of constructing Peacock Memorial Athletic Park, which was developed on a college-owned 16.5-acre tract at the southeast corner of North Eleventh Street and U.S. Highway 34. The park provided a new college baseball diamond and men's and women's soccer fields. Under construction for two years, Peacock Park required the removal of thousands of tons of earth from

*Formerly known as The Styx, Monmouth College's snack bar has been updated with an upscale look and a new name—Scotland Yard.*

PRECEDING PAGES *Completed in the spring of 2000, Peacock Memorial Athletic Park offers two regulation soccer fields—one for men and one for women—on its spacious grounds, just northeast of the main campus.*

RIGHT *David A. Bowers '60 reflects on his days as a college student at the 2001 dedication of the new residence hall that bears his name.*

the rolling site, landscape grading, and the creation of a holding pond.

With a gift from trustee Donald E. Fike, the baseball field was designated Glasgow Field in memory of Angela Glasgow '92 and in honor of her father, Terry Glasgow, Monmouth's longtime director of athletics, professor of physical education, head basketball coach, and head baseball coach from 1972 until 1994. During Glasgow's years as baseball coach, his Monmouth teams won 14 conference championships and compiled a 343–166–3 record.

A gated entrance to Bobby Woll Field, Boucher Plaza, was dedicated in 2000. The gift of Virgil "Tige" Boucher '32, a famed offensive guard and defensive tackle for the Fighting Scots football teams of the 1930s, the plaza memorializes his late daughter, Judy, and her husband, Joseph Chamberlain. Embellishing the plaza is a granite fountain with a rotating 800-pound red granite sphere crafted in China.

Immediately south of Peacock Memorial Park on North Eleventh Street is LeSuer Nature Preserve, a 1997 gift from former trustee William LeSuer '42 and Arlene Snow LeSuer '42. The former farmland is being restored to its original prairie, woodland, and wetlands condition. Bisected by Markham Creek, the preserve features three distinct ecosystems, with a one-acre parcel reserved for a sustainable organic produce farm. A public nature and walking trail through the site is being developed with interpretive plaques explaining the area's contrasting ecologies.

### Facilities for Living and Learning

The master planning process for the campus had identified the need for new student residence space. It had also recommended the demolition of 35-year-old Gibson Hall to make way for a recreation and wellness center.

In October 1999, the trustees authorized Metzger-Johnson Architects of Galesburg to begin designing a new 37,000-square-foot residence hall in the classical Georgian style of architecture prevalent on the Monmouth campus. Named in honor of college board chair David A. Bowers '60, who provided the principal gift, the coeducational suite-style residence hall opened in the fall of 2001.

As construction of Bowers Hall was being completed, work was already under way on the modernization of the 30-year-old Hewes Library, outfitting it with the latest information technology systems while increasing its overall aesthetic appeal and user-friendliness. Improvements included cutting 32 windows into the blank facades of the building to bring additional

## The Shields Collection

IN 1998, JAMES C. SHIELDS, a 1949 graduate of Monmouth College, presented to his alma mater his personal collection of art and antiquities, which started with a single mummified hawk five decades earlier and had grown to more than 600 pieces by the time of his gift. The James Christie Shields Collection contains an incredible assortment of artifacts that seem to transport the viewer to another place and time.

While cultures from all over the world are represented in the collection, most of the pieces are Egyptian and West African—the region of the world where Shields spent most of his childhood as the son of Presbyterian missionaries.

Shields was born in Addis Ababa, Ethiopia, and attended missionary schools in the Sudan and Egypt before coming to the United States in 1942. He served in the Navy during World War II and entered Monmouth College after his discharge. Following his graduation, he pursued a career not as an archaeologist or an art historian but as a high school English teacher, primarily in New York City. Shields collected whatever intrigued him, and as the number of items he found intriguing increased so did the collection. Watching his acquisitions accumulate, Shields also saw storage space in his apartment diminish. Every wall was lined with floor-to-ceiling shelves, every countertop was covered with artwork, and the floors became storage for some items. Shields realized it was time to do something with his art.

He knew that he wanted to donate his collection to an educational institution where others with a thirst for knowledge could experience that which had given him so much pleasure. His first thought was of the school in New York where he had taught for so long. It occurred to Shields, though, that the school was across the park from the Metropolitan Museum of Art, so it did not really have a need for the collection. Located four hours from any major city, Monmouth College seemed to be a much better choice.

Conversations that began in 1980 finally culminated in the complete donation in the fall of 1998. The collection now resides permanently in Hewes Library, where objects are displayed on a rotating basis.

*Representing the mythical antelope, Chi-Wara, who was believed to have taught agriculture to the Bamana people of Mali, this circa-1900 headdress was worn during the planting and harvesting dance.*

*A significant portion of the Shields Collection consists of ancient Egyptian artifacts, such as this model of a coffin from the 26th Dynasty (664–525 B.C.).*

light into the interior, building a new entrance on the east side of the building, installing a cafe, creating a high-tech electronic classroom, providing extensive Internet connections, and finishing the top floor with renovated art galleries and archive rooms. The library was also given a new heating and air conditioning system.

Renovation of Hewes Library was supported by a bequest from the Keith B. Capron estate, which was applied toward a challenge grant received from the Carver Charitable Trust, a major gift from trustee Ann Mack Collier '63, and an additional grant from the Caterpillar Foundation.

In August 2001, trustee and board vice president Walter S. Huff '56, who made a $5 million gift in 1983, presented Monmouth College with the largest gift in its history, $10 million, to be used for construction of the new recreation and athletic complex. The donation was the lead gift in a campaign to build a $21 million complex, named in memory of Huff's wife, Elizabeth. Incorporating the college's existing athletic facilities, the center will feature a natatorium, jogging and walking tracks, weight rooms, racquetball courts, aerobic exercise and dancing rooms, a fully equipped training room, new locker rooms, and indoor basketball, tennis, and volleyball courts.

The first component of the wellness center was created in 2000, when Isabel Bickett Marshall '36 provided funds for the Marshall Health and Fitness Center in Stockdale Center in honor of her late husband, Dr. James W. Marshall '36, and other members of the Marshall family.

To complete the modernization of the college's athletic facilities, property was acquired on the northwest corner of the campus for the construction of six tennis courts, practice fields for football, and additional parking.

Another element of the campus master plan was put in place in May 2001, when the college announced a lead gift from the Edward Arthur Mellinger Foundation for the renovation of the venerable college Auditorium. While retaining its original architectural design of 1896, the Auditorium's interior will be redesigned to be more accessible for college and community events. Plans included air conditioning, new main-level seating, a new sound system, and a complete renovation of the Auditorium's lower level with the addition of dressing rooms and remodeled practice rooms.

In March 2002, the Auditorium project moved toward completion with a gift from Arthur Dahl in honor of his late wife, Dorothy Peterson Dahl '40, a member of the college's board of trustees for 11 years. In recognition of Dahl's generosity, the building was renamed the Dahl Chapel and Auditorium. Louise DuBois Kasch '48 provided funds to renovate the performance hall, while Anne Kniss Lamprecht '49 and William Daniel '72 contributed to the refurbishing of the balcony and vocal rehearsal room.

Significant unrestricted gifts from former board chair Roger Rasmusen '56, trustee Frederick Wackerle '61, and former board chair Peter Bunce and his wife, Gail, have recently added strength to the college's overall efforts to upgrade its physical plant.

*Ground was broken for the new $21 million Huff Athletic Center during Alumni Weekend 2002.*

*The Monmouth Chorale, an elite 30-member a cappella choir under the direction of Dr. Perry White, is quickly establishing a national reputation.*

BELOW: *Former President George Bush addresses the 2000 commencement exercises.*

### Enriching the Student Experience

Rapid advances in funding and construction of new campus facilities during the Giese administration were matched by a pattern of steady growth in the size of the student body. Giese and others studying Monmouth's enrollment believed that a larger student body provides a broader and richer academic and social experience, and that this in turn translates into higher student retention rates.

Statistics bore out the president's position. By the fall of 1999, the retention rate rose to 92 percent, while enrollment had escalated by 82 percent in just seven years. By the fall of 2001, Monmouth's enrollment stood at 1,087 students.

Monmouth's favorable listings in national college guides continued. In 2000, Monmouth was included for the first time in the *Kaplan Newsweek College Catalog*. Based on a survey of 4,500 guidance counselors, the guide placed Monmouth among schools for the academically competitive student, schools offering the maximum amount of individual academic attention, and schools with notable study abroad programs.

In the spring of 2000, four Monmouth students arrived in Paris, the first to take advantage of a new off-campus program arranged between the college and the l'École Normale Supérieure Gestion et Commerce International, the premier private business college in France. Monmouth students also studied at the University of Reading's Centre for Children's Reading and Writing in England, at Kansai Gaidai University in Tokyo, and at the American College of Thessaloniki, Greece. Continuing a Monmouth tradition, faculty have recently taken students on privately arranged trips to such destinations as England, Germany, Greece, Italy, and Turkey, while student athletes have traveled to competitions in Paris, Barcelona, and Aruba. In 2000, trustee Harold Poling and his wife, Marian,

*Enthusiastic international students provide a festive accent to every homecoming parade.*

*Into the Twenty-first-Century 1994–2002*

*All-American sprinters Philicia Moredock '04 (left), Constance Jackson '02, and Jill Hoops '03 share the medal podium at the 2000 MWC Indoor Track and Field Championships. Jackson, who holds a record 29 Midwest Conference track and field titles, finished second in the nation in the 200-meter dash in 2001.*

*A tradition within the tradition of Monmouth's success in track and field is that the Scots perennially have a strong stable of sprinters. From left, the team of Ryan Moll '04, Vaughn Gray '03, Randy Williams '02, and Bryan Bittner '03 won the sprint medley relay in conference-record time at the 2002 MWC Indoor Track and Field Championships.*

RIGHT *Mark Allen '04 advances the ball during the first season of play at Peacock Memorial Athletic Park. Allen led the team in scoring during his freshman season and then played a vital role as the Fighting Scots qualified for their first national tournament in 2001.*

further strengthened international studies with a $3 million gift to help expand exchange programs and recruit international and minority students.

Volunteer social service also remained strong among Monmouth students. In 2000, students spent spring break cleaning up the Emerson Park neighborhood in East St. Louis. The previous fall, students joined in constructing a Habitat for Humanity home in Monmouth. Members of Greek organizations, approximately one-fourth of the student population, participated in social service projects. The three women's and three men's fraternities met community needs in a variety of ways, including holding a benefit concert for Jamieson Community Center, volunteering with the YMCA soccer program, and tutoring at the Warren County Public Library.

Traditional athletic programs continued to thrive, with a much richer variety of opportunities for both women and men. By 2002, Monmouth added men's and women's intercollegiate golf and tennis, bringing Monmouth's varsity athletics into exact balance, with nine sports each.

A new athletic balance was also evident in competition. The men's cross-country team won the conference championship in 1996, and the indoor and outdoor track teams won a combined 13 conference championships between 1995 and 2002. In these same years, Monmouth's women were achieving their own distinction. The women's indoor and outdoor track teams won a combined 11 conference championships between 1996 and 2002.

### Building a Curriculum for the Future

President Giese launched a review of the college's curriculum in the fall of 1999, when a task force was appointed under the leadership of physics professor and associate dean of the faculty Rajkumar Ambrose. "We will build on outstanding majors of the past, including the sciences, education, and business, while also strengthening more traditional liberal arts areas," Giese said.

The review was essential, Giese explained, for Monmouth "to keep a keen eye on our rapidly changing society—its technological advances and global opportunities and concern—and identify what academic areas may need to be

PRECEDING PAGES
*A spirited production of* The Merry Wives of Windsor *highlighted the 2000 Crimson Masque season. From left are Geoff Edwards '03, Andrew Rubia '02, John Stevens '00, Kyle Anderson '03, and Brandon Tweed '02.*

*Continuity is one of Monmouth College's defining traditions. A case in point is Mark Willhardt, left, who succeeded his father, Gary Willhardt '60, on the English Department faculty.*

enhanced, created, or restructured to keep our graduates in step with the professional competition they will encounter."

A grant from the Teagle Foundation of New York is financing a three-year process for organizing, planning, and implementing the new curriculum. In each phase of the process, teams of faculty and administrators travel to national conferences and consultations at peer institutions. Roundtable discussions evaluating experiences and findings follow each visit, and stipends are available for 12 faculty members to work intensively on course enhancement and design.

On the Monmouth campus, as on campuses all over the world, September 11, 2001, came as a shock to Monmouth students, who sat stunned before their TV sets as never before in their lives. A commemorative service was held, and classes explored the day's historical, political, and sociological impact. The Class of 2002, wishing to memorialize the tragic events of terrorism that clouded their senior year, erected a monument on campus in tribute to the victims and heroes of New York, Pennsylvania, and Washington, D.C.

On a much happier note, March 2, 2002, marked the 100th birthday of Monmouth's legendary music instructor Grace Gawthrop Peterson. A 1922 graduate of the college's Conservatory of Music who taught piano and voice at Monmouth for 50 years, she was honored with a gala tribute at Galesburg's restored Orpheum Theatre.

## Monmouth's Next 150 Years

Monmouth College entered the twenty-first century with strengths in each of the areas defined by President Giese's strategic initiatives. The residential and recreational life of students was improved by the renovation of McMichael Residence Hall and Stockdale Center, the construction of Bowers Hall, and the creation of new athletic facilities on campus and at Peacock Memorial Athletic Park. Learning and career opportunities were enriched with the renovation of Hewes Library, the Mellinger Center, and the Wackerle Center, and the expansion of international studies.

An influx of new faculty and scholars—47 percent of the college's faculty was new since 1997—brought professional expertise and innovative perspectives to the classroom. Generous support from donors and alumni increased the college's permanent endowment to more than $50 million. All these advances were accompanied by the steady growth of Monmouth's admission and retention and an enlarged reputation for liberal arts education among its academic peers.

Still more improvements were under way with the construction of the Huff Athletic Center, the renovation of the historic Auditorium, planning for the renovation of the

OPPOSITE PAGE *Nearly a century since it rose from the ashes of the tragic Old Main fire, Wallace Hall is an endearing and enduring symbol of Monmouth College. Before its massive columns, a new class matriculates each fall and a graduating class bids farewell each spring.*

*Twelfth president Richard Giese and his wife, Sandy, presided over Monmouth College's entry into the twenty-first century and its sesquicentennial celebration in 2002–03.*

Haldeman-Thiessen Science Center, and the reconfiguration of the college curriculum to meet the needs of future generations of students.

### Into the Future

Classical philosophy—one of the foundation stones of a liberal arts education—warns against making a final judgment about an individual's happiness until life is over. The same is certainly true about institutions, and Monmouth College's life is far from over. What judgments can be made, then, about the institution at age 150?

Perhaps we can do no more than Marcus Aurelius, the Stoic philosopher, who opened his *Meditations* with a profound reflection on the people who had made him the man he had become: his father and mother, his brothers and sisters, his teachers, his friends, and his associates. Especially significant were his teachers—selected by his parents for the excellence of their knowledge and, above all, their humanity.

For an education is more than learning facts and mastering techniques. It is the building of a human being whose life is worth celebrating.

Monmouth College has had its successes in building human beings. Ask its graduates. Ask those who contribute time and money so that others may have a presence similar to theirs. Ask yourself.

Monmouth's third president, Thomas Hanna McMichael, once noted that progress and improvements were possible because "old friends stood true and new ones were found." McMichael's words still ring true. This book celebrates those friendships, and in doing so it celebrates all those who have contributed, in large ways and small, to Monmouth College's first 150 years.

## Faculty and Staff with 20 or More Years of Service to the College

Allison, David C.
Professor of Biology
1962-96

Arnold, George
Vice President for Academic Affairs; Dean of Faculty; Professor of Education
1974- present

Austin, T. Merrill
Director of Musical Conservatory
1901-32

Babcock, Betty
Cashier
1974-95

Baird, Maude Edgerton
Assistant Librarian
1930-50

Ball, Elwood H.
Assistant Professor of Music; Dean of Men; Dean of Students
1953-83

Barr, Eva Louise
Professor of German and Spanish
1915-40

Bennett, Catherine
Secretary to the President; Secretary to the Business Manager
1968-91

Beveridge, Hugh R.
Professor of Mathematics; Dean of the College
1929-61

Blackstone, Lois
Office Manager; Treasurer; Assistant to Librarian; Librarian
1923-74

Blum, Harlow
Professor of Art
1959-99

Bowman, Milton L.
Professor of Biology; Registrar
1959-65, 1968-82

Brett, Cecil D.
Professor of Government and History; Director of East Asian Studies
1963-83

Buban, Steven
Professor of Sociology
1977-present

Buchanan, J. Dales
Religion
1923-46

Buchholz, Robert H.
Professor of Biology
1950-94

Burkitt, William
Painter, Decorator
1968-97

Campbell, Jennie Logue
Lady Principal; Professor of English
1874-89, 1896-1901

Cleland, Eva H.
Professor of English
1923-44, 1951-67

Cleland, John Scott
Dean of the College; Professor of Economics
1927-51

Condon, Jacquelyn
Vice President for Student Life; Dean of Students
1980-present

Cramer, Paul
Professor of Mathematics
1946-73

Crow, Mary Bartling
Professor of History
1946-85

Davenport, F. Garvin
Professor of History
1947-76

Davenport, Katye Lou
Instructor in Education
1949-55, 1957-77

De Young, James
Director of Theater; Professor of Communication and Theater Arts
1963-2002

Dober, Roy
Carpenter
1957-97

Donald, Dorothy
Professor of Spanish
1932-70

Fleming, David D.
Director of Development; Assistant to President; Trustee
1946-72, 1991-96

Finley, Lyle W.
Professor of Physics
1931-67

Fox, Bernice
Professor of Classics
1947-81

Garwood, Ruth
Professor of Spanish
1936-56

Gebauer, Peter A.
Professor of Chemistry
1975-present

Gibson, Emma
Professor of Latin, Dean of Women
1920-52

Gladfelter, Donald
Vice President for Finance and Business
1977-present

Glasgow, Terry L.
Professor of Physical Education; Athletic Director
1972-present

Graham, Russell
Vice President; Treasurer; Professor of Social Science; Librarian
1886-1925

Griffiths, Richard L.
Professor of Music
1967-98

Gustafson, Eleanor
Cataloger; Librarian
1963-94

Haldeman, William S.
Professor of Chemistry
1918-54

Hamilton, Martha Metzger
Assistant Professor of Art; Home Economics
1937-71

Hamilton, Thomas Hoffman
Professor of the Appreciation of Art; Director of School of Music
1932-57

Hastings, William
Professor of Psychology
1968-present

Hauge, Harris
Head Librarian
1963-91

Hogue, Mary Inez
Registrar
1923-52

Holland, Ceola
Head Nurse
1960-81

Hutchison, J. Calvin
Vice President; Professor of Mathematics, Natural Sciences, Latin, German; Librarian
1858-91

Jensen, Louenna
Bookkeeper, Accounts Payable, Purchasing
1978-present

Johnson, J. Prescott
Professor of Philosophy
1962-86

Kennedy, Adele
Professor of English
1946-77

Ketterer, John J.
Professor of Biology
1953-86

Kieft, Richard
Professor of Chemistry
1975-present

Kirk, Carolyn Tyirin
Professor of Sociology
1972-2001

Leever, Richard S.
Professor of English
1961-82

Lemon, J. Rodney
Professor of Political Economy and Commerce
1976-present

Liedman, Jean E.
Professor of Speech; Dean of Women
1936-73

Loya, Eileen
Secretary to President; Administrative Assistant to the President; Corporate Secretary
1952-81

Loya, Heimo A.
Professor of Music
1936-73

Marshall, James W.
College Physician
1948-73

Maynard, Milton Monroe
Professor of English, Education
1909-49

McClanahan, Thomas S.
Professor of Practical Surveying and Engineering
1873-97

McClenahan, Francis Mitchell
Professor of Physics and Geology
1924-49

McClintock, Roy M.
Professor of Government
1966-86

McCoy, Beth
Maintenance
1980-present

McCoy, Mary E.
Librarian
1936-57

McKelvey, Nelle
Secretary to the President; Office Superintendent; Treasurer
1911-37

McMichael, David M.
Business Manager; Vice President
1929-53

McMichael, Thomas Hanna
President; Professor of Bible
1902-36

McMillan, John H.
Vice President; Professor of Latin, Hebrew; Principal of Preparatory Department; Registrar
1886-1920

188    A Thousand Hearts' Devotion

McNamara, R. Jeremy
Professor of English
1964-95

McNall, Michael
Personnel Director
1980-present

Meliska, Charles J.
Professor of Psychology
1969-89

Nieman, George C.
Professor of Chemistry
1979-present

Pease, Harriett Kyler
Instructor in Art
1931-59

Peterson, Grace Gawthrop
Instructor in Music
1922-72

Petrie, Richard P.
Professor of Economics;
Director of Public
Relations, Director of
Admissions; Business
Manager
1929-53

Ralston, Harold J.
Professor of Classics
1946-70

Rankin, Glen D.
Director of Admissions;
Director of College
Relations
1957-86

Riggs, Edna B.
Associate Professor
of Music
1917-54

Robinson,
Luther Emerson
Professor of English
1899-38

Rodgers, Thomas H.
Principal of Preparatory
Department;
Professor of Mathematics
1864-98

Sanmann, Madge S.
Professor of Sociology
1949-69

Shaver, Glenn C.
Associate Professor
of Music
1925-53

Shawver, Benjamin T.
Professor of Chemistry and
Education
1946-74, 1975-85

Shoemaker, Homer L.
Instructor in Accounting
1961-91

Skov, Charles E.
Professor of Physics
1963-94

Sorensen, Francis W.
Professor of Education
1973-present

Sparling, Brigit J
Lecturer in English
1977-2001

Speel, Charles J. II
Professor of Bible
and Religion
1951-83

Spitz, Douglas R.
Professor of History
1957-96

Sproston, Michael
Associate Professor
of Music
1968-present

Stauffer, Frances
Secretary
1978-99

Stevenson, Anita Sue
Library Acquisitions
Manager
1980-present

St. Ledger, Dean
Superintendent of Buildings and Grounds
1957-95

St. Ledger, Nancy
Secretary, Science and
Mathematics
1980-present

Sullivan, Judy Snyder
Records Secretary, Office
of Admission
1979-present

Swan, John Nesbit
Professor of Chemistry,
Physics; Librarian
1893-1915

Thiessen, Garrett W.
Professor of Chemistry
1930-67

Thompson, Samuel M.
Professor of Philosophy
1926-72

Tinkham, Carolyn
Secretary: Student
Center, Physical Plant, Student Affairs
1981-present

Urban, Jacquelyn
Lecturer in Modern
Foreign Languages
1980-present

Urban, William L.
Professor of History and
International Studies
1966-present

Van Gundy, Justin Loomis
Professor of Greek
and Latin, Librarian
1914-36

Wallace, William
Professor of Communication and Theater Arts
1979-present

Walterhausen, George L.
Professor of Art
1966-2001

Weeks, J. Stafford
Professor of Bible and
Religion, Dean of the College
1959-86

Weir, Frank M.
Penmanship,
Bookkeeping
1855-90

Welch, Lyle L.
Professor of Mathematics
1979-present

Whaling, Dorothy
Assistant Treasurer, Controller, Assistant Registrar
1937-66

Whiteside, Carol
Secretary
1969-present

Willhardt, Gary D.
Professor of English
1967-2000

Williams, Ruth M.
Professor of Speech
1923-47

Wills, Donald L.
Professor of Geology,
Business Manager
1951-84

Wilson, John H.
Professor of Latin, Mathematics, Greek; Librarian,
Treasurer, Principal of
English
1861-1901

Winbigler, Alice
Professor of Mathematics, Astronomy;
Dean of Women
1879-1929

Woll, Robert G.
Professor of Physical Education; Athletic Director
1935-75, 1976-80

Wright, A. Dean
Professor of Psychology
1970-91

*This list was compiled from records and, in some cases, recollections available at the time of publication. It should be noted that professional titles varied over time and that every attempt has been made to be accurate.*

## Acknowledgements

This book is dedicated to the memory of Joanne Dutcher Maxwell '53, a college trustee who chaired the committee responsible for its production and writing. She offered invaluable advice, both as an alumna with personal insight to key chapters of Monmouth College history, and as a writer, editor, and publicist, which was her lifelong profession.

The idea to publish a new history of Monmouth College in connection with the sesquicentennial was suggested by President Richard Giese. Throughout the project, he provided the support and inspiration necessary to make it a reality. A book of this magnitude also requires a significant financial investment, and Don Gladfelter, vice president for finance and business, worked diligently, not only to secure the necessary funds, but to provide thoughtful fiscal oversight and direction.

The Monmouth College archives, from which the majority of the photographs and documents reproduced in this book are drawn, were made accessible through the generosity of curator Professor Stacy Cordery, and head librarian Richard Sayre, who went out of his way to accommodate almost daily visits to the archives in the face of major construction during the library renovation.

Any comprehensive history relies heavily on the scholarship of previous historians. A significant portion of this book is based directly on the work of the late Garvin Davenport, who wrote the book *Monmouth College: The First 100 Years* in conjunction with the 1953 college centennial. Produced under budgetary constraints, what that book lacks in girth, illustrations, and design is more than made up in concise historical scholarship and literary style.

A great debt of gratitude is owed to Professor Bill Urban, whose seminal history published at Monmouth College's 125th anniversary shed important new light on the personalities who comprised the faculty and administration during the formative years of the 1920s through 1960s. His extensive research, professional wisdom, and quiet guidance were invaluable.

No work of this scale could be completed without the assistance of readers, who carefully reviewed the initial drafts and offered helpful suggestions for content and style. Deserving of particular recognition are David Fleming '46, a former Monmouth College administrator and trustee, and Louise Lauder Roos '48, who has an abiding love for college history, particularly relating to Kappa Kappa Gamma and the women's fraternity movement. Jane Mears Warfield '56, the curator of Holt House, was also very helpful in opening its Pi Beta Phi archives for research.

Much of the day-to-day work in managing this project was the responsibility of the College Relations Office. Thanks to Dick Valentine, vice president for external relations, for allotting the many hours of staff time necessary. Thanks also to Barry McNamara, associate director of college communications, who assisted with the writing of sidebars, Dan Nolan, assistant director of college communications, and to interns Marybeth McGregor '01 and Brandi McCoy '02.

The project also benefited from the generous support of others in the college community. President Emeritus Bruce Haywood, longtime presidential assistant Eileen Loya, and professors emeriti Harlow Blum and Gary Willhardt all agreed to share their unique perspectives on Monmouth's history.

The formidable task of consolidating existing scholarship and original research into an engaging new text was ably accomplished by Daniel Meyer of the University of Chicago, who served as the principal writer. The book's striking design was created by The Grillo Group under the direction of Maria Grillo and Julie Klugman.

Finally, it is impossible to understate the college's gratitude to Kim Coventry of The Coventry Group, who managed the project from beginning to end. Her expertise in all aspects of publishing, from initial concept to final proofs, was invaluable. She graciously allowed Monmouth College to put its own unique mark on the book, stepping in only to offer advice or admonitions when professionalism dictated.

# Index

*Page numbers in italics refer to illustrations.*

Academy Building, 5, 7, 8, *8*
Academy, The. *See* Monmouth Academy
Acheson, Robert, 68, *107*
ACM, 105
Addams, Jane, 36
Adeleye, Gabriel, *159*
African American Alumni Network, 159
Aletheorian Society, 22, 24, 34, 35, 68
Allen, Mark, 184, *184*
Allison, David, 128, *128*, 145, 157, *157*
Alpha Tau Omega, 123, *150*, *151*, 175
Alpha Xi Delta, 68, 112, *124*, *125*, 126
Alternative Spring Break, 172
Amateurs des Belles Lettres, 22, 24, 35, 68
Ambrose, Rajkumar, 158, 184
American College of Thessaloniki, 181
American Foundation for Management Research, 131
Amy, William O., 142, 143, *143*, 146, 157
Anderson, Ellen, *23*
Anderson, Kyle, *182*, *183*
Angilly, Arthur O., 55
Anniversaries
  75th, 78
  125th, 141
  130th, 147
  Centennial, 103, *103*
Argonne Semester Program, 106, 128, *128*
Arkis, Ellen, *133*
Armsby, Margery, *61*
Armstrong, Jerry, *133*
Arnold, George, 158, 174
Art Center, 130, *130*
Art Department, 23, 24, 105
Art gallery. *See* Len G. Everett Gallery
Associated Colleges of the Midwest, 105
Assiut College, 84, 88, 91, 103, 159
Athletic center. *See* Huff Athletic Center
Athletic Conference of the Middle West, 57, 60
Athletic field, 36, *36*, 37, 71, 143, 144, 154. *See also* Bobby Woll Athletic Field; Peacock Memorial Athletic Park

Athletics, 32, 36, 42, 56, 57, 69, 71, 73, 86, 87, 110, 113, 115, 133, 135, 144, 145, 147, 148, 149, 161, 162, 175, 178, 184. *See also individual sports*
Atlas, 12, 51
Auditorium, *29*, 31, 33, 36, *44*, *45*, 51, 52, 55, 143, 180, 187. *See also* Dahl Chapel and Auditorium
Austin Hall, 94, 112
Austin, T. Merrill, 72, 73, *73*

BAAC
  *See* Black Action Affairs Council
Bagpipes, 72, 91
Baird, Jeanette, *75*
Baird, Kenneth, *75*
Baird, William, *75*
Baker, Ron, 148, *148*
Ballad, Bob, 123
Barks, Paul, 128
Barnes, Robert, *85*
Barnes, Wallace, 97
Barracks, The. *See* Academy Building
Barracudas, 133
Barr, Eva Louise, 110
*Barron's 300 Best Buys in College Education*, 158
*Barron's Profiles of American Colleges*, 172
Baseball, 37, 50, 56, 71, 145, 148, 162, 178
Baseball, women's, 149
Basketball, 37, *37*, 56, *56*, 71, 72, 87, *87*, 88, 113, *113*, 115, *134*, 135, 145, 148, 161, *161*, 162
Basketball, women's, *30*, 31, *40*, 41, 42, 148, 149, 161, *161*, 162
Bayliss, Joan, *107*
Bell, C. Clifford, 57
Bell, Steve, 160
Bennett, Mary Louise, 25
Bersted, George, *87*
Beste, Eugene, *71*
Beta Kappa, 69, 71
Beta Phi of Theta Chi, 69
Beta Theta Pi, 24
Beveridge, Dorothy, 154
Beveridge, Hugh R., 154
Beveridge Rooms, 154
Bigger, Matthew, *9*
Binary Program, 88
Biology Department, 33, 75
Bittner, Bryan, *184*
Black Action Affairs Council, 153, 159
Black, Andrew M., *11*
Black, Robert, *85*
Blue Key, 119, 141, 173
Blum, Harlow, 105, 158, 175

Board of Foreign Missions of the Presbyterian Church, 55
Bobby Woll Athletic Field, 143, 144, 145, 178
Bookstore, 112, 126, 144, *144*
Boone, Gilbert Ebbett, 127, *127*, 175
Boone House, 127, *127*, 175
Boone, Katharine Phelps, 127, *127*, 175
Boone Oriental Library and Fine Arts Collection, 127
Boruff, Clair, 89
Boucher Plaza, 178
Boucher, Virgil "Tige," 73, 178
Bowers, David A., 169, 170, 178, *178*
Bowers Hall, 166, *167*, 169, 185
Boxing, 71
Boyd, Hanna, *25*
Bradley, Mark, 147
Bretnall, George Herbert, *46*, 47
Brett, Cecil, 127
Bridge, Ninth Street, 42, *42*
Bronze Turkey, 72, 115, 160, *160*
Brook, Libbie, *25*
Brook, Zelpha, *61*
Brown, Donna, 156
Brown, James R., 5, 7, *7*, *9*
Bruen, Ada C., 24, *25*
Bruen Hall, 95
Brunke, Karen, *124*, *125*
Bryan, William Jennings, 36, 74
Buchanan, J. Dales, 78
Buchanan, Mrs. J. Dales, *78*
Buchholz, Robert, *126*, 128, *128*
Buckert, Kim, 149, 161, *161*, 162
Bunce, Gail, 180
Bunce, Peter H., 140, 142, 147, 180
Burlington Northern Foundation Faculty Award for Teaching Excellence, 147, 158
Burlington Railroad, 7, 35, 121
Burrello, Mary Lou, *124*, 125
Burton, Charles, 161
Bush, George, 181, *181*

Cahoon, Ivan, 86
Campaign for Monmouth College, 164
Campaigns, 12, 21, 51, 52, 56, 84, 122, 126, 131, 140, 141, 143, 147, 154, 157, 164, 169, 170, 174, 180

Campbell, Margaret, 69
Campus master plan, 174, 175, 178, 180
Cannon, Civil War, 43, 97, 97, 103, *103*, 106
Canopus Stone, 27, *27*
Cap, centennial, *100*, 101, 103, *103*
Cap, freshman, 69, *69*, *100*, 101, 103, *103*, 114, 115, *115*
Capron Classics Room, 146, *146*
Capron, Keith B., 146, 180
Capron, Minnie Billings, 146, 164
Carius, Brant, 162
Carlstrom, Kim, *143*
Carnegie, Andrew, 51
Carnegie Library, 51, *51*, 52, 54, 62, 104, 111, 112, *116*, *117*, 119, 123, 126, 154, 170
Carr, Daryl, 156
Carter and Bauer, 20
Carver Charitable Trust, 180
Case Institute of Technology, 88
Caterpillar Foundation, 180
Caterpillar Inc., 165
Cedar Creek, 43, *43*, 97, *97*, 106
Cedar Creek Church, 6, 43
Ceilidh, 173
Celebrating the World, 161
Celebrations, 75, 78, 170, 173, 185. *See also individual celebrations*
Center for Cultural Diversity, 159
Chamberlain, Joseph, 178
Chamberlain, Judy, 178
Chapel, 21, 104, *104*
Chapel Choir, 91
Chapel service, 102, 104, 122
Chapman, John, 162
Chatfield, Charles, 111
Chautauqua, 74, *74*
Chemistry Department, 75, 88, 89, 91, 106
Cherries Jubilee Festival, 140
Cherry, Emma Jean, 103
Choir, 72, 73, 75, 91, *98*, *99*, 101, 102. *See also individual musical groups*
Chorale, 73, 91, 181, *181*
Choral Society, 73, 91
Chorus, girls', 90
Civil Rights, 104, 129, 130, 131
Civil War, 13, 17, 18, 19, 20
Clarke, W. M., 56
Classical Course, 23
Classics Program, 146
Class rivalries, 97, 114

Cleland, Eva Hanna, 78, *78*, *107*, 123
Cleland Hall, *122*, 123
Cleland, John S., 78, 123
Cleland, Robert, *85*
Cochrane, John C., 121
Coeducation, 22, 23, 24. *See also* Women students
Cogswell, Richard, 158
Coleman, Bennie, *134*, 135, 148
College Addition, 20, 21
College chaplaincy, 172
College Choir, 102
College Concert Series, 91
College Senate, 104
Collegians, 90
Collier, Ann Mack, 180
Colonial Hotel, 35, 127, *127*
Color rush, 114
Community service, 172
Computers, 156
Conaway, Cheryl, 159
Concert Band, 91
Concert Choir, 73, 91
Condon, Jacquelyn, 174
Conglon, Cheryl, *133*
Congressional Medal of Honor, 19, 154
Conservatory of Music, 72, 73, 90, 185
Cooksey, Ben, 128, *128*
Corbett, Harvey Wiley, 55
Corgnati, Leino, *73*
Crabtree, Edith Reese, 103
Craig, Roberta, *61*
Craine, Beth, *61*
Creswell, Ruth, *61*
Crimson Masque, 73, 75, 111, 184
Cross country, 162, 184
Cross country, women's, 162
Cross, Deletra, *152*
Crow, Mary, 107, 142, *142*, 147
Cupola bell and clapper, 21, *21*
Curriculum, 23, 32, 33, 88, 104, 105, 107, 110, 115, 128, 141, 142, 143, 146, 157, 162, 163, 164, 184, 185, 187
Curtis, Robb, 147
Cusack, John, 56
Czechoslovakia, 161

Dahl, Arthur, 180
Dahl Chapel and Auditorium, 180
Dahl, Dorothy Peterson, 180
Daly, Lindy Simmons, *78*
Dances, 68, *68*, 75, 78, 94, 173
Daniel, William, 180
Darwinism, 33, 75
Davenport, F. Garvin, 5, 103, 105, 107

Index  191

Davis, Edwin, *71*
Dawson, Marcia, *124, 125*
Day, Mary, 148, 149
Delta Tau Delta, 24
Demonstrations, *118*, 119, 129, *129*, 130, 131
Depression, The, 78, 83, 86
DeuPree, Virginia, *133*
Dew, Bob, *71*
Dew, Leroy, *71*
De Young, James, 111, 158
Dickey, Robert, *71*
Dining Hall, *168*, 169
Distinction Program, 162, 163
Dobbins, Terry, *133*
Dolphins, *133, 133*
Donald, Dorothy, 105, 107, *107*, 164, 165
Dorothy Donald Chair for Romance Languages and Literature, 164, 165
Doty, Art, 111
Douglass, Lucile, *61*
Douglas, Stephen A., 12
Duff, Margaret Evans, *76, 77*
Duncan, James K. L., 19, *19*
Dunlap, Robert "Bobby," 154
Dunlap, Shirley, 95
Dunlap Terrace, 154, 165
Dyni, Anne Quinby, 121

Ealy, Eric, 161
Earp, Francis Louis "Jug," 56, *56*, 86
Earp, Wyatt, 56
East Asian Studies Program, 105, 127, 128, 159, 175
East Hall. *See* Austin Hall
Eccritean Society, 24, 35, 36, 68. *See also* Philo
Eckhard, Martie, *143*
l'École Normale Superieure Gestion et Commerce International, 181
Ecology Field Station, 128, *128*
Economics Department, 107
Education Department, 88
Edward A. Mellinger Teaching and Learning Center, 175, 185
Edward Arthur Mellinger Foundation, 175, 180
Edwards, Geoff, *182, 183*
Edwin A. Trapp Jr. Professor of Business Administration, 164
83rd Regiment of Illinois Volunteer Infantry, 18
11th Street Ball Park, 36, *36*, 37
Emerson Park, 184
Endowed faculty positions, 146, 147, 164, 165, 172

Endowment, 12, 17, 21, 42, 78, 139, 147, 164, 165, 174, 185
Engineering Department, 88
English Department, 88
Enrollment, 78, 107, 110, 115, 122, 123, 129, 131, 132, 133, 141, 147, 163, 164, 165, 172, 181
Erodelphian Society. *See* Philo
Erskin, James E., 34
Eta Sigma Phi, 146
Eva Louise Barr Language Laboratory, 105, 107, *108*, 109
Evers, Lorance, *71*
Extra-Curricular School, 128

Faculty, 78, 107, 110, 123, 132, 133, 157, 158, 159, 161, 163, 164, 165, 185. *See also individual faculty*
Faculty Long-Range Planning Committee, 107
Faculty Senate, 128, 131
Festival of Life, 173
Festival Olympics, 173
Fidler, John, *85*
Field hockey, 149
Fike, Donald E., 178
Financial aid, 141, 164, 165
Findley, Scott, *57*
Fine Arts Building, 112
Fine Arts Department, 55
Finley, Lyle, *78*, 104, 105, *105*
Finley, Mrs. Lyle, *78*
Finley, S. H., *78*
First Illinois Cavalry, 19
Fleming, David, 122
Fleming, Mary, *133*
Flint, Harrold P., *107*
Football, 37, 56, 57, *58, 59*, 60, 71, 72, 73, *73*, 86, 87, 115, 133, 135, *135*, 145, 147, 148, 160, *160*, 161, 162, 178, 180
Ford Foundation, 105, 127
Forrestal, James, 96
Forrest, Nathan Bedford, 18
Fort Donelson, 18
Fort Henry, 18
Fort Sheridan, 60
Fort Sumter, 18
Forward to the 21st Century Campaign, 164, 170
Foster, James, 112
Fox, Bernice L., *146*, 146
Fox, Kim Buckert. *See* Buckert, Kim
Fraternities, 24, 25, 68, 69, 70, 96, 110, 123. *See also indivdual fraternities*
Fraternity Complex, 122, 123, *123*, 126

Frazer, Charles, *71*
Freed, Catherine Moore "Kitty," *138*, 139, 140
Freed, DeBow, 27, 121, *138*, 139, 140, 142, 143, 145, *148*, 156, 164, 174, *174*
Freshman Honors Program, 128
Freshman Picnic, 144, *144*
Freshman Seminar, 143, 162
Freshman Walkout, 171, *171*
Friedrich, Karen, 148, 149
Fulsom, Ralph, 111
Fulton Hall, 55, 84, 90
Fulton, Samuel A., 84
Fundraising. *See* Campaigns

Gadske, Martha, *107*
Gainer, Frank, 56
Gambino, Anna, *124, 125*
Gerhart, Arthur, 75
German Club, 60, *60*
Ghormley, Harry K., 57, *58*
Gibson, Emma, *78*
Gibson, Frank, *71*
Gibson Hall, 122, 123, *123*, 158, 178
Gibson, Mrs., 103
Gibson, Robert Wesson, *100*, 101, 102, *102*, 103, 104, 105, 110, 112, 115, 120
Gibson, Sue, *124, 125*
Giese, Richard F., *174, 174*, 175, 184, 185, 187, *187*
Giese, Sandy, 187, *187*
Gillhouse, Tom, 148
Givens, Louis, *78*
Gladfelter, Donald, 174
Glasgow, Angela, 178
Glasgow Field, 178
Glasgow, Terry, 135, *135*, 145, 148, *148*, 162, 178
Glass, Martha, *61*
Glass, Thomas Beveridge, *46*, 47
Glee Club, girls', 90
Glennie Gymnasium, 144, 154
Glennie, Larry, 144
Glennie, Nancy, 144
Goldstein, Lorrie, *124, 125*
Golf, 148, 184
Golf, women's, 184
Gongwer, Howard, 111
Gonzalez, Arnoldo, 162
Gospel teams, 102, 104, 122
Government Department, 126
Graham, A. Y., 20
Graham, David, 20
Graham Hall, 112, 170
Graham, Jane, 23
Graham, Ralph, 112
Graham, Russell, 46, *47*, 50, 112

Graves, Steve, 147
Gray, Vaughn, *184*
Greek organizations, 24, 25, 26, 68, 69, 70, 71, 96, 110, *150, 151*, 184. *See also individual organizations*
Greenhouse, 128
Grier, Ada Bruen, 22, 84
Grier Hall, 55, 84, 86, *86*, 94, *94*, 96, *96*, 170
Grier, James Alexander, 84
Grier, James Harper, 22, 24, 84, *84*, 86, 88, 91, 94, 103
Griffiths, Dick, *137, 138*
Grimm, Bob, 172
Grube, Sandra, *124, 125*
*Guide to 101 of the Best Values in America's Colleges and Universities*, 158
Gymnasium, 41, *44*, 45, 52, 55, 62, 69, 71, *71*. *See also* Glennie Gymnasium

Habitat for Humanity, 184
Haldeman-Thiessen Science Center, 104, 106, 122, 126, *126*, 128, 154, 187
Haldeman, William S., 75, 88, 89, *89*, 91, 103, 106
Haldy's Boys, 89, *89*
Hamilton, Roland, 56
Hamly, Wallace, *71*
Hanna, Eva. *See* Cleland, Eva Hanna
Hanna, J. Ross, 50
Hanna, Mary N., 32
Harding, Abner Clark, 5, 7, 8, 18, 20
Hart, Herbert L., 71, 72, 73, 86
Hartwig, Tina, 175
Hauge, Harris, 119, *126*
Hawcock, Emory, 79
Hawcock, Ernie, 79
Hawcock, Jennie, 79
Hawcock's Cafe, 79, *79*
Haynes, Roger, 161
Haywood, Bruce, 142, *142*, 143, 146, 147, 153, 154, *154*, 157, 158, *158*, 163, 164, 165, 170, 174, *174*
Heath, James, *71*
Hendricks, Damon, *152*
Herbert, J. B., 36
Herbsleb, James, 107
Herman, John, 162
Hermann, Harold, 72, *72*
Hershberger, David, 91
Hershberger, Floyd, 91
Hewes, Chester, 122, *122*, 126
Hewes Library, 27, 104, 116, 117, 119, 122, 126, *126*, 144, 154, 170, 172, 175, 178, 179, 180, 185
Hewes, Mabel, 122, 126

Hewes, Thomas Randolph, 126
Hewitt, Herbert E., 45, 52
Hickerson, Angie, 149, 162
Hickman, Morton, *71*
Hickman, Robert, *71*
Highlander Room, 154, 175
Hill, Benjamin, 107
History Department, 45, 126
*History of Monmouth College: Through Its Fifth Quarter Century, A* (Urban), 141, 142
"Hits and Misses," 90, *90*
Holiday Inn, 123, *123*
Holm, Susan F., 164
Holt, Doris, 72, *72*
Holt House, 25, 70, *70*
Holt, Jacob, 70
Homecoming, 107, *107*, 112, *112*, 181
Home Economics Department, 88
Homes, Richard, *107*
Honors Convocation, 163, 173
Honors Course, 23
Honors Scholar Program, 141
Hook, Deborah, *133*
Hookham, Virginia, *124, 125*
Hoops, Jill, *184*
"Hour of Charm," 90
Houston, Jeff, *161*
Hoyman, Earla, 75
Hoyman, Jane, 75
Hoyman, Scott, *85*
Hubbard, Harold, *71*
Hubbard House, 159. *See also* Center for Cultural Diversity
Hubbard, Marilyn Kessinger, 159
Hubbard, Willis, 159
Hubble, Emma Roberts, *78*
Huber, Gordy, *87*
Huff Athletic Center, 180, *180*, 187
Huff, Elizabeth, 180
Huff, Walter S. Jr., 147, *147*, 164, 180
Hunter, Donovan, 135
Hunt, Joan Phifer, 149
Huseman, Ruth, 172
Huseman, Sue Ann, 170, *170*, 171, 172, 173, 174, *174*
Hutchinson, Clara, *69*
Hutchinson, J. C., 50
Hutchison, Margaret Jean, *85*

Ichthus Club, 102, 104, 122
I. C. Sorosis, 25, *25*, 70. *See also* Pi Beta Phi
Ides of March, 173

Illiniwek tribe, 4
Illinois Bankers' Life Insurance Company, 86, 87
Illinois State Academy of Science, 104, 105
Independent organizations, 110
Institutional Development Committee, 157, 158
Inter-Collegiate Oratorical Association, 34
Interfraternity Council, 126
International Relations Club, 159
Inter-State Oratorical Association, 24
Irwin, Isabelle Rankin, 46, 47

Jackson, Constance, 149, 184, *184*
James Christie Shields Collection, 179, *179*
Jamieson, Ann, 149
Jamieson Community Center, 184
Jamieson, Howard, *85*
Jamieson, J. F., *76, 77*
Jamieson Settlement, 6
Japanese Studies, 105, 128
Jazz Band, 140, *140*
Jazz Combo, 140
Jazz Vocal Ensemble, 140
Jenkins, Matt, *164*
Johnson, Babara Watt, 172
Johnson, Franklin, 126, 144, *144*
Johnson, Leland, *71*
Johnson, Nellie Higgins, *76, 77*
Jones, Lesley, *124, 125*
Jones, Robert, *71*
*Journal of Baltic Studies, The*, 161
Julian, William B., 159, 163, *163*
Junior Chautauqua, 74

Kane, Kelly, 160, 161
Kansai Gaidai University, 181
*Kaplan Newsweek College Catalog*, 181
Kappa Alpha Sigma, 26, 68
Kappa Alpha Theta, 25
Kappa Delta, 68, 112, *173*
Kappa Kappa Gamma, 22, 25, 26, 42, 68, 69, *69*, 70, 103, 112
Kappa Kappa Gamma Foundation, 70
Kasch, Louise DuBois, 180
Kemp, Marybeth, 174
Kennedy, Adele, 107, *107*
Kent State University, 129, 131
Kern, Dorothy, 95, *95*

Ketterer, John, 107, 128, *128*, 142, *142*
Kieft, Richard L. "Doc," 143, *143*, 158
Kilgore, Emma, *69*
King, LeRoy, 87, *87*
Kite, Patricia, *133*
Kloeppel, Peter, 156
Knox College, 6, 12, 37, 115, 160, *160*
Knox Manual Labor College. See Knox College
Komatsu, Takashi, *91*, 127
Kongable, Clara, *34*
Kotsuji, Abraham, *120*
Kovacs, Pete, 113, 115
Krause, Nancy, *124, 125*
Kresge Foundation, 143, 157
Kucharz, Rich, 147, 148
Kyle, Joseph, *50*
Kyle, Stanley, *71*

LaFollette, Robert, 74
Laine, Louise, *133*
Lake, Ann, *124, 125*
Lamprecht, Anne Kniss, 180
Language Lab. See Eva Louise Barr Language Laboratory
Language Studies, 105, 110, 146, 159
Lansing, Gulian, 27
Larson, Chuck, 113
Lavery, Bill, 162
Lawn Tennis Association, *38, 39*, 41
Lee L. Morgan Professor of History and International Studies, 165
Lemon, Rod, 110, *110*
Len G. Everett Gallery, 154
LeSuer, Arlene Snow, 178
LeSuer Nature Preserve, 178
LeSuer, William, 178
Levita, Joe, 148
Libby, Jake, 162
Liberal Arts Festival, 91, 105, 111, 128, 159
Library, 21, *44*, 45, 51, *51*, 105, 112, *116, 117*, 119, 122, 123, 126, 154. See also Carnegie Library; Hewes Library
Li, Chenyang, 161
Liedman Hall, 122, 123
Liedman, Jean, 96, *96*, 112, 123
Lightner, Mrs. Harry, 72
Lilly Endowment, 157
Lincoln, Abraham, 12, 18, 67
Lincoln Elementary School, 90
Lister, Ken, 111
Literary societies, 22, 24, 34, 35, 45, 68. See also individual societies

Little Five, 57, 60
Little Nineteen, 57, 72
Little Theater, 73, 111, *111*, 157
Livingston, David, *107*
London Arts Program, 111
Long Island College Hospital, 55
Loomis, Pete, 121
Lowell, Jane Quinby, 121
Loya, Eileen Sandberg, 121
Loya, Heimo "Hal," 90, 91, *91*, 107
Lucas, Tim, 148
Luebke, John, 140
Lyons, Althea Cooper, 45
Lyons, Samuel Ross, 42, *42*, 45, 49

Madden, James G., 7, 20
Madden, Maria, 7
"Magic, Minstrels, and Merrymaking," 161
Majorettes, 91, 112, *112*
Manandhar, Rama, *120*
Manley, Harry, 127
Marching Band, 91, 112, *112*
Marcus Aurelius, 187
Marine Room, 79
Markham Creek, 178
Mark of Commendation, 95, 96
Marshall, Andy, 123
Marshall, Bert, 56
Marshall Hall, 69, *69*, 113
Marshall Health and Fitness Center, 180
Marshall, Isabel Bickett, 180
Marshall, James, 56, 69, 180
Marshall, Marilyn, *124, 125*
Martin, Ginny, 172
Martin, Mrs., *71*
Mason, Robert L., 159
Mason, Sandra, *107*
Mathematics Department, 45
Max Meadows, Va., 172
Maxwell, Judith, *124, 125*
Maxwell, Samuel Steen, 33
Maybelline Company, 122
Mayer, Catherine, *133*
May Fete, 61, *61*, 95, 173
May Pole, 61, 173
May Queen, 61, *61*
McAllister, James, 107
McBride, Jerry, *113*
McCain, Evelyn, *61*
McCartney, Margaret, *23*
McClanahan, W. Stewart, 107
McClanahan, John, 18
McClanahan, Mary, 75
McClanahan, Paul, 75, *120*, 122, *122*, 130
McClanahan, Thomas S., 22, *22*

McClaughry, Elizabeth Madden, 22
McClellan, Mary, *61*
McConnell, Robert, *71*
McCorkle, Helen, *61*
McCormick, Robert R., 146
McCoy, Clem D., *76, 77*
McCoy, Katherine Oliver, *76, 77*
McCoy, Mary, 154
McCracken, Thomas, *50*
McDaniel, Clyde, *71*
McFeeters, Milo, 103
McGaughey, J. A., 56, 57
McIntosh, Jack, *71*
McKee, Bob, *113*
McKenna, Frank, 123
McKeown, Everett, *71*
McLaughry, Catharine, *23*
McLoskey, Bob, *113*
McLoskey, Leo, *71*
M Club Hall of Fame, 73, *73*, 149
McMichael Academic Hall, 144
McMichael, David, 78, *78*, 91, *91*, 94
McMichael Home. See McMichael Residence Hall
McMichael, Jackson Burgess, 32, *32*, 34, 41, 42, 50, 54, 55, 91
McMichael, Minnie MacDill, 62, 68, *76, 77*
McMichael Residence Hall, 54, 55, 56, *56*, 94, 112, 170, 175, 185
McMichael Science Hall, 54, *54*, 55, 75, 97, 104, 144
McMichael, Thomas Hanna, 42, 46, 47, 48, 49, 50, *50*, 51, 52, 54, 56, *64*, 65, 67, 73, 74, *74*, 76, 78, 83, 84, 88, 91, *91*, 187
McMillan family, 175
McMillan, Frank, 89
McMillan, John Henry, 46, 47, 50
McMullen, Donald, 75
McNamara, Jeremy, 158
McNamera, Brooks, 111
Mead, Kim, 149
*Meditations* (Marcus Aurelius), 187
Megchelsen, Florence, *61*
Mekemson, George, *107*
Mekemson, Harold, *107*
Mellinger Center. See Edward A. Mellinger Teaching and Learning Center
Meneilly, Robert, 95, *95*
Meneilly, Shirley Dunlap, 95
Men's Glee Club, 73, 75

Men's residence halls, 57, 90, 112, 123. See also individual halls
Merrill, Glen, *126*
*Messiah* (Handel), 75, 98, 99, 101, 102
Metzger-Johnson, 178
Miami tribe, 4
Midwest Athletic Conference, 69, 72, 86, 87, 135, 147, 148, 149
Midwest Athletic Conference for Women, 149
Military service, 18, 19, 20, 23, 60, 62, *62*, 63, 80, 81, 91, 94, 95, 96, 129, 132
Millen, Samuel, 6
Miller, Beth, *143*
Minnie Billings Capron Chair in Classics, 146, 164
Minnie Stewart Foundation, 70
Mitchell, Juan, 162
Moffett, Eugene, 89
Moll, Ryan, *184*
Monmouth Academy, 5, 7, 9, 17, 43. See also Monmouth College
Monmouth Chorale, 181, *181*
Monmouth College, 14, 15, 22, *122*
 architecture, 7, 20, 36, 41, 45, 52, *53*, 54, 55, 63, 121, 178
 campus development, 7, 8, 9, 20, 21, 51, 56, 112, 113, 122, *122*, 123, 126, 143, 154, 165, 175, 180
 diversity, 159, 161, 165
 educational mission, 21, 23, 31, 32, 84, 107, 174
 financial condition, 12, 21, 42, 50, 78, 104, 132, 133, 135, 140, 141, 144, 147, 163, 164, 165
 founding, 3, 6, 7, 9, 78
 land acquisition, 8, 20, 37, 71
 liberal arts tradition, 104, 105, 107, 110, 115, 120, 139, 142, 143, 157, 158, 165, 184, 185, 187
 Presbyterian tradition, 3, 21, 23, 31, 84, 102, 104, 111, 115, 122, 172
 ranking, 158, 159, 172, 181
 relations with Monmouth, Illinois, 4, 7, 51, 131, 171
 relations with Presbyterian Church, 104, 120, 122, 129
*Monmouth College: The First Hundred Years, 1853-1953* (Davenport), 103

Index 193

*Monmouth Collegian*, 27
Monmouthiana Room, 154, 172
Monmouth, Illinois, 14, 15, 21, 34
 architecture, 33, *33*
 diversity, 159
 founding and development, 4, 10, 33, 34
 Presbyterian tradition, 6
 relations with Monmouth College, 4, 7, 51, 131, 171
Monmouth Plan, 164, 165, 172
*Monmouth Review Atlas*, 160
Moore, Betty, *124*, *125*
Moorehead, Agnes, 111
Moore, Josiah, 18
Moore, Ryan, *164*
Moredock, Philicia, *184*
Morgan, Lee L., 164, *164*, 165, 170
Morgan Room, 170
Morrison, Clyde, 13
Morrison, James, 13
Morrison, Marion, 5, 9, 10, 13, *13*, 21
Morrison, Marion Mitchell, 13
Morrison, Marion Robert. See Wayne, John
Mueller, Ken, *113*
Mueller, Kenneth, 97
"Musical Moods," 90
Musical performances, 73, 90, *90*, 91, 173. *See also individual musical groups*
Music Department, 23, 32, 34, 36, 72, 73, 75, 90, 91

NARU, 94, 95, 96
National Collegiate Players, 73, 75, 111
National Endowment for the Humanities, 146, 147, 157
National Intercollegiate Women's Prone Rifle Match, 115
National Register of Historic Places, 121
National Rifle Association, 106
Native Americans, 4
Natural history museum, 21
Naval Flight Preparatory School, 94, 95
Navy Academic Refresher Unit. *See* NARU
Niblock, John, 111
Nicholas, Albert, 97, *97*
Nichols, Rusty, *107*
Night Shirt Parade, 57, *57*
Noël, Roger, *161*
North Central Association evaluation, 141

Nottleman, Rudolph, *103*
Nursing Program, 88

Oberstar, Betty Weiss, 89
Occupational Therapy Program, 88
Off-Campus Study, 105, 159, 161, 181, 184
Old Academy. *See* Academy Building
Old Main, 5, 20, *20*, 21, *29*, 36, *36*, *44*, 45, *45*, 51, *51*, 52, *52*, 187
Olmstead, Silas, 43
Olmstead's Mill, 43
Olympics. *See* Scot-Olympics
Onken, Amy, 69
*Oracle*, 110, 126, 143
Oral History Project, 172
Oratorical contests, 34, 35, 36
Orchesis Club, 61
Orchestra, 91, *98*, *99*, 101
Orpheum Theatre, 90, 185
Owen, Charles A., *75*, 88, *88*
Owen, Charles Jr., 89
Owen, John, *75*
Ozburn, Jack, *71*

Paine, Harriet, 23
Palmer, George H., 19, *19*
Pan-Hellenic Center, 113
Parents Weekend, 123, *123*
Patterson, Alice, 76, *77*
Patterson, Clarence, *71*
Patterson, Florabel, 45, 46, *47*
Peacock, Betty, *175*
Peacock Memorial Athletic Park, *175*, *176*, *177*, *178*, *184*, 185
Peacock, Safford, *175*
Peanut Night, 35
Pelisek, Joe, *115*
Peoria and Oquawka Railroad, 4
Peterson, Grace Gawthrop, 72, 73, 74, 82, *82*, 83, 90, *90*, 157, 185
*Peterson's Competitive Colleges*, 159
*Peterson's Guide to Top Colleges for Science*, 172
Petrie, Richard, *107*
Phelps, Hugh N., *175*
Phelps, Norma, *175*
Phifer, Joan, *115*
Phi Gamma Delta, 24
Phi Kappa Psi, 24
Philadelphian. *See* Philo
Phillips, Frank, 88, *88*
Phillips, Virginia, *133*
Philo, 24, 34, *34*, 35, 36, 68
Philosophy Department, 88
Phi Sigma Alpha, 68, 69

Physical Culture Course, 37. *See also* Athletics
Physical Sciences Department, 33
Pi Alpha Nu, 91
Pi Beta Phi, 22, 24, 25, 26, 68, *69*, 70, 84, 112
Piggott, Robert, *107*
Pinney's Tap, 115, *115*
Pipe and drum band, 172
Pole scrap, 69, 114, *114*
Poling Hall, 170
Poling, Harold "Red," 95, *95*, 170, 184
Poling, Marian, 184
Porter, David, 19
Porter, A. N., 76, *77*
Porter, James C., 6, 7, 43
Preparatory Department, 9
Presbyterian Church, 6, 9, 26, 43, 50, 51, 102
 educational mission, 6
 Egypt, 75, 84
 missionaries, 75, *75*, 95, *95*, 103
 relations with Monmouth College, 104, 120, 122, 129
Presbyterian high school, 7. *See also* Monmouth Academy
President's mansion, 3, *44*, 45, 51, 63, 121, 174
*Profile of Monmouth College, 1954-1974*, 107
Protests. *See* Demonstrations
Prugh, Wiley, *85*
Psychology Department, 110
Puck, Barbara, *133*
Putting Students at the Center Campaign, 170
Pyatt, Karen Friedrich. *See* Friedrich, Karen

Quinby, Elizabeth, 120, 121, *121*
Quinby House, 120, 121, *121*, 139, 174
Quinby, Ivory, 3, *3*, 20, 21, 23, 120, 121, 174
Quinby, Ivory II, 121
Quinby, Ivory III, 121, *121*
Quinby, Mary, 121
Quinn, Janet, *133*

Radio station, 112, *112*
Ralston, Harold, 27, 97, *97*, 146
Ramsdale, Margaret, 107, *107*
Rankin, Douglas, 157, *157*
Rankin, Glen, *87*, 122, *122*, 123
Ranney, Durbin, *71*

Rare Book Room, 154
Rasmusen, Roger, 180
*Ravelings*, 110, *110*, 171
Rawlings, Floyd, 107
Rayniak, Susan, *133*
Recitation Hall, 1
Recruitment, 122, 123, 141, 163, 164
Red Barn East, 111
Reed, A. G., 57
Reed, Judy, 111
Reed, Mark, 161, 162, *162*
Reedy, Bob, 147
Reflections, 152, 153
Regan, James, *71*
Reichow, Bill, 133, *133*, 135, *135*, 147
Reid, Andrew Graham, 46, *47*
Reid, Malcolm, *71*
Reifinger, Aleece, 111
Reimers, Tom, *113*
Religion Department, 120
Religious organizations, 102, 104, 122. *See also individual organizations*
Rendezvous for Renewal Program, 132, 133
Reno, Dick, 156
REO Speedwagon, 173
Residential facilities, 112, 122, 126, 158, 169, 178. *See also* Men's residence halls; Women's residence halls; *individual halls*
*Review*, 12
Rice, William C., 4
Rifle team, 106, 115, 149
Riggs, Edna Browning, 73, 90
Rilott, Jim, *113*
Ritchie, Adam, 43
Rivoli Theatre, *82*, 83, 90, 171
Robertson, Heather, 149, 161, *161*, 162
Robinson, Glenn "Jelly," 71, *73*, 87, 113
Robinson, Luther Emerson 45, *46*, *47*, 66, *67*, 73
Robinson, Thomas, *71*
Rogers, Amy, 22
Rogers, Aniel, 43
Rogers, John, 45
Roosevelt, Teddy, 74
Ross, Robert, 7, *7*, 43
Rowan, Penny, 162
Rubia, Andrew, *182*, *183*
Russell, Dwight, *85*
Ruth Huseman Meditation Room, 175
Ruth L. Wells Foundation, 154

Sander, Roger "Sandman," 148
Sanders, Jack, *71*

Sanders, Kathy, *124*, *125*
Sanderson, Kenneth, *71*
Sanford, Hal, 111
SATC, 60, 62, *62*, *63*
Saville, Edgar, *71*
Schisler, Dan, 162, *164*
Scholarships, perpetual, 10, *10*, 12
Schoolhouse, one-room, 5, *5*, 9
Schrenk, Clara, *61*
Science curriculum, 33, 88, 89, 104, 110, 128
Science Hall, *44*, 45
Scientific Course, 22, 23
Scotland Yard, 141, 169, *175*, 175
Scotlight, 141, 173
ScotOlympics, 173, *173*
Scots Day, 172, 173
"Scots 'N Skits," 90
Scots Sing, 141, *141*, 173. *See also* Scotlight
Scots Weekend, 173
Scott, Ed, 161
Scott, John, 11
*Scribner's Magazine*, 27
Sears Roebuck Foundation Award for Teaching Excellence and Campus Leadership, 158
Secret societies, 22, 24, 25, 34, 70. *See also* Greek organizations; Literary Societies
Seiler, Bill, 148
Semester schedule, 163
Senate Scholars, 162
Senior College Program of Study. *See* Thompson Plan
September 11, 2001, 185
Sharp, Barbara, *133*
Shauman, Robert, *107*
Shaver, Glenn, 72, *75*, 75
Shaw, Gloria, *152*
Shawver, Benjamin, 88, 91, *91*, 107
Shields, James C., 179
Shields, Nelle, 76, *77*
Shippen, Bob, 123
Showalter, Paul, *120*
Shrauger, Sterling, *71*
Sienkewicz, Thomas J., 27, 146, *146*, 158, 164
Sigma Alpha Epsilon, 123
Sigma Chi, 24
Sigma Phi Epsilon, 123
Skip Day, 173
Skov, Charles, 128, *128*
Smiley, Christiana, 23
Smiley, Robert, *71*
Smith, Carlos, 159
Smith, Chester, 57
Smith, Glenn, 57
Smith, Joseph, 12
Smith, Linda, *143*

Smith, Roderic, *61*
Snell, Nancy, *124*, *125*
Soccer, 176, *177*, 178, 184, *184*
Soccer, women's, 162, *162*
Social and cultural life, 24, 25, 35, 36, 61, 68, 69, 73, 75, 79, 86, 90, 102, 104, 105, 110, 111, 112, 159, 173
Social Service, 172, 184
Sociology Department, 88
Softball, 148, 149, 161, *161*, 162
Sororities, 24, 25, 68, 69, 70, 110, 112, 113. *See also individual sororities*
SOS. *See* Students Organized for Service
Sound of Five, 132, *132*, *136*, *137*, 139, 140, 144, *144*
Spanish influenza epidemic, 62
Spaulding, Sue, *124*, *125*
Speech Department, 32, 34
Speel, Charles, 27, *120*, 142
Spencer, Karen, 148
Spitz, Douglas R., 158
"Spree-For-All," 90
Stanton, Elizabeth Cady, 22
Stanton, Scott, 144
Stegeman, Hermann J., 57
Stevens, John, *182*, *183*
Stevenson, Howard, *71*
Stevenson, Martha Louisa, 25
Stewart, Albert Fulton, *46*, *47*
Stewart House, 25, 70, *70*
Stewart, James, 70
Stewart, Mary Moore, 25, *25*, 70
Stine, Richard Dengler, 131, *131*, 132, 133, 135
Stockdale Center, 41, 141, *141*, 154, *168*, 169, 170, 175, 185
Stockdale, James B., 154
Storm, 112, *112*, 113
Strabley, Bob, *164*
Streakers Weekend, 173
Student Army Training Corps. *See* SATC
Student Association, 159
Student Center, 112, 131, 154. *See also* Stockdale Center
Student Government, 110
Students. *See also* Women students; *individual students*
 African American, 129, 153, 159
 diversity, 159, 161, 184
 Hispanic American, 159
 international, 159, 181, *181*, 184

Student Senate, 131
Students Organized for Service, 172
Student Union, 86, *86*
Studio Art Department, 105
Styx, The, 112, 141, 175. *See also* Scotland Yard
Summer School of Biology, 33
Surveying, 22, *22*
Swan, John Nesbit, *46*, *47*, 50, 54, 75
Swimming, 71, 144, 148
Swimming, women's, 149

Tait, Joe, 112, *112*
*Takin' It to the Limit* (Sound of Five), 144, *144*
Talent show, 113, *113*, 141, *141*
Tamagawa Gakuen, 127, 128
Tartan plaid, 72, *115*, 170
Task Force on Budgetary Planning, 132
Tau Kappa Epsilon, 69, 107, 123
Taylor, Warren, *73*
Teacher's Training Course, 23
Teaching and Learning Center. *See* Edward A. Mellinger Teaching and Learning Center
Teagle Foundation, 185
Technology, 169, 170, 175, 178, 185
Tennis, 72, 148, 180, 184
Tennis, women's, 72, *72*, 149, 184
Terrey, Neal, *71*
Terrones, Steve, 140
Theater, 73, 75, 111, 154, 157. *See also* Little Theater; Wells Theater
Theological Seminary of the Northwest, 11. *See also* Xenia Theological Seminary
Theta Chi, 69, 71, 95, 123
Theta Chi Mu, 68
Thiessen, Garrett "Doc," 75, 79, 88, 97, *97*, 104, 106, *106*, 115, 149
"This Is It," 90
Thomas, Norman, 91
Thompson, J. R., *50*
Thompson Plan, 88
Thompson, Samuel Martin, 75, 78, *78*, 88, *107*, 142
Thomson, William J., 12
"Three Macs," 113, *113*
3-3 Curriculum, 107, 120, 141, 143, 163
Tinker, Alice Jeanette, *46*, *47*
Tinker, Gene, *73*

Title IX Educational Amendments of 1972, 149
"Town Topics," 90
Track and field, 71, 113, 148, 161, 164, *164*, 184, *184*
Track and field, women's, 149, 161, 184, *184*
Trapp, Edwin A. Jr., 164
Trotter, George, 87, *87*, 170
Trotter, Maxine Murdy, 170
Tug of war, 114, *173*, *173*
Turnbull, David, 89
Turner, G. Edgar, *46*, *47*
Tweed, Brandon, *182*, *183*

*Udder Confusion* (Thiessen), 106
Umennachi, Julius, 159
University of Illinois research station at Havana, 33
University of Reading's Centre for Children's Reading and Writing, 181
"Up 'N Atom," 90
Upton, Vincent, *71*
Urban Studies, 105
Urban, William, 27, 97, 126, 128, 142, *142*, 147, 156, 158, 161, 165
U. S. Navy NP-1 Spartan Trainer, 94, *94*
*U.S. News & World Report*, 158, 172
U. S. S. *Fort Hindman*, 19, *19*

Valentine, Richard, 164, 174
Valley Beautiful, 61, 154
Van Gundy Hall, 95
Venters, Aaron, *164*
Verigan, Neil, 97, *97*
Vesper service, 102, 122
Vietnam War, 118, 119, 129, 130, 131, 132
Visiting Scholar Series, 141
Volleyball, 148, 149, *149*

Wackerle Center, 185
Wackerle, Frederick W., 170, 180
WACS, 95
Wahpeton-Sisseton National American Indian Reservation, 172
Waid, Andrew Jackson, 55
Waid, Dan Everett, 36, 41, *41*, 52, 54, 55, *55*, 69, 71
Waid, Eva, 55, 71
Waid Pool, 71
Walker, Rachel, *23*
Walker, Susan Burley, 25
Wallace, Cynthia, *133*
Wallace, David Alexander, 9, *9*, 10, 11, 13, 18, 20, 21, 22, 23, 24, 26, 32, 36, 45

Wallace, Elizabeth, 25
Wallace Hall, 43, 51, 52, 53, 54, 55, 61, 62, 69, 86, *86*, 94, 110, 112, 154, 170, *186*, 187
Wallace, H. F., *50*
Wallace, John, 56
Wallace, John F., 42
Wallace, Martha Findley, 10
Warneck, Bill, 123
Warren County Public Library, 184
Washington Semester, 105
Watson, Craig, 158
Watt, Mary, *61*
WAVES, 95
Wayne, John, 13
Weeks, Stafford, *120*
Wehrs, Sharon, *124*, *125*
Weiss, Andrew, 164
Wellness center. *See* Marshall Health and Fitness Center
Wells, Rebecca Porter, 154
Wells, Ruth, 154, 157
Wells Theater, 97, 111, 157, 165
Wharff, Hazel Hatch, *115*, 149
Wheat, Chris, 162
White, Esther, 158
Whitefield and King, 54
Whiteman family, 175
Whiteman, Ralph, 175
White, Mildred, *61*
White, Perry, 181, *181*
Willey, Helen Wagner, 157, *157*
Willhardt, Gary, 185, *185*
Willhardt, Mark, 185, *185*
Williams, Randy, *184*
Williams, Ruth, 73, 75, *75*, 111
Willits, Anna Elizabeth, 25, *25*
Wills, Jim, *126*
Wilson, Clyde, *71*
Wilson, John H., 23, *23*
Wilson, Loyd, *71*
Wimpress, Gordon Duncan, 120, *120*, 121, 122, 126, 129, 131
Wimpress, J. Margaret Skerry, 121
Winbigler, Alice, 45, *46*, *47*, 61, 75, 78, *78*, 84
Winbigler, Gordon, *71*
Winbigler Hall, 55, 84
Winbigler, John, *71*
Woll, Robert G. "Bobby," 71, 72, *73*, 87, *87*, 135, 143, 145, *145*
Women's Athletic Association, 133
Women's athletics, 41, 42, *115*, *133*, 148, 149, 161, 162. *See also individual sports*

Women's residence halls, *44*, 45, *45*, 96, *96*, 112, 123. *See also individual halls*
Women students, 16, 22, 23, 24, 25, 61, *92*, *93*, 95, 112, 149
Woodbine, The, 60, 62, 63, *63*, 69
Woodburn, James, 6
Worcester, George, *107*
World War I, 60, 62, 67, 91
World War II, 83, 91, 94, 95, 96, 114
Worley, John R., *87*
Wrestling, 71, 148
Wyant, Sarah, 131
Wyatt, Travis, 162

Xenia Theological Seminary, 11, 32, 50, 84, 102
Xi Gamma Delta, 69, 71

Yankee Doodle Boys, 90
Yap, Soon Chye, 159
Yarde, Bob, *113*
Yearbook. *See* Ravelings
YMCA, 41, 60, *60*, 62, 102, 104, 122, 184
Young, Alexander, 11, *11*, 20
Young, J. A., 20
Yugoslavia, 161
YWCA, 60, 61, 90, 102, 104, 122

Zartman, E. C., 36
Zellers, Parker, 111
Zeta Beta Tau, 63, 123, *126*
Zeta Epsilon Chi, 26
Zipse, Sharon, *124*, *125*

Index  195